BLACK LONDON

Other books by the author

Carrington: A Life

BLACK LONDON

Life before Emancipation

Gretchen Gerzina

RUTGERS UNIVERSITY PRESS
New Brunswick, New Jersey

© Gretchen Holbrook Gerzina 1995

First published in Great Britain in 1995
by John Murray (Publishers) Ltd.

First published in the United States in 1995
by Rutgers University Press,
New Brunswick, New Jersey

Library of Congress Cataloging-in-Publication Data

Gerzina. Gretchen.
 Black London : life before emancipation / Gretchen
Holbrook Gerzina.
      p.   cm.
 Includes bibliographical references and index
 ISBN 0-8135-2259-5 (alk. paper)
 1. Blacks—England—London—History—18th century. 2.
Africans—England—London—History—18th century. 3.
London (England)—History—18th century. I. title.
 DA676.9.B55G47 1995
 305.896'0421'09033—dc20
                                                    95-33060
                                                    CIP

Typeset in Bembo by
Rowland Phototypesetting Ltd.,
Bury St. Edmunds, Suffolk
Printed and bound in Great Britain by
The University Press, Cambridge

To Pat Kaufman and John Stathatos

Contents

Illustrations

C. Williams. Published February 1820 in *Caricatures*, Vol. X. Courtesy of the Trustees of the British Museum.

11. 'The Sailor's Description of a Chase & Capture'. Lieut. John Sheringham, R.N. Published 7 January 1822. Courtesy of the Trustees of the British Museum.

12. 'Gustavus Vassa, or Olaudah Equiano'. Anonymous *c.* 1789. Courtesy of the Photographs and Prints Division, Schomburg Center for Research in Black Culture, the New York Public Library, Astor, Lenox and Tilden Foundations.

13. 'Joseph Johnson'. John Thomas Smith. Published in *Vagabondia; or Anecdotes of Mendicant Wanderers through the Streets of London*, 31 December 1815.

14. 'Charles M'Gee'. John Thomas Smith. Published in *Vagabondia; or Anecdotes of Mendicant Wanderers through the Streets of London*, 31 December 1815.

15. 'The Sharp Family'. Johann Zoffany, 1779–81. Courtesy of the National Portrait Gallery, London and the Lloyd-Baker Trustees.

16. 'William Murray, Lord Mansfield'. J.S. Copley, 1783. Courtesy of the National Portrait Gallery, London.

17. 'The Generous Master or African Sincerity, a West-India Anecdote'. Argus del [C. Williams]. Published in *Caricatures*, Vol. X, 9 January 1819. Courtesy of the Trustees of the British Museum.

18. 'A Mungo Macaroni'. M. Darly. Published 10 September 1772. Courtesy of the Print Collection, Lewis Walpole Library, Yale University.

19. 'Slave Trade 1: Slaves in Bondage'. Anonymous, undated. Courtesy of the Trustees of the British Museum.

20. 'Slave Trade 2: In full enjoyment of liberty'. Anonymous, undated. Courtesy of the Trustees of the British Museum.

21. 'The New Union Club'. [Marryat] – G. Cruickshank (?). Published 19 July 1819. Courtesy of the Trustees of the British Museum.

22. 'The Country Concert'. C.L. Smith. Published 10 July 1794. Courtesy of the Print Collection, Lewis Walpole Library, Yale University.

Acknowledgements

I wish to thank the following people and institutions:

The Dean and Chapter of York Minister, for their kind permission to use Granville Sharp's letter book.

The Sierra Leone Collection, Special Collections, the University Library, the University of Illinois in Chicago, for the use of letters from Sierra Leone settlers.

The New York Historical Society, for the use of Granville Sharp's transcripts and notes on the court cases of Thomas Lewis and James Somerset, located in their 'B.V. Sec. Slavery' collection.

The New York Public Library, the Schomburg Center for Research in Black Culture, Astor, Lenox and Tilden Foundations, for the portraits of Ignatius Sancho and Olaudah Equiano.

The National Portrait Gallery, London, for the portrait of William Murray, Lord Mansfield.

For the use of the painting *The Sharp Family* by Johann Zoffany, I am grateful to the National Portrait Gallery, London and the Lloyd-Baker Trustees.

The Lewis Walpole Library of Yale University, Farmington, Connecticut, for the use of illustrations. Particular thanks to Joan H. Sussler, Curator of Prints.

The Trustees of the British Museum, for the use of illustrations from the Department of Prints and Drawings.

The Earl of Mansfield, for the use of the portrait of Lady Elizabeth Finch Hatton and Dido by Johann Zoffany.

The Trustees of the Wedgwood Museum, Barlaston, Staffordshire, for the photograph of the Slave Medallion by Josiah Wedgwood.

The Public Record Office, London, for the use of materials on the Committee for the Relief of the Black Poor.

The many libraries which assisted in my research, especially the Houghton Library and Widener Library of Harvard University; the British Library; the University of Texas at Austin; and especially the library and interlibrary loan office of Vassar College.

This book could not have been written without those whose important work preceded it, particularly Peter Fryer, Folarin Shyllon and James Walvin.

Special thanks to those editors who believed in this project: Grant McIntyre, Kate Chenevix Trench and Leslie Mitchner.

CHAPTER ONE

Paupers and Princes: Repainting the Picture of Eighteenth-Century England

One morning in 1765, Granville Sharp literally fell over the man who would change the course of not only his life but also those of thousands of black people in England. Going to visit his physician brother William at Mincing Lane, off Fenchurch Street, he encountered a battered seventeen-year-old African slave named Jonathan Strong, who was seeking free medical help at Dr Sharp's surgery. His master had long treated him violently and now, pistol-whipped, lame, feverish and nearly blind, Strong had finally been turned out into the streets as useless and nearly dead. Dr Sharp admitted him into St Bartholomew's Hospital and months later, when he had recovered, the brothers found a position for him with a local apothecary.

This happy resolution ended two years later when Strong's previous master discovered him running an errand for his new employer. Seeing him fit and healthy he arranged for Strong to be kidnapped and jailed, preparatory to being sold and shipped to a Barbados plantation. West Indian slavery meant almost certain early and painful death, and in desperation Strong sent for Granville Sharp from his imprisonment at Poultney Compter (or Counter), not realizing – or perhaps not caring – that Sharp had forgotten who he was.

When Sharp arrived he was startled into a clear and sudden understanding of slavery in Britain which changed and challenged his world view. He had, of course, been seeing black people for most of his life, probably even in Durham, his childhood home, but it was not until they became unified and personified by one individual that they came into focus for him. Like one who buys a red coat and then discovers that everyone around him seems to be wearing one, Sharp's London seemed suddenly populated by thousands of black people living and working under a legal system which recognized most of them only as property and denied them the most fundamental of rights. He was no social activist, but a modestly educated clerk with a meticulous and highly developed religious sense which carried him into a relentless battle for justice. Yet he, like most abolitionists, never became a proponent of racial equality even while devoting his life to racial justice.

As with Sharp, once the lens through which we view the eighteenth century is refocused, the London of Johnson, Reynolds, Hogarth and Pope – that elegant, feisty, intellectual and earthy place of neo-classicism and city chaos – becomes occupied by a parallel world of Africans and their descendants working and living alongside the English. They answer their doors, run their errands, carry their purchases, wear their livery, appear in their lawcourts, play their music, drink in their taverns, write in their newspapers, appear in their novels, poems and plays, sit for their portraits, appear in their caricatures and marry their servants. They also have private lives and baptize their own children, attend schools, bury their dead. They are everywhere in the pictures we have all seen and the pages we have turned. They were as familiar a sight to Shakespeare as they were to Garrick, and almost as familiar to both as they are to Londoners today.

Once I became aware of this, London seemed to me, as it did to Sharp, to be suddenly occupied by two simultaneous centuries. Walking to my bank near Piccadilly Circus or my publisher in Albemarle Street, I crossed the street alongside fashionable ladies with their young African pages and macaronis with their black footmen. I saw them in the crowds of tourists and theatre-goers at Covent Garden or Drury Lane. They panhandled on Tottenham Court Road or near St Paul's, darted out of grocers' shops, hawked their wares on the sidewalks, lounged on corners. When I went home or out with friends in the evening I saw them returning to their families and neighbourhoods, entering their own clubs and pubs. So clearly had I come to see them that I was amazed when

2

I entered a well-known London bookshop one day, searching for the paperback edition of Peter Fryer's exhaustive *Staying Power: The History of Black People in Britain*, and instead of assistance received a stern look from the saleswoman. 'Madam, there *were* no black people in England before 1945,' she said.

London, like all old cities, prides itself on the way reminders of the past coexist with and inform the present. But here was a case of the present erasing the past. I would like to have asked the bookseller to occupy a dual state for a time, to walk through the London she believes she knows and to paint back into the picture the thousands of people her view of history has erased, a people whose 'presence here goes back some 2,000 years and has been continuous since the beginning of the sixteenth century or earlier.'[1] While nearly five centuries have passed since the beginning of that continuous presence, a vivid trail of diaries, memoirs, public records and pictures remains. The satirical prints sold by seventeenth-, eighteenth- and early nineteenth-century booksellers still appear in shop windows on the King's Road and in Bloomsbury; the dozens of novels containing black characters from the same period are still in many libraries. My task in this book is to reconstruct London, and indeed the entire country, by altering our vision.

It is perhaps more difficult to decipher and reconstruct the attitude of earlier white Britons toward these 'newcomers' (as they were seen) than simply to repaint the picture. For example, most historians give 1555, when five Africans arrived to learn English and thereby facilitate trade, as the beginning of a continual black presence in Britain. By 1596 there were so many black people in England that Queen Elizabeth I issued an edict demanding that they leave. At that time slaves provided a lifetime of wageless labour for the cost of the initial purchase, and increased the status of the owner. Alarmed that they might be taking jobs and goods away from English citizens and that 'the most of them are infidels having no understanding of Christ or his Gospel,' the Queen issued another ineffectual edict, then finally commissioned a Lubeck merchant, Casper van Senden, to cart them off in 1601. '[I]f there shall be any person or persons which are possessed of any such blackamoors that refuse to deliver them,' the Queen

3

wrote, other citizens were to notify the government of their presence.[2]

Van Senden and the Queen waited in vain, for black people were by then firmly ensconced in Britain's houses, streets and ports and portrayed on its stages. Many still believe Queen Elizabeth to have been an opponent of slavery because she may have expressed concern about the fast-developing slave trade, even while simultaneously authorizing and bankrolling Sir John Hawkins, a man who later added a shackled African to his coat of arms, to compete with the Portuguese and Spanish for this lucrative market. He had already been doing so for over thirty years.

As early as the beginning of the sixteenth century black entertainers had begun to appear in Scotland. Imported by the royal courts they quickly became not only popular but fashionably essential in England as well. Elizabeth herself, like her father before her, brought into her court an African entertainer and a page, making it 'clearly difficult for her to take a stand against the employment of Blacks when monarchs and their court favourites had themselves seen fit to find a niche for them at court.'[3] In any case her own propagation of the English slave trade led inevitably to the increase of the Afro-British population, and the use of black servants and entertainers by royalty and nobility filtered down to much less affluent households and establishments. As long as black people were seen as fashion accessories, and as long as ownership of them was encouraged their numbers inevitably increased. James I continued the fashion in his more licentious court, where 'conspicuous fashionable consumption was flaunted, and Negroes, as part of that fashion, became more in evidence' – he had a group of black minstrels and his wife had black servants.[4] Whites 'blacked up' for roles as Africans in plays and masques. The theatrical draw then, as later, was in the visual contrast and spectacle, but also probably in the assumption that more behavioural and verbal freedom could occur under the guise of a 'black' skin.

Shakespeare understood something of the position of black people in Europe and of European reactions to them. Relying on his audiences' racial understanding, an awareness (for all its reductiveness) that has later been forgotten or dismissed, 'he was able to play upon the overt and subconscious reactions of English-men to the wider social implications of black humanity.'[5] Those implications were linguistic as well as dramatic, for as 'Ethiope' or 'blackamoor' the African became part of the everyday language of Englishmen.[6] When Shakespeare wrote *Othello* he was not, as past critics have argued, particularly 'confused' about racial identi-ties even though he, like subsequent writers, took great liberties in portraying racial difference on the stage. He too would have seen black people on the streets of London for most of his adult life, and so would his audience. Racial jokes and word play were well within their experience and understanding.

Those linguistic repercussions have other implications as well. The roots of many English names come from the word 'Moor': Moore, Blackmore, Morris, Morrison, Murray, Morrow and others probably derive from Moorish ancestry as well as owner-ship. Morris dancing may have a similar source. Heraldry gives dozens of examples of Negro heads on coats-of-arms. More than simply working their way into the language, such examples prove the intricate weaving of Africans into a developing sense of an English identity in which, as Stuart Hall says, 'images produce and sustain an uncodified but immensely powerful conservative sense of Englishness.'[7] The English only began to see themselves as 'white' when they discovered 'black' people.

Within Shakespeare's lifetime, however, the British involve-ment with the triangular trade – the exchange of goods and slaves between Britain, Africa and the Americas – began. It was a trade which permanently transformed the economies of all three areas. As the development of British colonies in the West Indies boomed, so did the black population of Britain as planters returned home with their black servants. In 1768 Sharp and others put the number of black servants in London at 20,000, out of a total London population of 676,250. (Others, depending upon the year and the source, put the figure somewhere between 10,000 and 30,000, although the accurate figure is probably closer to 15,000.) These numbers were augmented by sailors, by students sent to study in Britain, by musicians who had become *de rigueur* in English mili-tary and domestic orchestras and bands, later in the century by refugees from America who had fought on the loyalist side in exchange for promised freedom in Britain or land in Canada, and finally by the natural growth of the community.

By the eighteenth century the black population in England, particularly in London, had indeed become a community, with a concern for joint action and solidarity. When in 1773, for example, two black men were confined to Bridewell prison for begging, more than 300 black people not only visited them but provided for their economic and emotional support. In the later eighteenth century there were black pubs, churches and community meeting places, changing the picture of isolated individual domestic servants and roving beggars on London streets to that of a thriving and structured black community. At the same time there was a huge upswelling in the British abolitionist movement which kept the issue of slavery in the public eye through boycotts, newspaper articles and petitions. There was also an increasing number of accomplished blacks resident in Britain such as George Bridgtower, the concert violinist who knew Beethoven; Ignatius Sancho, who corresponded with Laurence Sterne; Francis Williams, who studied at Cambridge; and Ukawsaw Gronniosaw, grandson of an African king, who escaped from slavery and married an English widow, and later published his memoirs.

This growing presence challenged the English sensibilities about race and fairness and xenophobia at a time when interest in Paine's *Rights of Man* and *The Age of Reason* jostled with the financial and material rewards of slavery. To deal with this contradiction a whole intellectual industry of justifying slavery was necessary, finding exhaustive expression in David Hume's assertion of Negro inferiority, in Bryan Edwards' and Edward Long's treatises on the West Indies, running straight through to Carlyle's infamous *Discourse on the Nigger Question* ('. . . if the Black gentleman is born to be a servant, and, in fact, is useful in God's creation only as a servant, then let him hire not by the month, but by a very much longer term,' he wrote in 1849). Necessary to these theories was a history of belief about black people themselves which was often expressed by dramatic oppositions. Pro-slavers portrayed black people as vicious, stupid and improved by slavery; abolitionists erred on the side of sentiment to portray them as docile and innocent. Somewhere in the middle lay reality, what this book intends to explore.

Then as now however, reality battled with popular culture, and despite daily evidence to the contrary it was often popular culture that won. Newspaper advertisements to sell or retrieve slaves began appearing in the port cities of Britain in the seventeenth century. From a 1696 *London Gazette*: 'Run away from Captain John Brooke of Barford near Salisbury, about the middle of August last, a middle-sized Negro Man, named Humphrey, aged about 30, in a dark brown Cloath Coat with hair Buttons . . .'. An advertisement in a 1709 edition of *The Tatler* offered 'A Black boy, twelve years of age, fit to wait on a gentleman, to be disposed of at Denis's Coffee House in Finch Lane, near the Exchange,' and the *Liverpool Chronicle* offered in 1768 'A Fine Negroe Boy, of about 4 Feet 5 inches high. Of a sober, tractable, humane Disposition, Eleven or Twelve Years of Age, talks English very well, and can Dress Hair in a tollerable way.' Advertisements such as these abounded in the press for well over a hundred years. Despite the assertion in *The Gentleman's Magazine* in 1763 that the sale of a black boy by auction with the rest of his late master's belongings was 'perhaps the first instance of the kind in a free country,' such sales were in fact open and commonplace in England.[8]

A person could read these advertisements and sensational stories of revolts on West Indian plantations quite coolly in the morning newspaper, and then shed tears that evening over similar situations presented on stage. A slave sold in a coffee house in Liverpool, or run off from a master in Bristol, or paraded with padlocked collar in London, ironically aroused far less public sympathy than a white man or woman pretending to be a black person in the theatre. Aphra Behn's controversial story of the enslaved African prince *Oroonoko* was popular when it was published in 1688, but it was wildly successful when Thomas Southerne turned it into a play and transmogrified the black wife Imoinda into the daughter of a Frenchman. The theatre-going public was quite accepting of racial mixing when sentiment, honour and questions of class were involved. Thomas Morton deviated only slightly from the *Oroonoko* model in his opera *The Slave* which featured a fierce but honourable African slave defending the lives of a quadroon slave, her white lover and their child during a slave rebellion and its subsequent suppression. Like *Oroonoko* it took place in Surinam and pitted the natural fidelity of black against the unnatural artifice of white. Such displays appealed to the better instincts of white Britons, in some ways allowing them to ignore the conditions of slavers at home.

The most famous example of this was the story of Inkle and Yarico, presented as an opera by George Coleman in Covent Garden in 1787. This story became a touchstone for the complicated dealings between black and white, where love and honour – all the finer instincts so dear to the public – were pitted against social and commercial gain. The audience was willing to forgive the most egregious errors in geography and anthropology in which Africa and America were confused, and American Indian and Negro were interchangeable, in favour of the moral issue of broken promises and fidelity. Inkle, an Englishman on his way to Barbados to marry an heiress, is stranded in North America with his servant Trudge. Both are rescued by two black women, Yarico and Wowski (the former speaks perfect English even though Inkle and Trudge are the first white men she has ever seen), and fall in love. In Barbados Inkle changes his mind and arranges to sell Yarico while his more honourable servant Trudge remains faithful to Wowski. In the end Inkle is punished not for his attitude toward slavery, but for his broken promise to the woman who saved his life. The English governor of Barbados himself arranges the weddings between black and white, but it is a white serving-girl who has the final song:

> Let Patty say a word –
> A chambermaid may sure be heard –
> Sure men are grown absurd,
>   Thus taking black for white;
> To hug and kiss a dingy miss,
> Will hardly suit an age like this,
> Unless, here, some friends appear,
>   Who like this wedding night.

Vindicating a woman's honour, no matter whether English or African, was at the heart of the play's success, but the exotic and distant location of the opera diluted its arguments on behalf of racial equality.

What happened when such plays were set in Europe? Henry Bate's comic opera *The Black-a-moor Wash'd White*, featuring white actors playing blacks, caused a terrible riot which Garrick himself had to quell when it appeared at the Theatre Royal, Drury Lane on 22 January 1776. Apparently a political satire about foreign control over Britain (perceived here perhaps as the power of white West and East Indians' influence), the play involves an eccentric nobleman who dismisses his white servants 'and is determin'd to replace them with a suite of Blacks' because he believes his wife and daughter to be involved with the same young man and interested in others. The young man in question disguises himself as a Negro, appropriately named Amoroso, to gain entrance to the house, and much is made of his masquerade. As a black man, he is 'a woundly fine One! And with a Jacket for all the world lac'd like a Magpye!' and speaks in a dialect full of words like 'Massa'. When the only remaining white servant catches him hand in hand with the fair young Julia there are numerous references to 'Blackamoor Devils' and Othello and Desdemona. The speech that probably provoked the riot is one in which the white servant, horrified, exclaims that 'the times are turn'd topsey turvey, that white Englishmen should give place to foreign Blacks!' and sings the following ballad:

> Must a Christian man's Son born & bred up
> By a *Negar* be flung in disgrace?
> Be a sham'd for to hold his poor head up
> 'Cause as how he has got a white face?
> – No never mind it little Jerry
> Let your honest heart be merry;
> British boys will still be right
> 'Till they prove that *black is white*!

This almost literally brought the house down.[9]

Garrick also produced *High Life Below Stairs* which featured two black servants played by white actors. Written by Townley but often mistakenly attributed to Garrick, it was an indictment of class rather than racial offences. Isaac Bickerstaffe's 1768 opera *The Padlock* was also successful in a European setting, and also avoided the issue of miscegenation. A typical farce in many ways, it has a central black character who speaks squarely against slavery. He is rude and sometimes drunken, but is allowed to declaim against the beatings he receives from his 'Massa' who 'lick[s] me every day with [his] rattan', and gets the final word in the last scene. His stock slave name of Mungo became a byword in late eighteenth-century political circles when a Colonel Barré applied it in a 1769 debate to Jeremiah Dyson, who apparently did the government's dirty work. The name stuck and afterwards Dyson generally was caricatured and cartooned as a black man, often in the guise of Soubise, the pampered slave of the Duchess of Queensberry. Mungo also became a synonym for any rude and forward black man in Britain, as with the anonymous 1792 engraving 'The Rabbits', in which a black man sells rabbits to a white woman who holds one disapprovingly by the hind legs. 'Be gar Misse dat no fair,' Mungo says to her. 'If Blacke Man take you by Leg so – you smell too.'

Other slave portrayals found their way more or less crudely into print and public conversation. When the Prince of Wales fell in love, or at least dallied, with a mulatto woman on his way home from the Americas, the popular artists wasted no time in christening her "Wowski" after the character in Coleman's opera and drawing them lying together in a hammock with her breasts exposed. The engravers and writers knew in these and other cases that they could 'rely upon a general understanding of the significance of [their] ideas and terminology . . . When evoking African or black imagery, writers were in effect appealing to the conscious and subconscious responses of white people recently made aware of the enormous differences between black and white.'[10] When, for example, as early as 1690 Dryden wrote a prologue to Beaumont and Fletcher's *The Prophetess*, he joked that English soldiers under William III in Ireland should 'Each bring his love a Bogland captive home; Such proper pages will long trains become;/With copper collars and with brawny backs,/Quite to put down the fashion of our blacks.' The audience easily understood not only the commonly repeated comparison of Irish to Negroes, and the allusion to black slaves' padlocked collars, a fashion which supported a whole industry of metalworkers and jewellers, but of the common use of black people as ornaments themselves.

Even while black people in general and black slaves in particular fell into certain proscribed types of representation, however, one of the common reactions to their plight was an ironic and unabashed bathos. Never was this better demonstrated than on Wednesday, 9 May 1759, when the theatre-going public of London was treated to a double drama. Two Africans, one of them a recently rescued enslaved prince, attended a production of Thomas Southerne's adaptation of *Oroonoko* at the Theatre Royal, Drury Lane. The young men received a standing ovation as they entered, and during Oroonoko's final speech, all eyes were on them as much as on the actors. The recent captives wept at the play's conclusion, but the audience wept even more in watching them do so. Here were theatre and transference at their finest, and London lapped it up. An English actor could induce catharsis in an African by pretending 'to be' someone like him; the audience could view both scenes simultaneously, and applaud both, then read a description of it the next week in *The Gentleman's Magazine*.

This prince, William Ansah Sessarakoo, was constantly in the news, and he and his companion were in demand everywhere. Their story inspired poetry and drama, and a fifty-three-page history, *The Royal African: Or, Memoir of the Young Prince of Annamaboe*. Briefly the facts were these: the young prince had been sent to London for education and, like the legendary Oroonoko, had been deceived by the ship's captain who 'instead of performing his promise, sold him to a gentleman in London.'[11] The prince's father commanded a powerful African trading area, and both French and English companies were courting his favour. To ensure continued trade, the French had invited one of his sons to Paris, where he stayed for some time learning French political and economic practices. Not to be outdone, the English later proposed the same thing for William, who already spoke English and considered the English traders his mentors and friends. Greed got the better of the English ship captain, and he decided instead to settle the king's debt to them by selling the prince in Barbados, where the ship next sailed on its triangular route. France and England were then at war, with battles between their ships taking place off the coast of Annamaboe (Ghana today); both countries wanted the king to choose a European national alliance. His fury with the English over their duplicitousness in selling William first led him to choose the French, but he later changed his mind when the English agreed to retrieve the young man and take him and another young African from Barbados to London as promised.

Few cases of slavery aroused English public indignation and excitement as much as this one. Nicknamed 'Cupid' by the English traders in Africa because of his sweet and trusting personality, William became an immediate favourite with everyone. Sentimental poems about him appeared almost immediately, addressed from him to a fictitious African lover named 'Zara', and from 'Zara' back to him. Samuel Johnson referred to this and similar cases when he wrote that 'In our own time, princes have been sold, by wretches to whose care they were entrusted, that they might have an European education; but when once they were brought to a market in the plantations, little would avail either their dignity or their wrongs.'[12] The Africans' desire for European education and their exotic nobility were irresistible to the public, which had a sentimental bent coupled with a righteous indignation, but this passion seemed reserved for those Africans who were 'wrongly' enslaved. As Wylie Sypher later put it, 'few besides anti-slavery crusaders seem to have paid much attention to the 14,000 Negro servants in England. But your free-born Briton could feel for a prince, particularly a prince in distress.'[13] In eighteenth-century Britain issues of race also involved issues of class, and both were fodder for high and low drama.

Sometimes the schemes to educate Africans as go-betweens for trade backfired, and the cost of maintaining them in England exceeded expectations. Yet despite one letter of 1755, to the governor of Cape Coast Castle from the 'Company of Merchants Trading in Africa', complaining that two black students 'have cost above £600 for Education, maintenance &c. since their being in England,' it was a common practice, according to one slave ship captain, for 'merchants and commanders of ships to Africa, to encourage the natives to send their children to England; as it not only conciliates their friendship, and softens their manners, but adds greatly to the security of the traders.'[14] Soon African leaders regularly began sending their sons to England, as they had already done to Portugal and Spain, to learn some of the ways of the Europeans with whom they traded. Christopher Fyfe estimates that in 1789 there were approximately 'fifty boys and twenty-eight girls in Liverpool, London, Bristol and Lancaster, all from the Sierra Leone region'.[15] Some of these (mostly young men) were dispatched to a variety of small schools around Liverpool to learn English and other useful commercial skills, while later in the century others were sent by missionaries to London for more comprehensive educations. There was also a third group of black students, for some West Indian planters sent their biracial as well as their white children to England to be educated. (This is the precedent for Rhoda Swartz in Thackeray's *Vanity Fair*.)

Like Oroonoko and the young prince of Annamaboe, it was not unusual for unscrupulous ship captains to view their African charges as financial opportunities rather than as commissions, and to sell the young men. Because of a situation similar to this, the English discovered in 1733 that there were already well-educated Africans. Taught by his father, a Muslim imam of royal lineage, a young man named Job ben Solomon was captured in Gambia in 1731 and sold for £45 in Maryland. Desperate, he sent a letter in Arabic to his father via London, where General James Oglethorpe took it to Oxford to be translated. 'The translation pleased him so much, and gave him so good an opinion of the man,' noted *The Gentleman's Magazine* later, 'that he directly ordered him to be bought from his master' and carried to England.[16] When he arrived in London two years after his enslavement, Job could translate between Arabic and English and was taken up by the English nobility. He stayed fourteen months and was continually 'lionized and fêted by polite society, treated as an equal by some of the country's greatest scholars and heeded by the nation's élite . . . A handsome, congenial man, Job was besieged by invitations from all quarters, notably from the Court. City merchants, scholars, philanthropists, aristocrats and those who were merely curious, vied with each other to sample the unusual spectacle of a scholarly African in their midst.'[17] Novelists were quick to incorporate characters based on him in their works, and Hannah More, Joseph Lavallé and Henry Mackenzie among others used actual and invented rescued princes in their works.

Audiences then, both literary and theatrical, were accustomed to seeing actual black people in the theatre as both subject and spectators. They also knew them as musicians and performers at fairs, not only in the metropolis but also in such places as Lancashire and Dublin.[18] The theatre in eighteenth-century London not only presented people the way they were but the way they wished to be. It allowed a move from mere representation to metaphor, often against a backdrop of a black presence at home and abroad. Let us start our tour in Covent Garden, at the Theatre Royal.

Around and inside this theatre, like that in Drury Lane, a crush of people scrambled for tickets, seats and attention. Onstage were performers as well as high-paying customers, who sometimes sat close enough to converse with the actors, be seen by the audience, and even cross in front of the action to meet friends. Orange sellers' wares caused a continual rain of peel from the boxes and galleries on to those in the pit. There were ladies accompanied by ornately outfitted black boys who carried their pillows and opera glasses, and more ordinary people, including servants both black and white with the time and the shilling necessary to sit in the cheapest seats in the upper gallery.[19] We know from Ignatius Sancho's letters that independent black people also attended the theatre. Aided by his friend David Garrick, the hugely famous actor and theatre-manager, Sancho even made an abortive attempt at acting the role of Oroonoko in the 1760s.

Outside the building hawkers and pickpockets flourished, as did prostitutes. *Harris's List* and other catalogues recorded them and their bordellos. Not only were there black prostitutes, driven like their much more numerous white counterparts to the profession by poverty and desperation, there was at least one, probably more, all-black brothel. (It was an age of specialization in this regard – there were also brothels specializing in flagellation and homosexuality.)[20]

In summer there would in all likelihood be a fair nearby; they lasted from two to six weeks and drew thousands of revellers to their performances and booths. Leaving Covent Garden for

Smithfield there was Bartholomew Fair where, as at Southwark Fair, all walks of life came together, although the pleasure gardens of Ranelagh and Vauxhall were more to the taste of the upper classes. These fairs featured acrobats, puppeteers, rope dancers, jugglers, magicians, many of whom were black. For evidence we have pictures like Hogarth's 1733 painting of Southwark Fair where, amidst the rough-and-tumble of crowds and performers, two figures are prominent in the centre foreground: a tall and elegantly dressed white woman beating a drum, and in front of her an ornately dressed black boy blowing a trumpet as he marches along. A detail from Rowlandson's 'Show Booths of the Fair' shows people on the swing-boat ride, some of them getting ill; in front of them is a black man who works at the fair. Black fairground performers were likely to elicit amused references to 'the devil on two sticks', an obvious allusion to both their colour and their agility whose origins lie in early presentations of the devil as black. Visitors would also have been fascinated by such exhibits as George Alexander Grattox, 'The Spotted Negro Boy'. A 1731 fair in Bristol featured a shaved bear, wearing a checked coat and trousers and seated in a large chair, called 'an Ethiopian savage'.[21]

Towards St James's, Pall Mall and the Strand, the visual contrast between black skin and white skin became obvious. This was the heart of appearance-conscious London, where the crowding, crime, smells and unsanitariness of ordinary life were at first less noticeable. Here the wealthy could afford to replace their rotted teeth with those pulled from the mouths of poor children; to wear over unwashed skin elaborately embroidered clothes costing what would support a destitute family for a year or two, while their pockets were being picked of handkerchiefs and watches; to buy and sell black people and flaunt their ownership while arguing the abstractions of liberty in coffee houses. If London was in the eighteenth-century a city of contrasts, then St James's in its unreal ostentation was its microcosm.

Nowhere does this study in extremes show itself better than in the deliberately exaggerated differences of skin colour. That white women complemented themselves with black pages is well known; the darker the skin the more valuable the child, and the more elaborate and expensive the livery purchased to set it off. Given classical names like Pompey and Caesar, they were dressed in brightly-coloured silks and satins, silver padlocked collars, and feathered turbans. They walked behind their ladies, and 'it was the duty of the little negro boy, in the service of the lady of quality in the last century, to attend his mistress's person and tea-table, to carry her train as she moved to and fro, to take charge of her fan and smelling-salts, to feed her parrots, and to comb her lap-dogs.'[22] Clothing, always a marker of class, by its very opulence ironically indicated the lowliness of the slave's position even though he may have been treated as a pampered pet. His function was just as frivolous as his appearance, and as hers. In an often deadly concession to physical contrast, many women exaggerated their fairness by painting their skin white with a poisonous lead-based make-up.

William Combe, in his satirical novel *Devil upon Two Sticks in England*, mentions a 'charming woman in deep mourning, followed by a black boy, in a fantastic livery',[23] and Charles Dunster's poem 'St James's Street' similarly discusses the folly of fashionable women accompanied by the black boys they owned:

> E'en now they come. Before them onward march
> In garb of State, with each his lofty Cane,
> His fierce-cocked Hat, and Bouquet blooming bright,
> Their powder'd Footmen. – Sometimes at their head,
> Index of Rank or Opulence supreme,
> A sable Youth from Æthiopia's climes,
> In milk-white Turban dight, precedes the Train. –
> The Fair herself, in narrow compass press'd,
> (While much of outward ornament her Chair
> Boasts, not unconscious of its Tassels gay,
> Its jetty Varnish, and gilt Coronets
> Which shine o' th' top), in posture comfortless
> Rides pinion'd, while her Hoop's reverted sides
> With whalebone strong her elbows cramp'd confine.
> Her head meantime sinks down, nor dares assume
> Its wonted port. The little vehicle
> Admits not that the lovely Nymph within
> Should sit erect when to her native Height
> She adds three feet of various Ornament . . .[24]

16

The Character of a Town Misse, published in 1675, stated that the 'fashionable high-class whore of the period' (Fryer's definition of a 'Town Miss') 'hath always two necessary Implements about her, a *Blackamoor*, and a little *Dog*; for without these, she would be neither *Fair* nor *Sweet*'.[25] The black page appeared in all types of artistic productions. Painters loved them for the visual contrast and drama they lent to portraits, and the subjects loved what the inclusion of them in their portraits said about their own economic status. Engravers and caricaturists loved them for the way they silently pronounced judgement on social and political vanity. In the several versions of the cartoon 'Heyday, is it my daughter Anne?' a mother stands amazed at the outrageously high hair of her citified daughter. The daughter's black page seems to reinforce her vanity yet he gapes at her openly.

Hogarth used black pages relentlessly in his visual attacks on white duplicity. In picture after picture they attest to the infidelity, crudeness and vanity of the people who owned them. It is from the caricaturists, says one nineteenth-century writer, 'that we can learn so much about a nation's manners and customs, ways and fashions, and other interesting matters too trivial for record at the hands of dignified history.'[26] He writes with painful nostalgia about eighteenth-century black London that was picturesque and flamboyant, in his hands itself a caricature.

The negro coachman, a very portly person, with powder over his curly pate; the negro footman, in a brilliant livery, stately of port and stalwart of body, if somewhat unshapely as to his nether limbs; in how many illustrations of social life do not these worthies appear? Then there is a splendid negro, wearing an embroidered Oriental dress, a member of the band of the Grenadier or Coldstream Guards, who plays the cymbals, gesticulating vivaciously – partly, it must be, owing to excessive enjoyment of his situation – with his fellow performer, of similar complexion and costume, who plays an instrument that has vanished with its sable professor; a brazen structure, tree-shaped, with bells depending from its branches. Other negroes there are who sell songs, sweep crossings, knit nightcaps and stockings, and manufacture garden-nets – stout negroes, indeed, of all kinds . . .[27]

17

He yearns for a past the scope of which he gets right but which he interprets incorrectly. For him the black inhabitants of eighteenth-century London come to stand for its entirety, metonyms of a colourful and jolly time unlike his own. The black men and women he envisages are enthusiastic and happy in their enslavement, delighting in their own vividness, eager to please and easily pleased.

> Some of us must surely possess youthful reminiscences of these Cæsars and Pompeys of the past. How they grinned! How they shone! How picturesque they were! They glorified the livery they assumed; they sublimated their plush. There was no killing their complexion; the brighter were the hues brought to bear upon it, so much the blacker, and, therefore, the better it looked. A negro might wear a dress made of the flamingo's feathers – he would set them off, as they would him.[28]

In attempting to recall childhood's colourful innocence, he reduces black people to children. His Negroes have rolling eyes, flashing white teeth and 'ebon face[s]' which 'gleam'.[29]

None of this was real life, of course. The underside was in Africa, on slave ships, and in the Caribbean and the Americas. The livery and the turbans resulted from the slave trade, New World slavery, and a plantation economy. Trade had brought silk and cotton to English backs, coffee, tea and sugar to their tables, and a romantic primitivism to their art and literature. But the tea, the sugar they stirred into it, and sometimes the very cups themselves existed because of the forced labour of black people, and the reminders of this inequality were around them daily. England itself provided plenty of contrasting scenes, reminders that the evils of West Indian slavery could be transported along with material goods.

In other areas of the country there was quite another aspect of black eighteenth-century life. All those runaways and castoffs had to go somewhere, and out of necessity many gravitated to white slums. In 1783 this poverty-stricken population was drastically augmented by black immigrants from North America, those who had fought for Britain in the American war and now arrived for their promised freedom. The black soldiers of revolutionary America – some 20 per cent of all who fought in that war, on both sides, were black – became beggars in London. For poor blacks there were few options. The itinerant of any race had little hope of steady employment. As early as 14 September 1731, blacks were forbidden by the Lord Mayor's proclamation to learn trades. It was a time when tradesmen were strictly regulated in all English cities in an attempt to protect local business and discourage migration. Lord Mansfield, who later had to preside over the Somerset suit brought by Granville Sharp to challenge slavery in Britain, repeatedly ruled that 'black servants were not entitled to wages or poor law relief' because 'the statutes do not relate to them, nor had they them in contemplation.'[30] There was a real possibility of starvation and homelessness in England. If, like Jonathan Strong, a slave ran away from his or her owner, there was a danger of recapture and the prospect of a worse enslavement, even perhaps early death, in the West Indies. Thomas Day's famous poem 'The Dying Negro' told the true story of the suicide of a black man stolen from England and from his English wife, who shot himself on a boat on the Thames rather than face slavery.

Some poor blacks found shelter in the areas of St Giles or Seven Dials, St Paul's, Ratcliff and Limehouse,[31] and along the Wapping riverside.[32] Since St Giles was also the patron saint of beggars, there was something of a pun in naming of this particular population 'St Giles' blackbirds'. Derelict tenements in these neighbourhoods were known as 'rookeries', not because of their black residents but because of the crowded nests they resembled. Housing, when it existed at all for poverty-stricken Londoners of any race, was dismal. The stench of London at this time is well-documented and a Dr Willan, writing in his 1801 *Diseases in London*, describes the housing and sanitary conditions of poor neighbourhoods vividly:

. . . from three to eight individuals of different ages often sleep in the same bed; there being in general but one room and one bed for each family . . . The room occupied is either a deep cellar, almost inaccessible to the light, and admitting of no change of air; or a garret with a low roof and small windows, the passage to which is close, kept dark, and filled not only with bad air, but with putrid excremental effluvia from a vault at the bottom of the staircase. Washing of linen, or some other disagreeable business, is carried on, while infants are left dozing and children more advanced kept at play whole days on the tainted bed: some unsavoury victuals are from time to time cooked: in many instances idleness, in others the cumbrous furniture or utensils of trade, with which the apartments are clogged, prevent the salutary operation of the broom and white-washing brush and favour the accumulation of a heterogeneous filth.[33]

These were not racially defined ghettoes. Black people forced to live in such areas shared these unsanitary conditions with poor whites who made up the majority of the population.

A more personal account of black poverty in England comes in the heartbreaking plea for help in *A Narrative of the Most Remarkable Particulars in the Life of James Albert Ukasaw Gronniosaw, an African Prince, as Related by Himself*. If the English loved a good rescue and an educated exotic, not all literate and freed Africans were treated so generously. Published in 1814 in Leeds, this short autobiography (later used as the basis for Caryl Phillips' novel *Cambridge*) outlines his capture in Africa as a boy, his slavery, Christian conversion, education and manumission (granting of freedom) in New York, and subsequent poverty in England.

In London he first lodged in Petticoat Lane, one of the areas Dr Willan mentions as containing some of 'the wretched inhabitants' of poor London. Like the buildings Willan mentions, this one housed textile workers whose rooms were also their sweatshops; here the looms of silk weavers contributed to the noise from the overcrowded buildings and streets. Unlike the entirely negative picture Willan paints, Gronniosaw found the place friendly and welcoming, even though London (and Portsmouth where he first landed) was filled with people eager to fleece newcomers. His landlady, 'a gentlewoman', introduced him to a female weaver who 'smiled upon us, and I loved her from that moment. She asked me many questions; and I in return talked a great deal to her . . . I began to entertain a good opinion of her, though I was almost afraid to indulge this inclination, lest she should prove like all the rest I had met with at Portsmouth, &c. and which had almost given me a dislike to all white women.'[34] He travelled to Amsterdam, where he was encouraged to marry a Dutch servant who 'was willing to accept of me,' but remained faithful to his weaver, Betty, and returned to marry her.[35]

Interestingly, the minister and other members of his London church objected to this marriage not because of Gronniosaw's race but because of the wife's financial situation. Elizabeth was a poor widow 'in debt, and with a child, so that they persuaded me against it out of real regard to me.'[36] He paid off her debts and they married, and their marriage would have been a happy one except for gruelling poverty. They removed to Colchester but the conditions for the working poor led to a series of lost jobs. Employers could let workers go at will, even during the bitterest winters, and pay what they pleased. Even though both husband and wife worked hard at whatever jobs they could find, in Colchester, Norwich and Kidderminster, and though Gronniosaw was often treated kindly by employers, a periodic lack of work and a refusal to beg led them and their children to the brink of starvation. When one of their children died, they were thwarted by local laws which refused burial to nonparishioners and the unbaptized. His final paragraph outlines their subsequent difficulties: 'my wife by hard labor at the loom, does every thing that can be expected from her, towards the maintenance of our family; and God is pleased to incline his people to yield us their charitable assistance, being myself through age and infirmities able to contribute but little to their support. And as poor pilgrims, we are travelling through many difficulties, waiting patiently for the gracious call, when the Lord shall deliver us out of the evils of this present world, and bring us to the *everlasting glories* of the world to come.'[37]

Gronniosaw's story is remarkable less for the light it sheds on racial issues than on ordinary English life at that period. We would expect in such a tale overwhelming problems of race, but these rarely figure. Mixed-race marriages tended not to be seen as problematic to the English because they primarily occurred among the lower working classes. The American academic Benjamin Silliman was appalled to see on Oxford Street 'a well-dressed white girl, who was of ruddy complexion, and even handsome, walking arm in arm, and conversing very sociably, with a [black] man, who was as well dressed as she, and so black that his skin had a kind of ebony lustre.'[38] Coming from a country where such relations were considered legitimate cause for murder, he seems to be as upset by the black man's wealth as by the miscegenation. The real fear here was that if black people weren't forced to quit England 'the natural beauty of Britons' would be ruined by 'stain and contamination'[39] caused by 'the Morisco tint'.[40] Philip Thicknesse noticed that in 'every town, nay in almost every village, are to be seen a little race of mulattoes, mischievous as monkeys, and infinitely more dangerous.'[41]

The cases of inter-racial marriage are far too common to delineate here, for the high proportion of black men to black women in Britain made it inevitable that some men would look to white women for companionship. That the latter were not averse to such unions is visually clear in the prints and engravings of Hogarth and Rowlandson, among numerous others, as well as in novels and plays, and that race was secondary, to the working class at least, is also clear from Gronniosaw's story. Instead he gives us a picture of the formidability of life for the working poor. Food, housing, work, medical care, burial – these fundamentals were often inadequate, sometimes non-existent. When we read about the concentration of thieves in poor slums, we must remember that these districts were also populated by those whose only recourse to starvation and death was frequently theft, prostitution and beggary.

According to novelist Elizabeth Helme's 1761 guidebook to London we find no fewer than seventeen streets, lanes, alleys, courts and yards named after black people. There were eight Black Boy Alleys (off Chick Lane, Barnaby Street, Rosemary Lane, near Peter's Hill on Thames Street, and in Southwark, Lambeth and Saltpetre Bank), a Black Boy Court off Long Acre, a Blackmoor's Head Yard near St James's Square, a Blackmoor Street in Claremarket, and Blackmoor's Alleys in Farthing Fields, Green Lane in Wapping, and St Martin's Lane off Charing Cross. Defoe, who wrote so contradictorily about black people in his various novels and pamphlets, had a publisher located on one of these. One of the most famous areas for thieves in London was the interestingly named Blackboy's Alley, even though proportionately few of the English criminals there were of African origin. There are records of black criminals hung or imprisoned from time to time.

As was customary at the time, many street names derived from the large, colourful and sometimes dangerously hung signs of local businesses. The trade in black people and the fruits of their labour was big business. Because they were viewed as picturesque and easily identifiable, it is no wonder that they were frequently displayed on signs and the cards of commercial traders offering such products as 'Black Boy and Sugar Loaf' along with various other tobaccos. Where signboards helped identify the unnamed and unnumbered addresses of London they also came to identify the entire street. London, 'if not actually "swamped" . . . by flesh-and-blood blacks, was "swamped" by *images* of blacks. London in the eighteenth century was *visually* black in this respect.'[42]

Not all such street names derived from shops and commercial enterprises. Surely some of them came, like the names of other streets and lanes, from one-time residents. Perhaps the saddest of these was Black Mary's Hole, 'a few straggling houses near the Cold Bath fields, in the road to Hampstead', wrote Elizabeth Helme. It was named for 'a Blackamoor woman called Mary, who about thirty years ago lived by the side of the road near the Stile in a small circular hut built with stones'.[43] The story of how Mary got there is lost. It could be the end of a history of abuse or the beginning of a lonely and destitute freedom.

But there is also plenty of evidence of a thriving black community in the period and of black people who achieved a comfortable and even, by contemporary standards, prosperous level of life. These 'met, lived, and entertained themselves in little black enclaves within the city of London. The houses of well-placed Negroes often became a focal point . . .'[44] This community was made up of those who 'one after the other, fled from bondage, heading for the poor alleyways and warrens of London. These runaways formed the kernel of a very distinct group of Blacks who were free and largely self-sufficient. In the course of the eighteenth century around this group there developed a free black community.'[45] It wasn't only escaped slaves who made up this community. Former slaves gained their freedom through legal

23

channels and as a result of charitable masters, or arrived as free people in the first place, or made up vital members of musical groups, particularly military bands (one was even a friend of Mozart). The renowned shopkeeper and former slave Ignatius Sancho was not the only black to be befriended by the rich and famous: the Prince of Wales himself had a well-to-do black friend about whom, sadly, little is known.

Reconstructing this community is far more difficult than recounting individuals mentioned in newspaper advertisements, wills and memoirs. At a time when literacy was low but advancing among the rank-and-file, it is no surprise that a population newly escaped from slavery would leave little written record. Much of what we can discover is in the form of educated whites' reactions to the growing black population rather than from blacks themselves. Even so, what glimpses we have speak volumes. A newspaper article from 1764 refers to 'no less than 57 [black] men and women' who held a party filled with music at a Fleet Street pub.[46] Dozens of black people sat in the gallery at the famous Somerset suit in 1772, and hundreds celebrated afterwards at a Westminster pub, charging admission. Edward Long, a notorious racist, complained after the Somerset trial that not only was the black population of England growing, but that they were encouraging and helping each other.[47] Philip Thicknesse, an overt racist and recognized in the press and in political cartoons as an eccentric, complained in 1778 that 'London abounds with an incredible number of these black men, who have clubs to support those who are out of place.'[48] In other words, not only must a viable communal network have existed, but it could be quickly and effectively mobilized for the purposes of social and political action, even at a time when their political clout seemed non-existent.

The fact that the black population was steadily increasing and an active black community was forming probably accounts for the developing fear of the black presence in Britain. Sir John Fielding, in his *Extracts from . . . the Penal Laws*, worried in 1768 that black people were becoming inappropriately influenced by notions of equality once they got to Britain.[49] Reactions such as these, unlike those of Elizabeth I, preceded a sudden influx of black immigration in 1783 and were the result of black people talking to each other in substantial numbers and acting in concert.

The burgeoning of the black population during an already vital and shifting century makes this particular period interesting. The century begins, for the purposes of this book, somewhat before 1700 and ends close to the beginning of Victoria's reign in 1837, coinciding with the end of slavery in the West Indies. Over this period we can watch English racial attitudes evolve from a kind of naïve – and not necessarily benign – curiosity into surprisingly modern and complicated beliefs about race. Captain Hugh Crow, who commanded the last slave ship to leave Liverpool, genuinely liked Africans even while believing that transporting them into slavery was reasonable and godly. Time and again, during the long press for abolition of the slave trade and then slavery itself, humanitarianism lost to commerce under the guise of phil-anthropy. After the slave trade ended and, later, slavery itself, and planters ceased to return to England with their black retainers, the Victorians gradually lost the black presence their predecessors had known. Like Carlyle, some became genuine racists, but when Harriet Beecher Stowe's sentimental abolitionist novel *Uncle Tom's Cabin* appeared in America in 1851–2, it started an English craze: they papered nursery walls with 'Topsy' wallpaper, bought Topsy dolls, and developed plays centred on the novel and its characters. The nostalgic Victorian writer quoted earlier exemp-lifies this romanticized view.

When we think about the often cold-hearted eighteenth-century view of slaves and slavery, we should recall that it was a cold-hearted and violent era. Travel between cities was infrequent, slow and extremely dangerous, and highwaymen and footpads abounded after dark. Especially among footpads who had no horses on which to escape, murder commonly accompanied rob-bery. Even the linkboys hired to accompany people home in the unlit city streets could not be entirely trusted. Corporal punish-ment was the norm, with flogging and hanging not only typical punishments but public entertainment. Those put into stocks often died at the hands of a zealous public which pelted them with everything from vegetables and mud to rocks. Particularly in the earlier part of the century witches were still feared and drowned, and those convicted were sometimes burned alive.[50] Prisons were so disease-ridden that inmates often died before trial or release. Indeed, official visitors to such places carried their own disinfectant and had to avoid contaminating others for hours after they left. Child labour was unregulated, and in certain London parishes infant mortality was astoundingly high. Cockfighting replaced bear baiting as good fun. Middle- and low-income families often lived in one room, with no windows for ventilation and light, and with only a single change of clothing, if that. Chamber pots were placed in dining rooms, even among the well-to-do. Offal and sewage were disposed of in the streets, and vegetables, pure milk and uncontaminated water were almost unheard of in the centre of large cities.[51]

Given all this, the complacent attitude towards slavery becomes part of the general fabric of life. Sentiment and fashion notwithstanding, slavery developed hand-in-hand with trade which brought variety and luxury even to ordinary lives. Rum and sugar replaced mead and honey, and few wanted to go back to a time when such things were unavailable even though they remained precious and expensive (one common servants' perquisite was the right to sell a family's used tea leaves). Cotton, because it was easily washable and cheap, made it possible to own changes of clothes and to clean one's clothing and sheets. Wealth poured into the ports of Liverpool, Bristol and London. If slavery made such things possible, the common attitude seems to have been, then so be it; life was hard for everyone. Judges were unwilling to rule on the side of human rights when the national economy and a great deal of human comfort seemed to depend upon its avoidance. As long as they appeared to have no voice or power, black people's enslavement could be viewed as an improvement not only over their former unchristian state, but over the difficult lives of millions of white English citizens.

Who were these men and women, chosen to serve not in spite of but because of their race? Did they have friends, wives and husbands, a community? What did they wear, whom did they serve, to what did they aspire? If servitude and illiteracy allowed few white English-born to leave lasting records of their lives, how much more difficult must it have been for those for whom English might well have been a second language, and England a second or even third homeland. With very few exceptions we know little about black people of the eighteenth century through their own voices, words or desires. There is a disjuncture between what was said about them and what they must have felt about themselves as insiders who were also outsiders, about the centuries-long struggle for control over their movements, about the routine of their daily lives.

Each time a letter or memoir mentions a momentous occasion at which a 'faithful black' was present, we must put words into silent mouths and question the participant's or critic's interpretation of action or motive. Even such a painstaking historian as J. Jean Hecht reads Jack Russell's comment in 1751 that 'Mr. [Samuel] Eyre's Black turns out badly and [I] believe he intends sending him immediately, without any of his friends will accept of him'[52] and automatically interprets it as a character deficiency on the part of the slave.[53] Like Hecht, the prolific scholar M. Dorothy George wrote sympathetically about black people in eighteenth-century Britain, yet also was able to characterize the filth of London streets before the Paving Acts as 'suggest[ing] a colony of Hottentots'.[54] Reade, the biographer of Francis Barber, Samuel Johnson's well-known servant, presents him with boundless compassion yet nonetheless refers to him as a 'nigger boy': ('and it must be remembered,' he adds, 'that negroes remain "boys" until the utmost period of decrepit longevity').[55] He has 'a negro's simple brain'[56] even though there is an attempt to present him as intelligent. In trying to determine the date of Barber's marriage to a white woman Reade justifies his conclusion by saying that 'we do not associate the negro temperament with long engagements.'[57] Reade was writing in 1912, at a time when the comfortably assumed 'we' of author and audience excluded people like his subject. More recent historians have done a better job of placing the black people of Britain squarely into the picture of the times and avoiding such racial pitfalls. They have given us a far more comprehensive frame; the next step is to imagine more fully representative lives. As Aesop's Lion said to the Man, 'There are many statues of men slaying lions, but if only the lions were sculptors there might be quite a different set of statues.'[58]

How then to present fully the black inhabitants of eighteenth-century England? The voices we have are primarily those of people who were not only literate but who had the leisure to record their lives and responses. Many white people left paper trails about themselves and those around them, but black people who could read and write or who impressed white people enough to be written about must represent a much larger group of forgotten souls. For this 'privileged' group – for privilege is a relative term – much of their lives took place below stairs. They sometimes were even able to move into economic and social independence. They were not, particularly in the last quarter of the eighteenth century, necessarily representative of the average black person in England any more than a valued footman was representative of the average indentured servant; they were simply far more likely to be noticed, written about or painted by those in the public eye. The difference between what whites said about blacks and what black people had to say about their own lives amongst white people must have been enormous. I wish I had said to that ponderous bookseller what Richard Holmes writes in *Footsteps*: 'that the past is not simply "out there", an objective history to be researched or forgotten, at will; but that it lives most vividly in all of us, deep inside, and needs constantly to be given expression and interpretation.'

> . . . the lives of great artists and poets and writers are not, after all, so extraordinary by comparison with everyone else. Once known in any detail and any scope, every life is something extraordinary, full of particular drama and tension and surprise, often containing unimagined degrees of suffering or heroism, and invariably touching extreme moments of triumph and despair, though frequently unexpressed. The difference lies in the extent to which one is eventually recorded, and the other is eventually forgotten.[59]

Jack Beef, Francis Barber, Elizabeth Clements, Olaudah Equiano, Ignatius Sancho, Jonathan Strong, Henry Soubise, and others: these are the black people whose lives we follow in the following chapters, and whose stories give us an entirely different viewpoint on eighteenth-century English society.

CHAPTER TWO

High Life below Stairs

Perhaps it is because readers are accustomed to stories of slavery in the Americas that stories about slavery in Britain have such an ability to surprise. We imagine large plantations, even though quite a number of American slaves lived on small farms, and in towns and cities. We assume them to have lived in all-black enclaves with little daily contact with whites unless they were house slaves. To envisage them in London and around the towns of England is a big leap, and yet there they were, both in the community at large or individually in domestic service, military service and schools. The daily details of their lives have been gleaned by studying what their owners or employers have written about their own lives, then enlarging those rather sketchy outlines into something more comprehensive. The lives of most black people were an odd mixture of isolation and assimilation, of separation from each other and the larger society while being connected to both. Yet, as the following examples of male domestic servants demonstrate, although they may have been separate in some respects, we can move from one to the next like stepping stones across the country, piecing together a network of affiliations, both white and black.

Jack Beef was the servant of the magistrate John Baker, who resided both in England where he served as a barrister of the Middle Temple and on St Kitts in the Leeward Islands where he was Solicitor-General. Baker kept a diary of rather terse entries for over twenty years, beginning in St Kitts at the end of 1751. Most of his notations concern business, but on occasion they allow tiny but memorable glimpses into the life of the oddly-named Beef and others like him.

Baker's story is full of deaths. He lost children and two wives, and his neighbours in England and the West Indies died with sad regularity. These tragedies make for sorrowful reading, perhaps because of the very reticence with which he records them. But he was also regularly responsible for the deaths of black people in the Caribbean, where the threat of slave revolts made all crimes committed by blacks capital offences. On 11 April 1752 Baker calmly records that he '[t]ried Mr. R. P[ayne]'s negro Will for breaking open his drawer and stealing about £60 out. Condemned and hanged,'[1] and when on 8 September 1753 'Mr. Wharton's overseer [was] found strangled this morning in a tub,' punishment was swift: only two days later 'Mr. Wharton's negro man, Devonshire, tried and hanged for killing Runnells, his master's overseer.'[2]

Despite the cost of replacing slaves black lives were cheap under West Indian slavery. On 30 July 1752 Baker's 'negro wench Lais died at three', and it was only a week later that she was replaced by '[t]hree negros [*sic*] of Jemmy Gardner bought for me at Nevis on Tuesday'[3] for £70.[4] (This makes Will's earlier theft nearly the value of three female slaves.) Over the period of one year early in Baker's diary, January 1754 to February 1755, entries see-saw between the value and worthlessness of black lives:

January 21, 1754: Commodore Browne brought back the negroes that ran away with Priest's little schooner.

January 23: This morning tried the negroes that ran away with Priest's schooner.

January 26: Mr. John Mills's Mingo and Mr. Payne's Cabenus executed this afternoon.

January 28: Mr. Wells etc. negro sale – some Ibbo [*sic*] negroes sold at £32 sterling – what madness! Better-looking, seasoned negroes at the same time sold for £50 currency, etc., at least 55.

February 4: Daphne brought to bed of a son.

February 11: Sent by Mr. Ryan's sloop Mr. Losack's and my report to the General of condemned negroes.

April 4: Sent away Fortune, whom bought of James Hazell . . . to St^e Croix.

August 8: Called down from Assembly to a letter from Thos. Cadwalader about negro man Sam pretending to be free.

October 20: Arrived this morning the 'Indian Prince' [a slaver].

February 21, 1755: A mulatto child of Samuel Mathews, the mason, left alone (about a year old) part eat and killed by the rats in the night.[5]

In this context of retribution, the struggle for freedom, birth and death, Jack Beef first makes his appearance in the diary, when he is sent to fetch another slave, 'Mr. Gardner's Nerrode', in May 1754,[6] and the following February is mentioned as returning with letters from a trip to Montserrat.

His wide-ranging freedom of movement stands out and raises questions among the stories of slaves stealing boats and money in order to flee, of running away, of feigning freedom. Why did Nerrode need to be fetched, and how did Beef feel about having to do it? How did it happen that he could travel to other islands on routine business matters for his master, and once there never 'pretend to be free'? Slavery gave rise to such paradoxes: as a master and a magistrate Baker must simultaneously have expected that most slaves would attempt to flee and yet Jack Beef would not; otherwise daily business – the point of slavery after all – could not be conducted.

Life in St Kitts was full of odd contradictions. Beef and a white apprentice named William Laurence went 'galloping' on horses while shiploads of Africans arrived in the port. (William was later thrown by his horse and killed.) Baker had 'Mingo' hanged 'for a riot' and 'Othello' was given 'a severe whipping for lying out, and Tycho a smart one for concealing it'. He sentenced a slave to death in the morning and went to a play that same evening. He had 'Mr. Gallwey's Chocolate [hanged] for theft' and his body thrown into the sea, while Beef sailed to Nevis and back to fetch his master's bottled beer.[8] Baker reported that 'Friday, one of my new negroes, died this morning' and '[n]ew negro, Sunday, went away,' while 'at two this morning, happening to go down, found negroes gaming in the kitchen.'[9] He may have been startled to find them gambling, but the modern reader surely wonders who renamed them, and how Jack Beef felt about 'the dance with negro wenches' that several white men of Baker's acquaintance had 'in Nutter's house in College Street'.[10] Baker himself never expresses an emotional response to the numerous executions he orders in

St Kitts, even though in London a few years later he writes with an almost tangible shudder of 'Golden Square – horrible scene – execution.'[11]

It is when Baker removes his household back to England that Jack Beef's varied skills and his importance to the entire Baker household become manifest. Far from being the familiar picturesque page carrying a pillow behind a lady of fashion, Jack has a crucial and trusted position in the family. When Mrs Baker, always referred to as 'Uxor' in the diary, is out of town and needs clothes, it is Jack who delivers them. When Baker leaves town Jack not only accompanies him, but also rides his horse, stays in the same inn, and goes ahead to make arrangements. And when the Bakers' sons Tom, Bob and Jo go to school, Jack goes in the post-chaise too. His relationship with the boys was especially close. More than once he visits them on his own, and when Jo runs away from school Jack Beef fetches him back, reinstalls him and stays overnight with the boy.

Beef's position was like one depicted in Cruikshank's engraving 'Home from School – or the commencement of the Holidays'. Three children race into the outstretched arms of their mother and younger brother in the drawing room. Even the dog is overcome with excitement and anticipation, and a parrot on a perch spreads its wings and opens its beak wide with seeming pleasure. The scene is echoed in two drawings on the wall: 'Harvest Home' depicts music and dancing, and 'The Happy Return' depicts reunited lovers. The whole scene of joyous reunion is observed from behind a doorway by a smiling black servant, who probably like Beef had fetched them safely home.[12] A matching engraving depicts everyone's sorrow when the next term begins and the children depart.

There is no doubt that Beef was Baker's right hand, and that this involved more than just running errands. The equestrian skills learnt in St Kitts became essential in England, and indeed the references to Jack's function as a horseman multiply during these years. Baker writes that 'I went on to town in chariot and Jack Beef sur mon cheval';[13] 'I rode to Town on grey horse, and Jack Beef on hired one';[14] 'Walked to Southward where Jack Beef met me with horses at Spurr Inn';[15] 'Dined Mr. Phipp's. Uxor, Patty and Mrs. Mason in chariot and Jack Beef à cheval';[16] 'Went [this morning] Jack Baker on grey horse, Jack Beef on little one, Uxor and I and Tom in chariot . . . to Windsor.'[17] 'Mr. Jack Johnston and I and Jack Beef together to March's Maidenhead Bridge, où supt and slept';[18] '. . . soir saw "Hamlet" and "Lottery" at Covent Garden. Slept at Golden Cross Inn as did Jack Beef';[19] 'Went Hide [*sic*] Park Corner où Jack Beef brought horses and rode home.'[20] Jack was on the road constantly and had his share of accidents: he was nearly killed in a fall in 1761.[21] In 1762 he had another bad fall.[22]

Far more surprising than that he should be thrown from time to time is that he was responsible for buying and selling the horses and that many of his errands were business ones. When Baker leaves his son Jo at Chichester, he rides home on a horse Jack bought for him;[23] when they return for a three-year period to St Kitts, Beef sells a black horse for two guineas.[24] When his son Tom falls seriously ill at Eton, Baker sends 'Jack Beef to Twickenham for money etc.'[25] He operated exactly as would a trusted white servant, even complaining when another servant returns home drunk.[26] He often travelled and slept away from home on his own, although most frequently when he was on business for the Bakers. He had his own horse, although it almost certainly was not his to sell or trade, and went 'out with hounds'.[27] Proud of Beef's talent for cooking turtles, Baker loaned him to a mayor in 1761 and to Sir T. Heathcote in 1763.[28] In 1762 Jack 'bottled off port-wine at Mr. Jones's.'[29] Clearly he was indispensable.

Far from being dressed in rags, Beef wore a livery measured and made by Baker's own London tailor.[30] From other notes we know that he got a new hat in 1760,[31] and a fustian frock coat in 1770.[32] This kind of outfitting was expensive and involved a certain degree of risk. Slaves and other servants frequently absconded with clothes purchased by their masters, and highway robbery and theft was rife. Defoe's Moll Flanders, a fairly typical petty thief, stole clothing and jewels from children, silk handkerchiefs from gentlemen, and fabrics from shops and homes. Someone like Jack Beef, who frequently travelled by himself on lonely roads, dressed well and often carried money, was a target for thieves. And indeed, in 1762 he was involved in a 'scuffle with men on horseback coming out [of] Southampton, lost his wigg [*sic*]'.[33]

Sir Joshua Reynolds' black servant had a similar experience which landed the thief in the Old Bailey under a death sentence. It seems he stayed out late with companions after seeing a guest of Miss Reynolds' home, and was locked out of the house. He was forced to spend the night in a dosshouse, where a thief brought in by the night constable cut through his pocket with a pen-knife and stole his watch and money. When the Reynolds' servant awoke and alerted the house they found the missing items 'in the possession of the unfortunate wretch who had stolen them.' The servant was bound over to prosecute and the thief received a death sentence. (This could not have occurred in the Americas, where no black could testify against a white.) Sir Joshua discovered the facts of this incident while reading his morning paper at breakfast and, angered to see that the escapades of his household staff had been made so public, he managed through friends to get the death sentence changed to transportation, and 'ordered fresh clothing to be sent to him, and also that the black servant as a penance, as well as an act of charity should carry to him every day a sufficient supply of food from his own table.'[34] To the modern reader the fact that Beef and Reynolds' servant could stand as witnesses against their attackers is perhaps less startling than the fact that they wore wigs and pocket-watches at all.

It comes as no surprise then that Baker, riding beside this sleek and capable man, should exclaim one day upon observing a bedraggled group of 1,400 soldiers followed by their shivering wives and children, 'Good God! What gentlemen are the negroes in W. Indies to these!'[35] Or, when he visits Prussia without Beef in 1760, that he should write, 'There came over the Ferry a number of peasants who are like our ancient villains [*sic*] in England, the first slaves I have seen in Europe, but nothing so easy and happy as those in America of the black line are.'[36] To Beef, who witnessed the endless punishments and executions of 'easy and happy' slaves in the West Indies, such glibly expressed thoughts would have carried enormous ironic weight. Certainly Beef could not help but be aware of his own relatively comfortable position in the

Baker household, but just as certainly he knew that unmanumitted (owned) servants, who received no wages, were ultimately less free than the poorest European peasants.

For all this information about his movements we know next to nothing about Beef's personal life. Appearances suggest that he was a faithful servant holding an important position, for Baker mentions no other servants with any regularity. If Beef resented his enslavement, for all his freedom of movement, Baker certainly never records it nor does he indicate an awareness of it. For him Beef's life was one of luxury when compared to those around him. There are, however, indications that although he could not express such things to his owners, there were in fact people to whom Beef could speak, and with whom he socialized. A few passing comments open a window into a more private world. Baker moved in élite intellectual and artistic circles, and was friendly with Hogarth, Garrick and Reynolds, among others. On 1 August 1759, he mentions that 'Jack Beef waited con [with] horses Mr. Garrick's – I came home.'[37] While the Baker entourage stays in Southampton, Jack Beef goes 'to town p[ro] diversis.'[38] Nearly ten years later Baker writes, 'came away between 10 and 11 – walk'd home thro' Smithfield and Snow Hill, Fleet Market, Fleet Street and Strand; (found Jack Beef gone out to a Ball of Blacks).'[39]

In these brief remarks we can glimpse a bit of Beef's other life. We know that Beef had a social life, that he amused himself in town – probably not alone – and that he was part of a network of black Londoners. Baker expressed no real surprise that Beef had a private life among other black people, even though 'black community life tended to be beyond the sight and hearing of curious white society'.[40] He had after all seen the gamblers in his own kitchen at St Kitts and was used to seeing groups of slaves together.

Not all whites knew that their black servants had black friends, though. A friend of Samuel Johnson's was startled when, in the doctor's absence, he discovered Francis Barber with 'a group of his African countrymen . . . sitting around a fire in the gloomy anti-room; and on their all turning their sooty faces at once to stare at me, they presented a curious spectacle.'[41] Like most outsiders to the Afro-British community, the Revd Baptist Noel Turner was amazed to discover that it even existed. Undoubtedly he was accustomed to seeing black servants all over England in ones and twos, and to considering them only as they were attached to individual households.

But as households were connected to each other, so were servants. James Doyle's painting, *A Literary Party at Sir Joshua Reynolds'*, shows the members of Johnson's famous club; in the picture Johnson, Reynolds, Garrick, Goldsmith, Boswell and others are at table being waited on by a black man (probably the same one robbed and forced by Reynolds to be charitable to the thief). Below stairs at the same time undoubtedly were some of the other black menservants. Whenever Jack Beef stayed behind at Garrick's to watch the horses, he certainly met friends. He undoubtedly knew Reynolds' servant, and probably Francis Barber as well. He may even have known Ignatius Sancho, a free black who was friendly with Garrick. When the well-to-do socialized above stairs, their servants did so below stairs, participating in a parallel social life.

It was not only below stairs and in 'gloomy anti-rooms' that they met. At the gathering in 1764 of fifty-seven black people mentioned in Chapter 1, they 'supped, drank, and entertained themselves with dancing and music, consisting of violins, French horns, and other instruments, at a public-house in Fleet-street, till four in the morning. No whites were allowed to be present, for all the performers were Blacks.'[42] Nearly 200 attended the black ball held in a Westminster pub after Mansfield's decision on the Somerset case.[43] Although the white community expressed some amusement at the idea of a black social life, such a life was vibrant. If servants like Beef were accustomed to making such arrangements for their masters, they were surely capable of making them for themselves.

It was not only with other blacks that black servants socialized, either. After a prolonged stint back in St Kitts, the Baker household returned to London and Beef's English amusements resumed. He attended both the 'Ball of Blacks', and also went to the theatre with Baker's other servants. He and the maids watched Garrick perform from gallery seats given them by a Mrs Swinburne.[44]

Garrick, a consummate entertainer, seems to have been a favourite with servants. Once he deserted his friends after dinner, and later was discovered 'fully occupied in amusing a negro boy who was a servant in the family, by mimicking the manner and noise of a turkey cock, which diverted the boy to such a degree that he was convulsed with laughter, and only able now and then to utter, "Oh, Masser Garrick! You will kill me, Masser Garrick!" '[45] Two months later the entire Baker family went to see a play at Covent Garden, and the staff sat in the gallery again.[46] Years earlier Baker mentions having friends to dinner, and that the guests' numerous servants, including a black maid, also dined there.[47] Baker attends church with the four female servants,[48] the 'servantes' go 'pour un ride to Romsey' and Jack Beef goes 'con elles',[49] so we know that his social companions were both black and white, male and female.

It is in popular rather than in 'high' art that we get glimpses of the servants' life, particularly when it concerned people like Jack Beef. 'High Life Below Stairs', a 1774 engraving by Joseph Bretherton, shows three lazy servants refusing to answer their master's bell, each telling the others to go. Coachman, in a wig, says 'You go,' to the cook. Cook replies, 'Hang me if I go.' On her right is Kingston, the black servant in his natural hair, who points to Cook and says, 'Mollsey, Pollsey go.' The subtitle of the engraving is 'As t'was represented at Cashiobury the seat of The Earl of Essex'. It was later reproduced with a new caption which read 'Blackee you go!' from the coachman; 'Sambo, answer the Door —' from the cook, and 'Cookey, you go!' from the black man. Although the composition of the picture remains the same in both with the cook defiant and alert in the centre and the two men lolling close-eyed on each side of her, the black servant is at once obviously at the bottom of the pecking order, but also able to pass the task back to the others. The earlier version avoids all racially-specific names, making the three servants equal below stairs.

David Garrick produced James Townley's farce of the same name, in which these characters appeared. Often mistakenly attributed to Garrick in published editions, this play, like the often expressed complaints about servants who aped the upper classes they served, concerns the pretentious social life of those below stairs. The servants adopt the titles of their masters – the duke's manservant is known as 'the Duke' to his peers and pretends to speak French, Lady Bab's maid is called 'Lady Bab', and the central figure is Kingston, 'a young West Indian of fortune' who, as a child in Jamaica, 'had a hundred blacks kissing [his] feet every day.'[50] When the Duke discovers that his servants of all races are taking advantage of him he disguises himself and attends one of their parties.

The dialogue in the engraving occurs in Act I, in which a sleepy and drunken Coachman and Kingston argue with the Cook over who is to answer the door:

> *Coach*: You go, cook; you go –
> *Cook*: Hang me if I go –
> *Kingston*: Yes, yes, cooky go; Mollsey, Pollsey, go –
> *Cook*: Out you black toad – It is none of my business, and go I will not.

There is also a black maid, Cloe, and against both of these black characters the other servants demonstrate their pretentiousness by racial denigration. When the servants decide to dance, 'Philip' pairs them off, ordering 'the two devils' to 'dance together'; when the 'Duke' kisses 'Kitty' there is 'kissing round – Kingston kisses Cloe heartily' and 'Sir Harry' exclaims, 'See how the devils kiss!'

From plays like this we would seem to learn something about the life of black servants in England, but the experience of playwrights above stairs does not necessarily reflect an intimate knowledge of those below stairs. Even so, the black people in the play belong to a class system that was just as rigid below as above stairs, and the repeated use of the word 'devil' reiterates the vulgar pomposity of those who pretended to be what they were not. The *dramatis personæ* for the 1782 Edinburgh production lists no actors for the roles of Kingston and Cloe and must have cut the satirical lines about black servants. Another two-act farce entitled *Bon Ton; or, High Life Above Stairs* mocked the salacious and greedy upper classes. A black servant named 'Mignon' also disappeared in the

1782 Edinburgh production of this production, where the two farces must have been presented as a double bill.

A 1799 engraving by Cruikshank is much more overt in its satirical intent. Here there are nine servants playing cards by a roaring kitchen fire. They are all well-dressed, sitting in elegant chairs; there is a cloth on the table. They ape the pastimes and manners of their masters upstairs, and flirt with each other ('John I am lew'd,' says a ladies' maid, leaning toward the man beside her) while ignoring a summons from upstairs. The black footman on the left of the picture is the only one standing, and as he spills wine from a bottle in one hand and from a tray of wine glasses in the other he says, 'Come Massa Coachee, wet your whistle with a Drop of *Black Strap.*' His livery is extremely ornate, with ruffles, epaulets and ribbons, and the implication is that even the servants have a servant. There is no chair for him at the table.

This picture is less a literal depiction of the function of black servants among their fellow servants, than an indictment of the pretensions of servants of this period. Its title, 'Loo in the Kitchin or High Life below Stairs', refers both to the name of the card game and to the 'lewdness' of their behaviour. Moving outside of one's class and adopting the mannerisms of those of a higher social station, particularly those mannerisms and behaviour by which some of the eighteenth-century upper classes were known, seemed to some social critics to be innately indecent. Servants often adopted 'much of the related social ritual' of their employers. A letter from a 1757 issue of the *London Chronicle* complains that the 'present Age are grown so unfortunately polite . . . that common Servants (I mean the female part of them) send Cards to one another to make up a Party at Whist, or pass an Evening . . .'[51] A writer to *Lloyd's Evening Post* complained more specifically that a servant of his 'had received a card reading: "Mr. Senegambia Mungo's compliments to Mr. John Ship, and should be proud of his company this evening at ——, Esqr's in Cheapside."' The servant explained that his host

> . . . was a black servant of Mr. ——, in Cheapside; that although an ignorant African, who could neither read nor write, he had all the

pride of an East-Indian nabob; that he had before lived in a Nobleman's service, where the Steward had been accustomed to have his
routs as well as his Master, and therefore thought he now had an
equal right to have his . . .

According to the writer, the invited servant

> . . . was introduced . . . by the Cook, who apologized for her greasy
> condition, by saying that, she was obliged to cook the supper; and
> that as her Master kept very few servants, she was forced to act the
> part of the Mistress of Ceremonies herself, it being very improper for
> 'Squire Senegambia to appear in that character. On entering the room,
> 'Squire Senegambia, who sate at the head of the table, rose, and saluted
> me, in broken English, with, ''Squire Ship, I am happy to be
> honoured with your company this evening . . .'[52]

The facetious tone stems directly from Townley's farce but this
is a third-hand tale, written to the newspaper not by the white
servant in his own words, but translated and perhaps embellished
by his master.[53] The further displacement from 'appropriate'
behaviour is exemplified by having a black act as host to whites,
be waited on by whites, while borrowing the language and mannerisms of upper-class whites.

Stories like this one, involving transgressions of the privileges
or necessities of several classes of white English people, were at
the heart of a call to limit the importation of black servants into
England. It was the Jack Beefs whom apologists for slavery like
the notorious Edward Long had in mind when they stated that
West Indian slaves were far happier and healthier than English
peasants. They were fed, clothed and housed, could sing and dance
all night and retire under palm trees in their old age, they argued.
Long cited the case of Francis Williams, the black classicist and
poet educated at Cambridge University, as a negative example,
for on his return to Jamaica where he was born a free black to
free black parents he set up a school and 'was haughty, opinion-
ated, looked down with sovereign contempt on his fellow Blacks,
entertained the highest opinion of his own knowledge, treated his
parents with much disdain, and behaved towards his children and
his slaves with severity bordering upon cruelty.' (He also quoted

David Hume as saying of Williams, 'they talk of one Negroe as a man of parts and learning; but 'tis likely he is admired for very slender accomplishments, like a parrot who speaks a few words plainly.')[54]

In contrast Long, like Baker, presented grim pictures of poverty in the British Isles, where the poor were unfed, unhoused, and subject to crime and disease. They utterly discounted the overwhelming evidence of cruelty and abuse on plantations and elsewhere (including England), the fact that the condition of slavery was not only unchosen but passed down through the condition of the mother in perpetuity.

While the general concern was that bringing unpaid black servants to England led to increased unemployment among white servants, since no slave required a salary, the real fear was that they would no longer consider themselves as slaves and might expect the rights afforded to white people. One writer to *The Gentleman's Magazine* of 1764 was quite clear on this.

> The practice of importing Negroe servants into these kingdoms is said to be already a grievance that requires a remedy, and yet it is every day encouraged, insomuch that the number in this metropolis only, is supposed to be near 20,000; the main objections to their importation is, that they cease to consider themselves as slaves in this free country, nor will they put up with an inequality of treatment, nor more willingly perform the laborious offices of servitude than our own people, and if put to do it, are generally sullen, spiteful, treacherous, and revengeful. It is therefore highly impolitic to introduce them as servants here, where that rigour and severity is impracticable which is absolutely necessary to make them useful.[55]

Senegambia, if his story were true, refused to 'put up with an inequality of treatment,' while Jack Beef as a respected footman faced little of it. However, each was only as useful as far as he knew himself to be subservient. Beef's very efficiency and efficacy depended to a large degree on belief in himself and in his abilities even though whites wanted it not to be so, and would have liked to have had it both ways.

Someone calling himself 'F. Freeman' wrote a similar letter to the *London Chronicle* a year later, decrying the importation of

'Negro and East India servants, who of late years are become too abundant in this kingdom.' He estimated their national population to be thirty thousand 'at the lowest.'

> These poor people are all, for the convenience or humour of their owners, brought into this kingdom slaves; and while they continue as such, it cannot be supposed their service does not ease their masters more in expence . . . and if they have become released from their state of slavery there can be no just plea for their being put on an equal footing with natives, whose birth-right, as members of the community, entitle them to superior dues . . . It may be serviceable to invite over those who practice useful arts, because we are benefited by their skill and labour; but as it is far otherwise with menial servants, or the mere instruments of our pleasures and amusements, as while resident here they live on the common stock, and when they go from us they lessen it; therefore they stand in the way of more profitable and useful natives, and serve to obstruct a far better population.[56]

He went on to propose a tax on black servants of forty shillings each, yielding the annual sum of sixty thousand pounds to be used toward paying off the national debt.

While the economic argument was most often put forward as a reason to curb the black population, the moral one was generally primary. 'Anglicanus' complained in 1764 that 'many have been perplexed how to satisfactorily get rid of them . . . and here have not known who would accept of them even as gifts, when they have once contracted habits that are the grounds of just dislike,'[57] but it was Sir John Fielding, brother of Henry Fielding the novelist and designer of the London police system, who put his finger on the real complaint. '[T]hey no sooner arrive here,' he wrote, 'than they put themselves on a Footing with other Servants, become intoxicated with Liberty, grow refractory, and either by Persuasion of other or from their own inclinations, begin to expect Wages according to their own Opinion of their Merits.'[58] Here then was the unexpected rub: black people in England began to consider themselves equal to white people of a similar class, and deserving of wages for their labour.

This was a two-edged sword. One final consequence of Beef's freedom of movement was that he died alone, away from Baker's household, at the lodging house of a barber, just as he was on the verge of real freedom. According to the editor of Baker's diary, '[i]t would seem that he had just left his master's service on January 2, 1771, and was about to return to the West Indies, a free man with his little savings.'[59] Sometimes ill (at which times Baker always sent for medical help), Beef felt unwell and laid down to rest after a good dinner. He died in his sleep. Baker went immediately to arrange his funeral, and notified Mrs Baker by post. Jack Beef was buried on 10 January 1771, next to the Foundling Hospital in London. Baker and a number of others, including a black man who was once their coachman, attended his funeral.

This much we know, but there is so much more we do not know, and it is in these gaps that the real biography of Jack Beef lies. Was he born in the West Indies, or brought in on a slaver? How did he come to have such a privileged position in the Baker household? Did he perhaps have a wife and children in the West Indies, brothers or sisters? If he had, it seems likely that Baker, despite his harsh notions of punishment and ease with the institution of slavery, would have tried to keep them together. Once, on their three-year stint back in St Kitts, a slave named Dorus told him that two of his brothers had arrived on a slave ship. Baker immediately 'went down and bought them, coachman and ploughman.'[60] What we do know is that Jack Beef had a lasting influence on Baker and his family. When Mrs Baker died three years later and her devastated husband had to send discreet news of it to a friend in Paris, he sealed the letter 'with a strange seal . . . the white one with a head once Jack Beef's.'[61]

When black servants remained in England, gained money and freedom, they were able to move into English society in ways which upset some and pleased others. Perhaps the best-known fact about Francis Barber, Samuel Johnson's manservant, is that he left money and much of his property to him in his will. Johnson's first biographer, Sir John Hawkins, was incensed by this and by the fact that Barber was married to a white woman and lived in an English town. Even more upsetting to him was that Barber had control over Johnson's manuscripts and a number of his artefacts, and that it was Barber whom Hawkins, a friend and trustee of Johnson's, had to petition for use of these items. This was power of a real and lasting sort.

There are gaps in some of the details, but Barber's biography is much more complete than Jack Beef's. We know that he was born in Jamaica to 'native' parents but brought to England sometime around 1752 by a Colonel Bathurst, who apparently owned a few slaves but abhorred slavery. Bathurst sent Francis to school at Barton in Hertfordshire, where he studied under the Revd William Jackson. How old Barber was at this time is unclear, even according to his own scattered evidence. When Bathurst died, he left Barber a legacy of freedom and twelve pounds. His son, Dr Richard Bathurst, asked Johnson if Barber could join his household, and Johnson agreed. He had recently lost his beloved wife and was gaining some financial and literary success for *The Rambler* and other works. At the same time he was so well known for his careless personal habits (Hawkins said that his 'great bushy wig, which throughout his life he affected to wear, by that closeness of texture which it had contracted and been suffered to retain, was very nearly as impenetrable by a comb as a quickset hedge . . . his external appearance was, not to say negligent, but slovenly, and even squalid')[62] that many were surprised when he decided to keep a servant. This was the beginning of a long and affectionate, although sometimes troubled, relationship.

Many have written about Barber, and nearly all of the accounts refer primarily to his position as Johnson's legatee. This is important of course, yet the approximately thirty-four years of their lives together made their relationship difficult to categorize as simply one of master and servant, or for the will to be seen as the last, perhaps irrational, act of a unique man. Johnson's concern for Francis was certainly paternal, and recognizing him as his heir put him in many ways on the footing of a favoured ward since Johnson had no children. Like Bathurst, Johnson sent Barber to a grammar school, also in Hertfordshire.

Yet it also seems entirely likely that Johnson's highly publicized aversion to slavery as well as his friendship with the Bathurst family made him leap at the chance to prove his convictions. Like those of Granville Sharp and Lord Mansfield, the two main protagonists in the James Somerset court case, Johnson's convictions and affections were unimpeachable, even though his feelings about black people as a whole were less clear. Johnson's friend Hester Piozzi, admittedly not the most reliable interpreter of Barber's actions, claimed that '[w]hen he spoke of negroes, he always appeared to think of them as a race naturally inferior, and made few exceptions in favour of his own; yet whenever disputes arose in his household among the many odd inhabitants of which it consisted, he always sided with Francis against the others, whom he suspected (not unjustly, I believe) of greater malignity.'[63]

Johnson never hesitated to voice his opposition to slavery, and his unequivocal quotations on the subject are well known. 'How is it that we hear the loudest yelps for liberty among the drivers of negroes?' he asked about the Americans.[64] He lifted his glass at Oxford and toasted 'the next insurrection of the negroes in the West Indies.'[65] He wrote in a letter that 'I do not much wish well to discoveries, for I am always afraid they will end in conquest and robbery.'[66] He closely followed the important Scottish case of the slave Joseph Knight, who wanted to sever his relationship with his former master, and produced an important opinion which is still reproduced in textbooks in America and Britain. 'The sum of the argument is this,' he wrote. 'No man is by nature the property of another: The defendant is, therefore, by nature free: The rights of nature must be some way forfeited before they can be justly taken away: That the defendant has by any act forfeited the rights of nature we require to be proved; and if no proof of such forfeiture can be given, we doubt not but the justice of the court will declare him free.'[67]

Barber came to Johnson free or was manumitted soon afterwards (the dates are unclear) and although we cannot be clear about his age or his earlier life, it seems that he 'grew up' in Johnson's home. His difficulties were those of a normal adolescent who wants to make an independent life for himself while Johnson, *in loco parentis*, wanted to see him safe and well-educated. Barber left Johnson twice, most likely out of boredom. The first time he went to work for an apothecary in Cheapside, upsetting Johnson who wrote to a friend in 1756 that 'my boy is run away and I do not know whom to send.'[68] Barber visited Johnson a number of times during this period, an indication that he did not wish to completely separate himself from his employer, before finally returning to Johnson's establishment.

He left again in 1758, for that most archetypal of youthful escapes, running off to sea. This time Johnson, with perhaps a less-developed sense of adventure, really was distraught, for he could imagine no worse place for anyone. Barber was young and slight of build and besides, he said, 'No man will be a sailor who has contrivance enough to get himself into a jail; for being in a ship is being in a jail, with the chance of being drowned.'[69] Many assumed that, according to the maritime practice of kidnapping men to serve in the navy, Barber had been pressed into service, but this was not the case. The life of a young man in service to a brilliant but academic lexicographer fulfilled few of his desires to live an active life; in contrast to Barber's, Jack Beef's life was a whirlwind of activity.

This time Johnson mobilized all of his contacts to gain Francis's release (even Tobias Smollett was marshalled into service on this occasion). Barber was on board the HMS *Stag*. Johnson wrote to a Sir George Hay in the Admiralty that 'I had a Negro Boy named Francis Barber, given me by a Friend whom I much respect, and treated by me for some years with great tenderness. Being disgusted in the house he ran away to sea, and was in the Summer on board the ship stationed at Yarmouth to protect the fishery.' Johnson asked for his assistance in retrieving Barber, adding that 'he is no seaman.'[70] It took time but he was eventually returned to Johnson.

This seemingly small episode, the last time Barber left Johnson's service until the latter's death in 1784, was a formative one whose importance has perhaps been overlooked. Johnson's hue and cry was nothing like the advertisements that appeared throughout the century offering rewards for runaway slaves.[71] Yet, while Johnson freely admitted his 'tenderness' and concern for Barber, he also indicated a kind of ownership. Barber was 'given him' rather than hired by him, although it seems probable that Barber received some kind of financial remuneration. At the same time, his tone is exactly that of a father who wants the prodigal to return home. The prodigal may have returned, and he certainly served him faithfully for the next twenty-five years, but years later Barber told Boswell that he did so 'without any wish of his own.'[72] He was free for a time to choose his own employment and the path of his life, but the world acknowledged Johnson's *de facto* ownership over him.

Life under Johnson was hardly one of confinement, however. Barber had a social life of sorts and ladies apparently liked him. Mrs Piozzi recorded a conversation with Johnson in which he declared that 'Frank has carried the empire of Cupid further than most men. When I was in Lincolnshire so many years ago, he attended me thither; and when we returned home together, I found that a female haymaker had followed him to London for love.'[73] When Johnson sent him to the grammar school in Bishop's Stortford, probably in 1767, he referred in letters to Barber's friends and amusements.

Francis was likely quite a bit older at this time than the other boarding students at the school and his social life there remains something of a mystery. The school faced near collapse when the headmaster died unexpectedly, but his widow Mrs Clapp took over in his place and kept Barber on as a boarder during holidays as well as during term. By 1770 he had been there three years, yet Johnson's letter to him on 7 December of that year reads like one to a child: 'Dear Francis, – I hope you mind your business. I design you shall stay with Mrs. Clapp these holidays. If you are invited out you may go, if Mr. Ellis gives leave. I have ordered you some clothes, which you will receive, I believe, next week. My compliments to Mrs. Clapp and to Mr. Ellis . . .'.[74] Barber was at this time at least twenty-five years old, and clearly in quite an odd situation. His fellow students were far younger than he and probably unlikely to invite him to their homes; the neighbouring houses might certainly have housed servants who would have made potential companions, but no mention is made of them.

While his later letters show him to be intelligent and articulate, he was held in a peculiar state of arrested development while at school. It is not clear exactly what his position was there. He studied, of course, but did he have any other functions in the household? He was, after all, Johnson's servant as well as his protégé, his 'ward' who was rarely allowed to return 'home'.

Had he been white one might conjecture that he took on the responsibilities of tutor to the younger boys (we see examples of this sort of arrangement in the works of Dickens and the Brontës), but this does not seem to have happened. Neither does he seem to have performed the tasks of a servant, although this is what his work would be on leaving school.

Barber returned to Johnson in 1772, five years after being placed at Bishop's Stortford. Hawkins, always uncharitable where Barber was concerned, wrote in his book on Johnson that Barber's 'first master had, in great humanity, made him a Christian; and his last, for no assignable reason, nay, rather in despite of nature, and to unfit him for being useful according to his capacity, determined to make him a scholar.'[75] Mrs Piozzi noted that he seemed to have learned little for all his time at school, but such schools required no government certification, offered questionable education and 'some of the men who conducted private schools would not a century later have been deemed fit to take the management of a charity school, for their extant letters and petitions abound with grammatical errors. Their pupils could not be expected to surpass them.'[76] Once back in London he received and answered letters for Johnson, took care of his manuscripts, and Johnson writes to Mrs Piozzi that Barber wanted to borrow her copy of *Evelina*, the new novel by Fanny Burney who was a regular visitor to the Johnson household.[77]

About Barber's marriage Hawkins is even less charitable. Four years after returning to Johnson's service Barber married – apparently with Johnson's blessing – and brought his white wife Elizabeth to live with him in Johnson's house. Although theirs seems to have been a marriage based on true affection, outsiders leaped to unfavourable conclusions. Hawkins concluded that Betsy, as Johnson always referred to her, was a prostitute, this being for him the only possible explanation for racial inter-marriage.

. . . It was hinted to me many years ago, by his master, that he [Barber] was a loose fellow; and I learned from others, that, after an absence from his service of some years, he married. In his search of a wife, he picked up one of those creatures with whom, in the disposal of themselves, no contrariety of colour is an obstacle. It is said, that soon after his marriage, he became jealous, and, it may be supposed, that he continued so, till, by presenting him with a daughter of her own colour, his wife put an end to all his doubts on that score. Notwithstanding which, Johnson, in the excess of undiscriminating benevolence, about a year before his death, took the wife and her two children, into his house, and made them a part of his family; and, by the codicil to his will, made a disposition in his favour, to the amount in value of near fifteen hundred pounds.[78]

Johnson's friend Hester Piozzi passed a similar judgement when, years later, she noticed Barber's daughter in Lichfield and remarked that she '*called herself* – & was *called* by others, the Daughter of Dr. Johnson's Negro Francis. She was rather a remarkably *fair* Girl, & approaching to pretty; but Frank tho' almost 15 years at *School*, never I suppose learned *much* of Natural History.'[79] She entitled this entry in her Commonplace Book '*Blackamour*', and like Hawkins did not understand that such a marriage could legitimately produce fair children. Even Johnson, who never seemed to doubt that the child was Barber's, wrote that 'Frank's wife has brought him a wench; but I cannot yet get intelligence of her colour, and therefore have never told him how much depends upon it . . .'[80] Reade jumps to Barber's defence, oddly enough, by offering this explanation: 'If her guilt were to be read in the light skin of her infant, we may be quite sure that Frank, temperamentally jealous and with the primitive passions of his race, would not be behind his master in drawing unfavourable conclusions . . . [Johnson] may have thought that it would be a good thing for the "wench" if she favoured her mother more than her father; and have realized that a white woman might feel less affection for a baby wholly black.'[81]

As further proof of Barber's marital unsuitability Mrs Piozzi offered one other anecdote:

On the birth-day of our eldest daughter, and that of our friend Dr. Johnson, the 17th and 18th of September, we every year made up a little dance and supper, to divert our servants and their friends, putting the summer-house into their hands for the two evenings, to fill with acquaintance and merriment. Francis and his white wife were invited

49

of course. She was eminently pretty, and he was jealous, as my maids told me. On the first of these days amusements (I know not what year) Frank took offence at some attentions paid his Desdemona, and walked away next morning to London in wrath. His master and I driving the same road an hour after, overtook him. 'What is the matter, child (says Dr. Johnson), that you leave Streatham to-day? *Art sick?*' He is jealous (whispered I). 'Are you jealous of your wife, you stupid blockhead?' (cries out his master in another tone). The fellow hesitated; and, *To be sure Sir, I don't quite approve Sir*, was the stammering reply. 'Why, what do they do to her, man? do the foot-men kiss her?' No Sir, no! – Kiss my *wife* Sir! – I hope not Sir. 'Why, what do they *do* to her, my lad?' Why nothing Sir, I'm sure Sir. 'Why then go back directly and dance you dog, do; and let's hear no more of such empty lamentations.' I believe however that Francis was scarcely as much the object of Mr. Johnson's personal kindness, as the representative of Dr. Bathurst, for whose sake he would have loved any body, or any thing.[82]

Evidence from those who knew Johnson and Barber well proves genuine affection existed between Francis and his employer. Mrs Piozzi recalled that when Johnson's cat Hodge 'was grown sick and old, and could eat nothing but oysters, Mr. Johnson always went out himself to buy Hodge's dinner, that Francis the Black's delicacy might not be hurt, at seeing himself employed for the convenience of a quadruped.'[83] When he was away for six weeks in 1776 he asked a friend to '[r]emember me kindly to Francis and Betsy,'[84] and in another letter in 1775 writes 'give my love to Francis.'[85] Boswell, who never shared Johnson's unequivocal aversion to slavery, always spoke kindly of 'good Mr. Francis'[86] and 'honest Francis'.[87] He was infuriated by Hawkins' 'opportunistic biography' of Johnson, which appeared rather too quickly after his death, and saw him as unreliable and vindictive, taking advantage of his position of executor to make use of Johnson's papers before turning them over to Barber, the 'residuary legatee, whose property they were.'[88]

There is some evidence that Hawkins tried to make off with other of Johnson's artefacts left to Barber, and resented the good opinion others held of him. 'I know it has been considered an offense of a heinous magnitude, to weight any claim against the merits of Mr. Francis Barber, merits that had no foundation, but in his consultation of his own interest or the perverseness of his admirers . . .' he wrote.[89] George Birkbeck Hill, who later edited Boswell's *Johnson*, comments succinctly that '[n]owhere does Hawkins more show the malignancy of his character than in his attacks on Johnson's black servant, and through him on Johnson . . . But Hawkins was a brutal fellow.'[90] Perhaps the strongest evidence of Boswell's willingness to accept Barber is in his referring to him with earnest politeness as *Mr* Francis Barber, an appellation which Hawkins used with great sarcasm, at a time when black men and women were commonly referred to by first name only.

Hawkins may have been upset that Johnson neglected his advice about Barber's annuity. When Hawkins told him that a generous legacy for a faithful servant in a good family was £50 a year Johnson replied, 'Then, I shall be nobilissimus, for I mean to leave Frank seventy pounds a year, and I desire you to tell him so.' In fact, he left him even more than that. After disposing of certain items and sums, his will stated that 'the rest of the aforesaid sums of money and property, together with my books, plate, and household furniture, I leave to the before-mentioned Sir Joshua Reynolds, Sir John Hawkins, and Dr. William Scott, also in trust, to be applied, after paying my debts, to the use of Francis Barber, my man-servant, a negro, in such a manner as they shall judge most fit and available to his benefit.'[91] Henry Angelo, writing of his father's career at Windsor as a riding and fencing master, confirms that it was not unusual for servants 'in certain old families' to be left enough to allow them to retire in comfort and 'respectable style.'[92] The only unusual fact about Barber's inheritance is that it was left to a black man.

Hawkins' remarks are particularly telling because of the link he makes between sexuality and what was to him the inappropriateness of giving Francis and Elizabeth Barber money; his leap is from her wrongly assumed infidelity to Johnson's wrongly placed financial generosity. Similarly, Hesther Piozzi's disparaging of Elizabeth Barber as a Desdemona persecuted by an irrationally jealous Othello led her to seek another explanation for Johnson's 'personal kindness.' And indeed, it is clear that in this case, as with many of the well-treated black servants brought into England, a deep-seated racial hostility, on the part of the monied rather than the serving classes, led them time and again to accuse of moral lapses those who were rewarded for their integrity.

The Barbers' morality was never in question by anyone who knew them, but Francis and Elizabeth and their three children were never destined to live a comfortable life. After Johnson's death they removed themselves to Lichfield, and found it difficult to live within the means that Johnson had provided. Some of this may be due to their inexperience in handling financial matters, and Barber seems to have drawn upon the executors for money rather more frequently than should have been necessary. But it was also true that they had three small children to support and that neither of them was in very good health. Barber refers in a rough draft of a letter to Bishop Percy in 1788 to the 'infirmatives' he and his wife have been suffering, 'together with those attendant on age', another clue that he was older than one might have expected.[93] He was advised to set up a book shop, since the literary life was one he was accustomed to and one which could afford him an income, if managed properly, but he did not take this advice.

Reade chalks up Barber's financial incompetence to the fact that 'Johnson's household was run on easy lines which can hardly have imbued him with sound theories of domestic economy,'[94] but when Francis and Elizabeth's son Samuel became a Methodist lay minister and his brief biography was written, it said that the Barbers 'were improvident, strove to make a figure in the world, lived above their means, and dissipated their property.'[95] After Barber's death Elizabeth and Anne, her 'fair' daughter, set up a small school and were regarded as upright and hard-working citizens. The Barber children married whites, as did their children's children. With the exception of Samuel Barber, the minister, they became manual labourers, blending with each generation further into the white English working-class population.

The story of Francis Barber demonstrates the difficulties that many white and black English found themselves in because of slavery, which held black people in situations of paternal or abusive control. Johnson's abolitionist stance and well-intentioned treatment of Barber was completely unlike that of Jack Beef, whose master bought, sold and condemned slaves. One wonders how different a man Barber might have been had he been allowed to remain on the HMS *Stag*, where he was apparently happy and an equal among seamen. Although the life was difficult and oftentimes brief for both white and black, there was an activity and camaraderie on board ship that Barber's London life lacked.

Francis was lucky to be able to reach adulthood in England, for the biggest difficulty facing young black males of the period was that they were prized for their youth and scorned for their manhood. The most common solution to adolescence was deportation; when they outgrew their usefulness as fashion accessories they were sold back into plantation slavery much as one would get rid of a difficult lapdog. Those who were allowed to remain in England were often apprenticed, sold or turned into faithful family retainers. The Duchess of Devonshire offered her mother an eleven-year-old boy because 'the duke don't like me having a black, and yet I cannot bear the poor wretch being ill-used; if you liked him instead of Michel I will send him; he will be a cheap servant and you will make a Christian of him and a good boy; if you don't like him they say Lady Rockingham wants one.' He was cheap, of course, because as a slave he required no salary, and the Duke didn't want a negro servant because it 'was more original to have a Chinese page than to have a black one; everybody had a black one.'[96] But the Sackvilles went one step further in depersonalizing their black servants by giving them the same name generation after generation: 'The black page at Knole,' wrote Vita Sackville-West, 'of which there had always been one since the days of Lady Anne Clifford . . . had always been called John Morocco regardless of what his true name might be.'[97] And sure enough the 1613 roster of attendants 'At the Long Table in the Hall' gives at the very bottom, in the kitchen and scullery, 'John Morockoe, a Blackamoor.'[98] Not all of them fared well either, for Sackville-West mentions casually that once the 'house-steward killed the black page in the passage.'[99]

The reason for getting rid of these young men or depersonalizing them had as much to do with sexuality as with ownership. They were developing into manhood when their value had been as asexual creatures who accompanied ladies. And indeed there were reports of white women who carried their affections for their black servants rather further than propriety tolerated. The historian Folarin Shyllon writes that

> In common with the great ladies of the period, Elizabeth Chudleigh [*sic*], the licentious Duchess of Kingston, had a black boy named Sambo as a pet. The Duchess had Sambo when he was five or six years old. She was so fond of him that she dressed him in elegant style, taking him with her to most of the public places she frequented, 'especially to the play, where he sat in the boxes with her.' But all good things come to an end, and as Sambo grew up, 'he was deemed at last too big to be admitted to those favours formerly enjoyed with his mistress.' Instead of riding in the coach, the black boy was obliged to mount outside. The Duchess now sent him to school, but 'he never learned anything.' Which is not surprising, considering the sort of life he had hitherto led. Sambo was now about eighteen or nineteen years old. He started staying out several days and nights at a time, and his haunts 'were chiefly in Hedge-lane amongst a set of whores and ruffians.' Clearly, Sambo had outgrown his usefulness, and in due course, he was dispatched to the West Indies and slavery.[100]

From this perspective, the paternalism of Johnson which denounced slavery and saw no difficulty in Barber's marrying and bringing his wife into the household, can hardly be faulted.

It was Julius Soubise whose life combined all of the elements of those privileged men discussed thus far. His story is a microcosm of eighteenth-century excess, made notable because of the elements of race and class. Like Jack Beef he was an equestrian, like Francis Barber he was an obvious favourite with his mistress and popular with women, like the 'Mr. Senegambia Mungo' of Cheapside complained about in *Lloyd's Evening Post*, he had an active social life which imitated that of men of fashion, and finally, like 'Sambo', the favourite of Elizabeth Cudleigh, his life changed dramatically as he went from boyhood to manhood.

Carried as a child from the West Indies to England by Captain Stair-Douglas of the Royal Navy, he was brought to the attention of Catherine Hyde, the Duchess of Queensberry, as being an unusually bright and personable boy. When she met him she was charmed and convinced the captain to part with him. The Duchess was one of the eighteenth century's most eccentric characters, even as a young woman. A beauty, she nonetheless dressed so simply – in country dresses and aprons – that she was refused entrance to fine houses by servants. She wore this garb even to the most elegant of balls, to the perpetual distress of her hosts. (Her childhood too was unusual; there was for example the horrific incident of a kitchen boy roasted alive on the spit and partially devoured by her mentally-impaired brother when the staff were preparing for a wedding.)[101] A patron of the playwright John Gay, she was commanded to stay away from Court by no less a person than King George II because she solicited subscriptions there for Gay's latest play despite its having been refused a licence by the Lord Chamberlain.

She was older when she took in Soubise and lavished upon him, apparently with the Duke's blessing, all the attention normally given to a son and heir. Soubise was even a great favourite with the maids, who were not overworked themselves and who called him 'the young Othello'. He had a leisured and splendid childhood, '[w]as engaging in his manners, and soon manifested a disposition for gallantry.'[102] Taught to fence and perhaps dreaming of one day becoming a general, Soubise attended Mr Angelo's *manège* where he excelled at riding and swordsmanship and where the Duchess came with her friends to watch him train. This attention, together with that of the other students of high-born families, caused him to exaggerate his pedigree. When the Duchess discovered that he was passing himself off as the son of an African prince she was appalled. '"O! is it so, Master Soubise?" said her grace. "I must lower your crest, I perceive."' She proposed to article him to Angelo as a riding and fencing assistant but Angelo, worried that the other students would be offended by his race, resisted. It was his wife who convinced him to go ahead, and to his surprise Soubise turned out to be extremely popular with the young noblemen. 'His manners were engaging,' wrote Angelo's son who knew him, 'and his good nature gained him the affection of everyone who came to the house.'[103] He played the violin, composed musical pieces, and later learned oration from Garrick, who befriended a number of black people. As part of his regular duties he accompanied the elder Angelo to Eton and Windsor as an usher, where his popularity increased.

At this point things began to get out of control. Soubise 'suddenly changed his manners, and became one of the most conspicuous fops of the town. He frequented the Opera, and the other theatres; sported a fine horse and groom in Hyde-Park; became a member of many fashionable clubs, and made a figure.'[104] Unknown to Angelo he lived a double life with secret private apartments full of hot-house flowers, a mistress and a hired coach, extravagant dinners for his hangers-on complete with claret and champagne, hosted at fashionable inns. 'He was equally expensive in perfumes, so that even in the lobbies at the theatres, the fops and the frail fair would exclaim, "I scent Soubise!"' noted the younger Angelo. 'He was no less extravagant in nosegays, and never seen, at any season, without a bouquet of the choicest flowers in his bosom. As general a lover as Don Juan, he wrote as many sonnets as Charlotte Smith; but not in that elegant writer's mournful strain – for he was as gay as a butterfly.'[105] When after two years the senior Angelo discovered these excesses his first impulse was to report Soubise to the Duchess, but he was amazed to find that all these bills were regularly discharged and a blind eye turned to his affairs.

Her leniency toward Soubise did not go unnoticed. Always an object of interest because of her eccentricities, both she and her protégé now became objects of satire. A famous 1773 engraving by William Austin portrayed the two of them engaged in a fencing match and titled it 'The D—— of playing at FOILS with her favorite LAP DOG MUNGO after expending near £10000 to make him a ——.' She sports a fencing mask and he is saying, 'Mungo here Mungo dere Mungo Every where above & below. Hah! What you Gracy tink of me Now.' In fact, Soubise became something of a staple metaphoric figure for eighteenth-century folly in prints and engravings. A similar engraving from 1787, 'The Major at Exercise', shows him boxing with a Major Coleraine even though Soubise had died before that (the exact date is unknown) and a book of drawings on 'macaroni' figures from 1772 shows him elegantly decked out with ruffles and sword as 'A

Mungo Macaroni.' For years extravagant and pretentious political figures like Jeremiah Dyson were satirized in engravings as Soubise, with black faces and in luxurious attire.

This attention only made the Duchess stronger in her support of Soubise, but if a report in *The Morning Post, and Daily Advertiser* after her death in 1777 is to be believed, even she finally realized when he had gone too far. According to the newspaper,

> he enticed one of the house-maids under the pretence of her meeting with a country acquaintance, to call at a house in the Strand, where he had previously secreted himself, and having fixed upon a notorious bawdy-house for the accomplishment of his designs, threatened the girl to murder her, if she refused to yield up her person. – The girl immediately when she got home, made the Duchess acquainted with her melancholy tale; her Grace offered her money, and told her not to speak of it, and she would take care of her; but finding the girl determined to appeal to the laws of her country, she sent for S——, and having filled his pockets, she sent him off to Harwich, where he might either have the opportunity of escaping, or waiting till such time as the girl's resentment could be softened.[106]

This was a scene straight out of Richardson's *Pamela*, and soon afterwards Soubise was hustled off to India where he changed his ways. The Duchess and Duke saw to it that he established a riding school in Bengal, where in the end he successfully trained private students and received a large salary for breaking in horses for the government. The life that Angelo described 'as gay as a butterfly, and his day of sunshine almost as short' came to a sudden end. In trying to break a difficult Arabian horse one day 'he was thrown, and, pitching on his head, was killed on the spot.'[107]

The younger Angelo retained a delight in Soubise and a forgiveness that Ignatius Sancho, probably the best-known black man in eighteenth-century London, refused. It was to Sancho that the Duchess of Queensberry turned when Soubise proved too much for her to handle, apparently believing that because he had suffered from similar lapses as a young man and had since become a model citizen, admired by nobility and commoners alike, he could succeed with the young profligate where she failed. Sancho accordingly took him in hand, but with his eyes wide open. In a letter dated 14 February 1768, he wrote to a friend to help Soubise, but cautiously:

> There is sent out in the Besborough, along with fresh governors, and other strange commodities, a little Blacky; whom you must either have seen or heard of; his name is S——. He goes out on a rational well-digested plan, to settle either at Madras or Bengal, to teach fencing and riding – he is expert at both. If he should chance to fall in your way, do not fail to give the rattlepate what wholesome advice you can; but remember, I do strictly caution you against lending him money upon any account, for he has every thing but – principle; he will never pay you; I am sorry to say so much of one whom I have had a friendship for, but it is needful; serve him if you can – but do not trust him.[108]

Four years later Sancho was more pleased with Soubise's progress now that he was away from the temptations of London, but still found it necessary to send him a long and fiery letter about his past, his blessings and his vagrancies, especially in his unusual position as a black man privileged by some of the most distinguished people of his time. 'Happy, happy! what a fortune is thine!' he exclaimed. '– Look round upon the miserable fate of almost all of our unfortunate colour – superadded to ignorance, – see slavery, and the contempt of those very wretches who roll in affluence from our labours. Superadded to this woeful catalogue – hear the ill-bred and heart-racking abuse of the foolish vulgar.' As always, money figured into any discussion with or about Soubise, and he ended this letter with a financial lesson which Soubise, with his previously unlimited credit, sorely needed:

> I am pleased with the subject of your last – and if your conversion is real, I shall ever be happy in your correspondence – But at the same time I cannot afford to pay five pence for the honour of your letters; – five pence is the twelfth part of five shillings – the forty-eighth part of a pound – it would keep my girls in potatoes for two days. – The time may come, when it may be necessary for you to study calculations; – in the mean while, if you cannot get a frank, direct to me under cover to his Grace the Duke of ——. You have the best wishes of your sincere friend (as long as you are your own friend).[109]

Soubise was his special reclamation project, but also a thorn in his side. 'Hang him! he teases me whenever I think of him,' he confessed on 23 July 1777.[110] Acutely aware of their position as black men in English society, he worried as much about the example they set of black English society in general as he did about Soubise's own lapsed moral condition. Certainly his taking on of the younger man as a philanthropic and moral project stemmed from race, but his real concern was for the young man's reformation even while he despaired of its possibility. '– When you see S——, note his behaviour,' he wrote to a friend on 8 November 1772. '– he writes me word that he intends a thorough and speedy reformation. – I rather doubt him, but should be glad to know if you perceive any marks of it.'[111]

His last preserved letter to Soubise was written in 1778 to India, informing him of the deaths of both the Duke and Duchess of Queensberry. It was a long treatise, outlining a plan of moral action and offering advice. At the same time, it unflinchingly laid out the state of Soubise's reputation in England now that he had lost his patrons: 'You may safely conclude now, that you have not many friends in England – Be it your study, with attention, kindness, humility, and industry, to make friends where you are – Industry with good-nature and honesty is the road to wealth. – A wise economy – without avaricious meanness, or dirty rapacity, will in a few years render you decently independent.' He cautioned Soubise to read the Bible and to pay his bills; he owed money to a saddler ('It was borrowed money, you know') and to a Bond Street merchant but could count on receiving nothing from Sancho himself. '[W]hatever commissions you send over to me – send money – or I stir none –,' he wrote. 'Thou well knowest my poverty – but 'tis an honest poverty – and I need not blush or conceal it.'[112]

The Duchess of Queensberry could not have selected a more upright mentor for her young protégé, and Sancho's contribution to the picture of blacks in eighteenth-century Britain cannot be underestimated. No doubt the extremely successful posthumous publication of his letters in 1782 stemmed largely to his being, as the title page stated, 'An African', and therefore in the public's view similar to Samuel Johnson's proverbial woman preacher (one was less surprised to see her do it well, he claimed, than to see her do it at all). But it gave contemporary as well as modern readers a vivid and alternative portrait of a black man wholly at home in England and English society, while at the same time amusedly aware of his position as both insider and outsider. This was quite a different picture from those of either the suffering slaves abroad or the costumed pages at home, which were more in the way of theatre and needed realistic augmentation. And indeed, his life and letters considerably broaden the picture of eighteenth-century London life in general.

Sancho was born aboard a slave ship in 1729 and baptized almost immediately in Carthagena by the bishop. He was orphaned soon after – his mother died of disease and his father committed suicide – and brought to England at the age of two, where his master gave him to three maiden sisters in Greenwich. The Bishop had dubbed him Ignatius, and the three women added 'Sancho' after Don Quixote's companion. His life with them was unhappy, and they often threatened to return him to plantation slavery. Fortunately, as a child he was often admired for his quickness and good spirit and the Duke of Montague, who 'brought him frequently home to the Duchess, indulged his turn for reading with presents of books, and strongly recommended to his mistresses the duty of cultivating a genius of such apparent fertility.'[113] When life in Greenwich finally became unbearable, Sancho turned to the now-widowed Duchess who at first turned him away. She soon discovered that he intended to shoot himself rather than return to his previous mistresses, and took him into her household as a butler until her death, 'when he found himself, by her Grace's bequest and his own oeconomy, possessed of seventy pounds in money, and an annuity of thirty.'[114]

It was at this point that he strayed from the straight and narrow and, like Soubise later, squandered his money on gambling and women. He even, at Garrick's suggestion, attempted acting, playing Othello and Oroonoko, those two staple black characters of the eighteenth-century stage, but a speech impediment aborted his success there. When he lost his clothes at gambling he returned to service at Montague House under the Chaplain, where he reformed his life and married a West Indian woman named Anne.

Sancho loved his wife unabashedly. To one friend he wrote on 15 September 1770 that he hoped 'Mrs. Sancho will be as good as her word, and soon pay you a visit. – I will trust her with you, though she is the treasure of my soul.'[115] To Soubise he wrote on 11 October 1772 that he was 'heartily tired of the country; – the truth is – Mrs. Sancho and the girls are in town; – I am not ashamed to own that I love my wife – I hope to see you married, and as foolish.'[116] Anne and Ignatius Sancho opened a grocer's shop on Charles Street, Westminster, on 29 January 1774. There they worked together and received visitors of all ranks. When it was quiet Sancho sat at the back and wrote his famous letters, but his wife was also literate and discerning and they read and discussed his correspondence together. Over the years the steady arrival of five daughters and a son kept them busy but also delighted them. He referred to his family as 'the hen and chicks', the 'Sanchonets and Sanchonettas',[117] and nearly always appended his wife's greetings to his letters.

The visitors to the Sancho establishment and the people they visited were astonishing for a grocer and his family, let alone a black one. Garrick, the Montagues, and other well-known and high-born figures were his friends; he corresponded with Laurence Sterne whose *Tristram Shandy* he admired immensely. John T. Smith visited the Charles Street shop with his teacher, the sculptor Nollekens who, 'having recollected that he had promised [Sancho] a cast of his friend Sterne's bust', decided to deliver it. There they 'drank tea with Sancho and his black lady, who was seated, when we entered, in the corner of the shop, chopping sugar, surrounded by her little "Sanchonets"'. They discussed politics, and Smith also recalled Sancho speaking knowledgeably about art during a visit to Nollekens' studio.[118] Nollekens himself had a black servant, a woman named Elizabeth Rosina Clements, also called 'Black Bet' and 'Bronze', who 'went grey in the service of the thrifty Nollekens.'[119]

Sancho was the model for the character Shirna Cambo in the 1790 novel *Memoirs and Opinions of Mr. Blenfield*, in which he serves as wise man and adviser to a young man who, like Smith, was taken to visit him. During their friendship Cambo instructs Blenfield on filial duty, religion, literature, slavery and philanthropy. This novel is perhaps the first instance in English literature when white men visit a black family in their home as equals, and when black people are shown as integrated into the white English community. One scene takes place in an oyster club, where Cambo is a local favourite and sought-after companion. There they discuss Sterne and Burke and his is the voice of moral conviction, the impetus for the Blenfield's subsequent positive behaviour. 'Such were the general effects of all my visits to the house of this worthy man,' says Blenfield. '[I]t was the chief desire of his heart to scatter instruction by the most pleasing and insinuating subjects; for every decent merriment he had a smile, for every sorrow he had a tear: it was his good genius that rendered him the patron of the one, and the soother of the other; in his method he had educated his own family, wherein he lived to see and to admire the blessing of an extended circle, where virtue and all the softer characters of Christianity were engrafted and diffused.'[120]

In reality, as in the novel, Sancho was a corpulent character given to self-deprecating irony about his race. Explaining why he could never serve the parish offices, he writes that he is 'utterly unqualified through infirmities – as well as complexion. – Figure to yourself, my dear Sir, a man of a convexity of belly exceeding Falstaff – and a black face into the bargain – waddling in the van of poor thieves and pennyless prostitutes.'[121] He refers to himself variously as a 'poor Negro', a 'blackamoor', 'a poor African', 'a fat old fellow' and 'Sancho the Big'. He signs his letters to *The General Advertiser* and *The Morning Post* 'Africanus'. One is always aware when reading his letters of the extent to which he was aware of his race, or rather, the extent to which he kept it at the forefront because he knew others were aware of it. ('Your daughter Kate brought me your letter,' he wrote to Mrs H—— on 22 December 1771. '– she seemed a little surprised at my being favor'd with your correspondence – and I am sure wished to see the contents.')[122] His self-mockery was underpinned by deadly seriousness on slavery. Well aware that he had only through providence escaped West Indian slavery, he spoke against the 'peculiar institution' as it appeared in both the East and West Indies, 'a subject which sours my blood'.[123] On 4 May 1778 he cautioned a young friend off to a career in India not to make a fortune at the expense of the Indian people: 'I do not wish you half a million – clogged with the tears and blood of the poor natives.'[124] A religious man, he referred to Jesus as 'the Son of the Most High God – who died for the sins of all-all – Jew, Turk, Infidel, and Heretic; – fair – sallow – brown – tawny – black – and you and I – and every son and daughter of Adam.'[125] He read the latest books and pamphlets against the slave trade, some of them sent by friends. One he thanked 'for your kindness in sending the books – That upon the unchristian and most diabolical usage of my brother Negroes – the illegality – the horrid wickedness of the traffic – the cruel carnage and depopulation of the human species . . . The perusal affected me more than I can express; – indeed I felt a double or mixt sensation – for while my heart was torn for the sufferings – which, for aught I know – some of my nearest kin might have undergone – my bosom, at the same time, glowed with gratitude – and praise toward the humane – the Christian – the friendly and learned Author of that most valuable book.'[126]

Here and elsewhere appears in his letters what W. E. B. Dubois would much later refer to as the 'double consciousness' that was an inevitable part of the black experience, the simultaneous and sometimes conflicting awareness of being both a part of the political and social organism as a citizen, and of being a descendant of Africa. For Sancho this double consciousness was always close to the surface, even when expressing thoroughly British political and social views. He wrote, for example, one of the most immediate and impressive accounts still existing of the Gordon Riots (in which a black man took part), and his day-to-day accounts of English life shed light on the daily life of the ordinary Londoner in the late eighteenth century. Take, for example, the following:

. . . not five minutes since I was interrupted, in this same letter of letters, by a pleasant affair – to a man of no feelings. – A fellow bolted into the shop – with a countenance in which grief and fear struggled for mastery. – 'Did you see any body go to my cart, sir?' – 'No, friend, how should I? You see I am writing – and how should I be able to see your cart or you either in the dark?' – 'Lord in heaven pity me!' cries the man, 'what shall I do? oh! what shall I do? – I am undone! – Good God! – I did but go into the court here – with a trunk for the lady at Captain G——'s (I had two to deliver), and somebody has stole the other. – What shall I do? – what shall I do?' – 'Zounds, man! – who ever left their cart in the night with goods in it, without leaving some one to watch?' – 'Alack, sir, I left a boy, and told him I would give him something to stand by the cart, and the boy and trunk are both gone!' – . . . the trunk was seen pending between two in the Park – and I dare say the contents by this time are pretty well gutted.[127]

The distraught driver shows no surprise at encountering a black shopkeeper, and Sancho responds to him as a more than full equal.

However, while he was fully and comfortably incorporated into English life, there are also hints of the differences which he and his family must have felt because of race. They visit the theatre frequently without incident, he fishes in Scotland on an extended holiday, and he takes three of his daughters to Vauxhall for an evening in August 1777: 'Heaven and Earth! – how happy, how delighted were the girls! – Oh! the pleasures of novelty to youth!' Yet he adds, 'We went by water – had a coach home – were gazed at – followed, &c. &c. – but not much abused.'[128] He takes this as expected, but refers to England as 'your country' to a friend when he exclaims that the 'grand object of English navigators – indeed of all Christian navigators – is money – money – money . . .'[129] His needs and pleasures are far more modest. He delights in his daughters' birthday parties, his pipe (a brand of tobacco, 'Sancho's best Trinidado', was later named after him),[130] his friends' letters and visits, his wife's solicitude and intelligence, and good books.

Most accounts of Sancho's life and influence concentrate on his literary enthusiasms, for he is perhaps best known for his admiration of Laurence Sterne. He first wrote to Sterne in July of 1776, identifying himself as a black man who was also a great admirer of Sterne's writing, 'beseeching' him 'to give one half-hour's attention to slavery, as it is at this day practised in the West Indies.'[131] As it happened Sterne had just been writing the famous scene 'of a friendless poor negro-girl' which moved Toby to tears in *Tristram Shandy*, and a friendship by post began. Sancho emulated Sterne's literary style, especially in his propensity for dashes and exclamatory asides and practically the only remark one historian makes about Sancho is that his letters were a 'rather painful imitation of the manner of Sterne.'[132] He admitted that 'if I am an enthusiast in any thing, it is in favour of my Sterne,'[133] but there is also evidence, which most critics have ignored, that he was entirely self-conscious in his imitation, even exaggerating it for the amusement of his correspondents who were fully aware of his particular hobby-horse.

He took the works of other black writers, such as they were, far more seriously than his own, since he never wrote his letters for publication, although he did publish a book of his musical compositions. The American slave Phillis Wheatley became a sensation for her neo-classical poetry, taking England and America by storm; few previously believed that it was possible for a black person to have literary genius. She was lionized when she visited England, and in both countries a list of convinced subscribers was appended to the poetry, and the original edition of her work was prefaced by the testimony of the learned white men who had tested her abilities and attested to the authenticity of her poems. Her master and mistress in Boston taught her to read and write at an early age and gave her free reign in her learning, and took credit less for her erudition than for the fact of owning such a wonder.

Sancho admired her work, published in London in 1773, but censured her owner and subscribers. 'Phyllis's [*sic*] poems do credit to nature – and put art – merely as art – to the blush. – It reflects nothing either to the glory or generosity of her master – if she is still his slave – except he glories in the low vanity of having in his wanton power a mind animated by Heaven – a genius superior to himself,' he wrote on 27 January 1778. 'The list of splendid – titled – learned names, in confirmation of her being the real authoress – alas! shows how very poor the acquisition of wealth and knowledge is – without generosity – feeling – and humanity. – These great folks – all know – and perhaps admired – nay, praised Genius in bondage – and then, like the Priests and the Levites in sacred write, passed by – not one good Samaritan amongst them.'[134]

Sancho wrote letters nearly to the end of his life, recording his decline through fever, asthma, dropsy and gout, many of his symptoms probably brought on by obesity. He died on 14 December 1780 at the age of fifty-one, and was buried in the Broadway, Westminster.[135] His fame, such as it was, came post-humously; his passing was noted in *The Gentleman's Magazine*. When *Memoirs and Opinions of Mr. Blenfield* was published ten years later it offered this eulogy to 'Shirna Cambo': 'Myself and a few other of his friends paid him the last respect, and saw his family seated in the comfortable possession of what he had pre-served by fair dealing, during a life of domestic virtue and public rectitude. There are men to whom all praise is needless, before whose characters all panegyric is trifling and vain; such was the amiable, the excellent, the self-instructed Shirna Cambo! But the tears that followed his hearse are his best eulogy!'[136]

His letters were collected and published by one of his correspon-dents, Miss F. Crewe, in 1782, and sold so fast that the *Monthly Review* had to wait for the second printing the following year in order to review it.[137] There were over 600 subscribers to the book, including nobility, and Anne Sancho, who kept on their grocer's shop, received more than £500 for its publication. Their son Wil-liam republished the letters in 1803. Over a hundred years later, in a magazine article, 'Gillespie' drew comparisons between Samuel Johnson and Ignatius Sancho:

> Physically they were both corpulent and unwieldy in their persons; intellectually, they were giants, their minds ranging over a large area, and easily assimilating, and quick to appreciate the characters and facts which surrounded them. Socially, they were in their habits domestic, and in their aspirations noble. Johnson, however, had his biographer; it is regrettable that Ignatius Sancho did not meet with his Boswell.[138]

What do we learn from Sancho about black life in London? First of all, that it was entirely possible for a black family to exist in domestic harmony and with a sense of community with both white and black friends and neighbours. While perhaps his being black was at first a novelty for those who befriended him, for the most part those friendships lasted and grew into a new kind of racial harmony. The patronage of the rich and famous extended beyond the simple bequeathing of money to faithful servants and, if the author of *Memoirs and Opinions of Mr. Blenfield* is to be believed, white Britons were increasingly willing to be instructed by and learn from their black neighbours.

It seems too that there must have been other Sanchos and Beefs and Barbers, for any number of black slaves received their freedom and small legacies from less well-known masters. Not all of them would have been able to rise to the kind of independence these achieved, but to open a shop and settle into a community was occasionally possible and acceptable to the general population. There was, for example, a black man named Pompey, in service to a Colonel John Hill, who considered standing for the speakership of a parliament of footmen. In 1780, the year Sancho died, two black footmen duelled with pistols behind Montague House, and were seconded by two white footmen.[139]

What seems to make Beef, Barber and Sancho stand out is their level of education, at least in the cases of Barber and – although he claimed to be primarily self-taught – Sancho. We hear about these three now because the people who 'owned' or knew them gave us the legacy of their remembrance, in words and in visual images. Sancho was painted by Gainsborough, and there is some evidence that he also appears in Hogarth's 1742 *Taste in High Life*. Francis Barber was painted by Sir Joshua Reynolds, who like Hogarth often included black people in his art. The servant who nearly sent the thief to the gallows is likely to be the same man who appeared in some of Reynolds' portraits, when families who were sitting for their likenesses did not provide their own servants for the paintings. These portrayals are far from representative of the vast majority of black servants. Most lived in far less glory, working for far less generous masters and mistresses. In picture after picture they appear throughout the century, silent witnesses to and participants in eighteenth-century English life.

CHAPTER THREE

What about Women?

At the height of the late eighteenth-century struggle over the slave trade, the noted caricaturist Gillray published an engraving titled 'Philanthropic Consolations after the loss of the Slave-Bill'. In it two white West Indian men smoke and drink in their parlour with two bare-breasted black women; one of the women sits on a man's lap and is being fondled. Everyone, including the turbaned black boy who waits on them, is smiling. On the wall hangs a picture of Inkle and Yariko, from the opera by George Coleman, and a picture of Westminster Abbey. Gillray was satirizing how white creoles benefited from opposing abolition and made black women appear happy in their enslavement.

A few years later another print, 'The Happy Negro', romanticized Africa and motherhood. A black man sings that the 'white man's joys are not like mine', for although 'me is poor . . . me is gay':

> Me sing all day, me sleep all night;
> Me hab no care, my heart is light;
> Me tink not what tomorrow bring,
> Me happy so me sing.

Seated next to him are his wife and child in a conventional Madonna pose, wearing modest white gowns.

As the battle over slavery heated up, British factions promoted two opposing images of black women. To the promoters of slavery black women were sexual creatures, necessary to colonial labour and complicit in an open system of concubinage. To abolitionists they were wives and mothers torn from family and home. Both images relied upon the greed of the white man who on the one hand physically benefited from the sexualizing of black women and on the other, as the 'Happy Negro' sang was

> . . . full of care, his heart no light,
> He great deal want he little get,
> He sorry, so he fret.

Both had to do with a selectively politicized and economized morality but neither addressed the reality of black women in Britain.

From the earliest instances, the black female presence in Great Britain was conflated with a spectacle and pageantry which quite literally set the stage for their representation even to modern times. In the sixteenth and early seventeenth centuries black men and women and their painted white counterfeits appeared regularly in masques and pageants. Henry VIII and the Earl of Essex dressed as Turks for a court festival in 1510. Their torchbearers 'were appareyled in Crymosyn satyne and grene, liyke Moreskoes, their faces blacke', while six women appeared with 'their faces, neckes, armes and handes, covered with fyne pleasaunce blacke . . . so that the same ladies seemed to be nigrost or blacke Mores'.[1] The character of the Moor was used in such diverse productions as a London drapers' pageant in 1522, George Peele's 1585 pageant, Thomas Middleton's 1613 *Triumph of Truth*, and Anthony Munday's 1616 *Chyrsanaleia*.[2] The 'masque of Moors' became a genre in and of itself during the reigns of Edward VI, Elizabeth, and James I – there was even one just for female Moors in 1551 – and no costs were spared on display and costume.[3]

The most famous of these masques is Ben Jonson's *Masque of Blacknesse* from a pair of 'royall Masques, The one of Blacknesse, The other of Beautie' ordered by Queen Anne. She and her ladies performed it in 1605 and 1608, dressed in costumes designed by Inigo Jones. Earlier, actual black women performed in these productions. One hundred years earlier William Dunbar's notorious poem 'Ane Blak Moir' described a Scottish tournament of forty days' duration, presided over by a black woman 'recently landed furth of the last schippis'. First announcing that he has long written about white women and will now turn his pen to a black one, Dunbar unflatteringly describes Ann as having full lips, being like a toad to touch, with a cat-like nose and skin like a gleaming tar barrel. The jousters who fight hardest in the field get to kiss and embrace her, while the losers 'sall cum behind and kis hir hippis'. James IV spared no expense in outfitting her in gold, taffeta, gauze, damask and silk, all imported. At the end of the forty days 'there were three days of feasting, culminating in a display by a conjuror who caused a cloud to descend from the roof of the Holyrood-house banqueting hall and, as it seemed, snatch up the black lady so that she was seen no more'.[4]

This ribald and, to modern readers, offensive public display combined perceptions of black women which were common even at that early date and which persist till this day. Ned Ward mentioned a black female acrobat at Bartholomew Fair in *The London Spy* of 1698–9; a 'Countrey Fellow . . . Cackled' at '*the Devil going to Dance*'.[5] More positively, a black woman playing Polly in *The Beggar's Opera* in Lancashire was found 'excellent as to figure, and speaking, but remarkably so as to singing'.[6] By the eighteenth century such performances featuring black women were rare as they began to occupy a status even lower than that of the richly attired and ultimately expendable black page.

The practice of including black servants in portraits continued into the eighteenth century. At first featuring animals as the devotees of the subject, young black boys and sometimes girls took on that role. Mignard's *Duchess of Portsmouth* (1682) shows the pale and serene Duchess with her arm around her adoring 'pet black'.[7] In place of a slave's collar the girl wears a string of pearls which sets off her dark skin, and an expensive lace-trimmed dress. She holds a seashell full of pearls. Her hair is close-shaven, while her mistress's is arranged in soft curls. Wright's *Two Girls and a Negro Servant* has a similar portrayal, of a dark and short-haired girl kneeling to offer a basket of flowers to her two fair, long-haired child mistresses. Dabydeen claims that in the first type of portrait the '*aesthetic* image of Madonna and Child mirror the *political*, imperial notion of Mother Country and Child Colony', and that both types place white masters and black servant in positions 'of dominance and inferiority'.[8]

In early representations the slaves' pure, youthful and unconditional affection underscored their masters' apparent goodness

and purity. When their images appeared primarily in art and spectacle, their function was to provide a startling or amusing contrast
to white women. Like the young, dark and extravagantly decorated African boys so popular in the first three quarters of the
seventeenth century, black women were used in the popular media
of prints and engravings and fiction to complement those whom
they served. By the Elizabethan period white, 'particularly when
complemented by red, [was] the colour of perfect human beauty,
especially *female* beauty', an 'ideal already centuries old in Elizabeth's time'.[9]

In the more reform-minded final decades of the eighteenth century these representations reverted to the satirical extremes
common nearly 300 years earlier in Dunbar's time, which relied
upon the placing of a black woman into a traditionally white
woman's role. A Woodward Delin print from 1803, 'Advertisement for a Wife!!', shows a hypochondriacal man surprised at
home by a queue of women who have come to offer their marital
services. Among them is a black woman who finds 'Massa' a
'pretty man'. 'Advertise for a Wife!' exclaims the man as he leaps
from his armchair, 'I should as soon think of advertising for a
Death Warrant – Mercy on me there is a black among them . . .'
A coloured engraving from 1830 also shows the amusement
afforded by this role reversal when a heavy black woman sits
daintily in her mistress's finery, with a candle, bottle and wine
glass on the table next to her. From behind a curtain peek the
young ladies of the household who have apparently put her up to
the charade. 'You tink Massa Captin take me for young lady?'
she asks them. The caption is 'None but the brave deserve the
fair.' 'Massa Captin' probably indicates that he is a West Indian,
for it was a known fact that white male creoles commonly took
black women as their mistresses, with or without their consent.

In England itself, despite everyday interactions between blacks
and whites, discussion about black women and white men quickly
degenerated to its lowest sexual denominator.[10] In Gillray's 1788
drawing of the Prince of Wales and his Wowski, she wears western
clothes but is almost completely bare-breasted as they gaze into
each other's eyes. This undermines the innocent caption: 'Free as
the forest birds we'll pair together,/Without remembering who

our fathers were,/And in soft murmurs interchange our souls.'
That the prince had a black mistress caused no alarm, but

> For a gentleman to be caught in bed with a black woman, or for the
> black servant to gain the affections of his white mistress, was the
> height of social folly. Yet both frequently occurred, to the private
> amusement and public shock of society. Cartoonists and caricaturists,
> those graphic barometers of English society in the late eighteenth
> century, took great delight in bringing to their curious audience the
> saucy truth or mischievous innuendo of sexual relations between black
> and white. There were of course instances of happy, stable relations
> between black and white which managed to survive the pressures of
> society. But these were generally ignored as society of all levels fixed
> its sordid gaze on the more titillating aspects of sexual relations.[11]

To view the popular prints and novels, one would have thought
that the sexual relationship was the only one between whites and
blacks, but the 'titillation' stemmed as much from the crossing of
class lines as from racial ones. Black footmen might and did marry
white serving maids without eyebrows being raised, but anyone
marrying his cook, of whatever colour, committed a different,
and far worse, sort of social transgression.

John MacDonald, a white footman who wrote of his exploits
while serving and travelling with numerous masters, illustrates
this relative colour-blindness among the serving class. He mentions a black woman known as Sally Percival who lived in India
with a Dr Percival and their son. At the doctor's death she received
'her freedom and a great deal of money', but despite her wealth,
as she told MacDonald, she would have preferred the privilege of
real marriage. Without a hint of racial animosity but with a great
deal of gallantry MacDonald responded, '[I]f I was good enough
for you, I would propose myself for your husband'. He saw her
as entirely honourable and indeed superior to him, 'a good-natured
and good-tempered woman as ever lived, and had not the least
pride, though she was worth upwards of four thousand pounds
sterling'.[12] In his class, race was no impediment to marriage but
such a disparity in income was.

Sally's case was an unusual one, for her position left her with
money and status. The black prostitutes in London were less

lucky. Mostly forced into this profession by poverty or abandon-
ment by their white masters, they were in great demand by a
monied white clientele. 'Black Harriot' was stolen in Africa and
bore two children by a Jamaican planter who brought her to England then died of smallpox. Driven to prostitution to support
herself, she was attractive and educated, drawing a long list of
more than seventy clients, 'at least 20 of whom, according to a
contemporary account, were members of the House of Lords'.[13]
She was 'very alluring . . . tall, well made, and genteel . . .' with
'a degree of politeness [i.e. intellect], scarce to be paralleled in an
African female'.[14] The 1770s must have been a high point for this
sort of activity, for in addition to Sally and Harriot, Boswell was
informed by the Earl of Pembroke of the entirely black brothel
catering to the nobility. There was a Mrs Lowes in 1788 and a
Miss Wilson in 1793, both plying their trade in Soho to great
financial success, both known for their sweetness, beauty, and
intelligence.[15] In the early nineteenth century, 'Ebony Bet' worked
in a flagellation brothel.[16]

While the relations between young black men and their mistresses were confined to certain classes of people, those between
black women and their employers tended to occupy a more highly
charged sexual territory. The most common scenario for black
women involved arriving in England as part of the chattel and
entourage of returning or visiting white creoles, male and female.
The sexual liaisons of black women and white men in the West
Indies were well known and vilified in Britain, even though the
West Indians themselves saw it as a common enough, and perhaps
even necessary, component of life in the Caribbean. For the black
women who willingly entered into such relationships it was the
only sort of upward mobility and comfort available to them; for
those who did so unwillingly it was one of the greatest horrors
of slavery. There are numerous stories of black women who
destroyed the babies conceived in this way.

For white women in the West Indies and Britain, however,
the story was rather different. Novel after novel discussed the
widespread practice of black concubinage, frequently placing the
blame on the black women and deliberately ignoring the men's
transgressions. Jane West, under the pen name of 'Prudentia

Homespun', wrote *Advantages of an Education. Or, the History of Maria Williams* (1793) about a woman who left her daughter in England to avoid the dangerous climate and attitudes of the West Indies. Her husband, who had been there for several years, was becoming thoroughly dissipated, and her friends begged her to come to him. 'His faults,' one of her friends wrote to her, 'are no more than the common vices of the island.'

> The planters, generally speaking, countenance each other in irregularities, at which an English libertine would blush. The redundant fertility of these tropical climes, and the bad habits which slavery introduces, are not favourable to the cause of virtue. The lord of the soil, accustomed to the mean subservience of those around him, who think themselves honoured by being made the instruments of his crimes, soon overcomes every restraint of conscience, and pleads example to conceal, if not to extenuate his fault. Mr. Williams is less culpable than many others. But surely, Amelia, you have been blameably wedded to ease and indulgence in renouncing the matrimonial ties, rather than the enjoyments which your own country afforded.[17]

Daughters raised in the West Indies were seen by female novelists as facing the greatest danger of contamination from black people. Mrs Neville, in Helena Wells's *Constantia Neville; or, the West Indian* (1800), 'would have been perfectly happy, but for the black servants'[18] and she took pains 'to keep Constantia from the negroes (Mrs. Neville always having an English woman in her nursery)'.[19] According to her, Constantia 'could not comprehend that the superiority arises from our making her so much our companion, nor our fears for doing so, namely, the fear of contamination from the negroes, whose immoral discourse and corrupted dialect, if she had often heard it, unrestrained by our presence, might have had the most pernicious effects'.[20] She considers that 'the danger to females is . . . greatest' for in Barbados 'there was no instance of any resident having a white mistress; all men of fortune, who were not married, had their brown women; but such connections were kept among domestics, the issue of them brought up as slaves, and not unfrequently sold on the death of the master of the estate'.[21] Consequently it is in England that

Constantia first really encounters 'the issue' of such alliances and is shocked to learn that a wealthy young mulatto, the inheritor of his white father's fortune, had the audacity to address a white woman, but applauded the woman for refusing to compromise herself even in the face of such tempting wealth.

Conversely, it was also essential that black women be viewed as the allies of white women, in the West Indies and in Britain. Notoriously spoiled in both the East and West Indies, white women in the eighteenth century, like those in earlier centuries, frequently used darker, subservient women to elevate themselves socially and to appear fairer complexioned. Much more tangible than these aesthetic concerns were those of personal safety and welfare, for during the frequent slave revolts whites were often rescued by faithful blacks. It was to this as well as to the image of thwarted motherhood that abolitionists turned, but in England these faithful servants and their masters and mistresses had different relationships.

Drawn from the ranks of those whose masters no longer needed them, or those who were freed, or those who ran away when they arrived in Britain, this larger group became part of the silent serving class, taken advantage of by new employers who played on their fear of returning to even more horrible West Indian plantation slavery. One night in 1790 the moralist writer Hannah More watched in horror as a black woman 'was dragged out from a hole in the top of a house [in Bristol], where she had hid herself, and forced on board ship'. More wrote to Horace Walpole of her 'great grief and indignation'.[22] In 1792 another black woman was sold in the same slaving port for £80 and put on board ship where 'her tears flowed down her face like a shower of rain'.[23]

There were far fewer black women than men in Britain – an unequal market fuelled by the continuing demand for black boys. For every woman taken up by a slave dealer, former master or sexual client, many more performed the drudgery of daily domestic life and witnessed, perhaps even more than black men, the peccadilloes of private English life. 'Statute Hall for Hiring Servants' of 1770 depicts withered members of the upper class interviewing robust and desirable young male and female servants. In the background, in shadow, a black woman seeking employment observes them. 'The H–r–g–n Haram' from 1775 shows a young black woman standing in the background of a genteel brothel, and in 'Charms of Precedence' from 1795 a black serving woman's tray of food is overturned by gentlemen attempting to outdo each other in exaggerated *politesse*. The black woman or man as iconographic social conscience grew over the course of the century to be almost as common as the sexual figure, emphasizing the irony of the 'savage' English nobility observed by the 'moral' primitive.

A far smaller number than their male counterparts, black women's transference to Britain carried proportionately more weight. In 1785 so small a percentage of the black population was female that 'the consequences of this sexual imbalance were profound and far reaching, both for the blacks themselves and, in a wider context, for their relations with white society.'[24] Public perception replaced reality and affected black women even more than it did black men, even though their daily lives contradicted their representation in popular culture. As with young black men it was when they grew old, or were baptized, educated, or desired freedom that they became problematic and hailed less as a depiction of an orderly national condition than of a disorderly social one. When Dinah Black was sold by her mistress then rescued from a ship in Bristol in 1687, she took her mistress to court and won the right to earn her own living until the next session reconvened.[25] It was a small and temporary victory.

A similar but more famous case was that of Katherine Auker who went to court in Middlesex in 1690 to be released from her master. She had resided in England for six years where she was baptized, believing, like so many other slaves, that it automatically freed her. Her master and mistress 'tortured her and turned her out', and since they refused to give her a discharge she was unable to seek employment elsewhere. Her employers returned to Barbados but had her thrown in prison. 'The court,' writes Fryer, 'maintained a neat balance between property rights and the rights of the individual by ordering that she be free to serve anyone – until her master returned to England'.[26]

Granville Sharp, who so assiduously and successfully learned to use the courts for blacks' justice, took on the case of John and Mary Hylas in 1768. John arrived in England in 1754 with his mistress Judith Aleyne. Mary arrived the same year with her master John Newton; the two married in 1758 with their owners' consent. During the eight years of their marriage, John received his freedom, but in 1766 Mary's masters apparently changed their minds or needed money and had her kidnapped, taken to the West Indies and sold. John Hylas himself approached Sharp, who took on the case and wrote about it at some length in his letter book. Hylas was advised to sue for damages rather than recovery of his wife, and this was held against him. At the opening of the trial 'Sir Fletcher Norton first Council for the Defendant insinuated that [Hylas] did not want to have his Wife again, as he has asked for nothing but Damages, and consequently that the taking her away was no great loss to him,' Sharp recorded. 'Therefore (says he) we will meet you halfway if you will give up your action for Damages, we will restore the Woman to the Plaintiff'. Sharp called upon the Bible and early law to plead his case. According to both, he argued, a husband and wife were one, 'and if he be free, so must She likewise'.

The jury finally found for the defendant, but undercut this potentially important decision by awarding Hylas only a single shilling in damages. Sharp was infuriated, believing that Mary should not only be returned but that John deserved '£500 damages at the least, besides treble costs . . . as the first lawyer of the kingdom would be, if he should lose his wife in the same manner'.[27]

> The poor Man indeed was asked in Court, whether he would have his Wife or Damages. He replyed he desired to have his Wife.
>
> But why this cruel alternative? If he had a right to his Wife (which cannot be denied) he most certainly had a right to Damages also, in consideration of the Violent and unpardonable outrage committed against *himself* in the *person* of his Wife, for which no pecuniary allowance whatsoever can really make him amends . . .
>
> It was nevertheless, insinuated in Court, that Hylas had not much regard for his Wife; that he rather wished for Damages, than to recover the person (though he even proved otherwise) and therefore that the Damages should be proportioned to the loss which might appear to be sustained.[28]

The court had to consider both John's rights as a husband and Mary's position as a chattel, and questioned the possibility of marital fidelity and affection between black people.

Sharp knew, however, that more was at stake:

> Nevertheless before the Cause was opened, near even during the time that the Clerk was tendering the Oath to the Jury Sir Fletcher Norton came into Court and acquainted the Judge, that now the great important Question concerning the right of retaining Slaves in England was likely to come before his Lordship, signifying at the same time that it is a point of great difficulty, and that a judicial determination much to be wished for, or to that purpose &c.
>
> Sir Fletcher likewise observed afterwards, that there are now in Town upwards of 20,000 Negroes. I could have told him that there would soon be 20,000 more, [if] the important and difficult point, as he calls it, was . . . determined on his side of the Question, whereas if it was clearly proved on the other hand that Negroes become free on their landing in England, it is very certain that their West Indian Masters who are so tenacious of this kind of property would for the most part be prevented thereby from bringing them.[29]

Hylas, who merely wanted his wife back, was caught up in England's fear of taking on the larger question of slavery on British soil, which Fletcher undoubtedly hoped this case would determine. It did not, but Newton was ordered to return Mary on the next ship or within six months, 'whichever was earlier'.[30]

Fifty years after the James Somerset case in 1772 (see Chapter 4) the courts again tested whether or not residence in England conferred automatic freedom on slaves. Grace Allen spent a year in England with her mistress, but two years after their return to Antigua she was taken from her mistress by a customs officer who believed her former English residence made her free. Unlike the other cases hers was argued in the West Indies where it was decided and later upheld on appeal that she remained the property of her mistress. While pro-slavery interests celebrated, not everyone in England was pleased. The *New Times* considered her kidnapped, and saw the case as a battle between 'flesh and blood on one side, and perishable possessions on the other – the cause of

78

liberty and the cause of gold – God and Mammon. Which is best entitled to consideration?'[31]

What is interesting about these last two cases is that they were not brought by the defendants themselves. While Dinah Black and Katherine Auker sued for the restoration of their liberty and the right to support themselves, Mary Hylas and Grace Allen were not even present in England during the trials, nor could they bring legal action, for in the West Indies there was no such thing as slaves' rights. The white men involved in these two cases agreed to take them on in order to set precedents and in an attempt to resolve larger issues of black people's legal status left unsettled through the long history of their presence in Britain. The Black and Auker cases, as Sharp and others knew, did little more than keep two women employed and off the streets while the English judicial system wavered over problems of property versus humanity. Scotland had no such doubts; slavery was banned on its soil.

Little was to change in the eighteenth century, which saw Yorke and Talbot's precedent-setting 1729 decision 'that a slave, by coming from the West Indies, either with or without his master, to Great Britain or Ireland, doth not become free; and that his master's property or right in him is not thereby determined or varied' at one end, and at the other heard the Earl of Abingdon, discussing Wilberforce's bill against the slave trade, declare to the House of Lords in 1793 that 'Humanity is a private feeling and not a public principle to act upon. It is a case of conscience, not of constitutional right'.[32] By 1822, and even after Grace Allen's case, not much had changed in England to improve the position of black people despite the ending of the slave trade.

Even so, a number of black women able to remain in England achieved a reasonably comfortable life. Many were baptized, some of course hoping thereby to gain official freedom, but others out of true religious and communal feeling. Frances, a 'Blackymore maide', was baptized in Bristol in 1645. A 'Dark woman' named Ann Atkins was a member of the same church from 1677 until her death in 1695. A black woman was rumoured to haunt the area surrounding the west-country church to which she belonged.[33] A group of black parishioners turned out for a christening at the parish church of St Giles' in 1726, to the amusement of a writer for the *St. James's Evening Post*:

> 1st Came the reputed Father, a Guiney Black, a very clever well-drest Fellow, and another Black who was to be the Godfather. 2dly, The Midwife or rather her Deputy, a White Woman, carrying the little sooty Pagan, who was to be metamorphos'd into a Christian, 3dly, The Mother, who was also a Black but not of the Guiney Breed, a well shap'd, well dress'd Woman. 4thly, The two intended Godmothers, attended by 6 or 8 more, all Guiney Blacks, as pretty, genteel Girls, as could be girt with a Girdle, and setting aside the Complexion, enough to tempt an old frozen Anchorite to have crack'd a Commandment with any of them.[34]

The correspondent saves his admiration for the 'tempting' women. Indeed black women sometimes received as much or even more sympathy than did black men. A popular poem called 'The African Widow being the History of a Poor Black Woman' is one example:

> In London city once there dwelt
> A poor but honest pair,
> God blessed them with an infant child
> And she was all their care
> From Afric's far distant shores,
> To this good land she came,
> Friendless and poor alike unknown
> To fortune and to fame.

Oddly enough, despite the glowing and famous example of Anne and Ignatius Sancho, part of the novelty for eighteenth-century Britons was not in seeing black people individually, but in seeing black people marry and set up house together.

The everyday life of a black serving woman probably involved little of ceremony or community. For illustration we should turn to the life of Elizabeth Rosina Clements, the elderly black servant of the Royal Academy sculptor Joseph Nollekens, the same man who presented Sancho with the bust of his revered Laurence Sterne. Apparently a free woman, she worked for years in his house at number 28 Dean Street, Soho, for little remuneration besides shelter and minimal food. Nollekens' biographer, John Thomas Smith, describes her as

> . . . a woman possessing a considerable share of drollery; and from her complexion being of a chestnut-brown colour, somewhat tinctured with olive, she acquired from the shopkeepers, particularly those of Oxford-market, the nickname of 'Black Bet': but from the artists the more classical appellation of 'Bronze' . . . Indeed, she might very well call to mind the expression of Petrarch, who describes his female servant as being 'brown as a Libyan desert, and dry as a mummy'.[35]

Perhaps she was born in Britain, or perhaps she arrived there as a girl or young woman who, like Dinah Black or Katherine Auker earlier, was given the questionable opportunity to fend for herself. We know she was free because she received wages — although extremely meagre ones — from Nollekens and his wife.

Although he, like Samuel Johnson, belonged to Sir Joshua Reynolds' Literary Club which then met at the Turk's Head in Gerrard Street, Nollekens and his wife were notorious misers. There was never enough food in the pantry for a full meal. They stuffed their pockets with butter and sugar when they dined out and dinner guests, when they were unavoidable, shared with them a meal meant only for two: 'cheese [was] never allowed, nor seen in [Mrs Nollekens'] house, but at set dinners; when, as there was a partition in the old family tray, she generally sported samples of two sorts, taking particular care that they should not be too heavy for Bronze to put on over the head of her master', wrote John Thomas Smith in his recollections of the artist.[36]

> Poor Bronze, who had to support herself upon what were called board-wages, had barely a change [of clothing], and looked more like the wife of a chimney-sweeper than any other kind of human being. As for table linen, two small breakfast napkins and a large old tablecloth, a descendant in the family, which, when used, was always folded into four, was the whole of his stock; for he possessed no doileys; and Bronze declared to me that she had never seen such a thing as a jack-towel in the house, nor even the nail-holes where one had been. She always washed without soap: there were no hearthstones nor black-lead dust for the stoves; nor a cake of whitening for

81

the kitchen-grate; nor even a yard of oil-cloth to preserve the stones from grease, much less an old bit of bedside carpet, to keep the bones of poor Bronze free from rheumatism.[37]

Nollekens reportedly was so cheap that 'he absolutely suffered his own uncle and aunt to sell their beds to support them in water-gruel', although he later assisted them financially.[38]

Neither were the Nollekens noted for cleanliness or fashion. Smith recalled that Boswell, 'meeting him in the pit of the Pantheon, loudly exclaimed, "Why, Nollekens, how dirty you go now! I recollect when you were the gayest dressed of any in the house." To whom Nollekens made, for once in his life, the retort-courteous of "That's more than I could ever say of you"'. This disreputable state was not particular to Nollekens; Johnson was positively famous for it and Boswell himself 'certainly looked very badly when dressed; for as he seldom washed himself, his clean ruffles served as a striking contrast to his dirty flesh'.[39] While Nollekens rarely added to his wardrobe, his wife augmented hers by buying mismatched shoes second-hand, a fact obtained by her friends' maids 'who were encouraged to *pump* Bronze . . . and were also informed that her muffs and parasols were obtained in the same way'.[40]

Mrs Nollekens did not like Bronze, but needed to make use of her in these deceptions. She kept a finer change of clothing at her sister's house in order to attend card parties without her husband's knowledge.

> At these ceremonious card-parties, Mrs. Nollekens, who, the reader will recollect, played the strict Hoyle game, would remain till she found herself in possession of more than she sat down with, and then inquired if her servant were below. Poor Bronze then attended her to the upper chamber, where, after changing her dress, she remained in her camlet-cloak till the whole of the visitors were gone; and then the foot, which had been that evening graced with a silver-spangled slipper, was pressed into a wooden clog. Thus equipped, Mrs. Nollekens, on leaving the house, placed her delicately-formed arm upon that of her faithful servant; whose swarthy hue her mistress could scarcely by daylight bear to look upon, but upon these occasions she condescended to rest upon her with perfect confidence.[41]

What about Women?

It was Bronze who, 'labouring under a severe sore-throat, stretching her flannelled neck up to her mistress', announced visitors, and it was Bronze who, when Nollekens was bored in his studio, amused him by dancing with his cat.[42] And it was also Bronze who seemingly took every opportunity to report the idiosyncratic goings-on of the Nollekens household to other servants and to Smith. Indeed, there existed an equally irascible relationship between husband and wife and between Bronze and her master. If he screamed at her in front of his guests, as he was wont to do (she declared that 'No one could eat till he was red in the face at master's table'),[43] 'Nollekens ordered Bronze out of the room, saying "he never liked that woman – her mouth looked so much like the rump of a chicken"'[44]

John Thomas Smith, who later became Keeper of Prints and Drawings at the British Museum, began his career as an artistic apprentice and protégé to Nollekens. Under the guise of an amused bystander he reported his activities, and by the time he wrote the sculptor's biography freely referred to him as 'simple and half-witted'[45] and 'little more than one remove from an idiot'.[46] As an old woman and a black woman, Bronze had little choice but to remain where she was, but she herself was far from perfect. Even the sympathetic and indebted Smith admitted that 'she was not over-cleanly in her domestic habits or person' and that 'in her grey-haired state, became addicted to drinking'. Nollekens' nurse in his final months refused to eat any of the food Bronze prepared. Still, at the end of his life, it was Bronze and not his other attendants with whom 'Mr. Nollekens made the most free . . . he listened to her silly nonsense with the full expectation of hearing what she had often said, and then would joke in his way in return'.[47]

Bronze was allowed a few liberties. She and the one other servant in the house alternated Sundays off, which gave them a one-day holiday in every fourteen days. Even this was granted for ironic reasons: 'it was Mr. Nollekens [sic] opinion, that if they were never permitted to visit the Jew's Harp, Queen's Head and Artichoke [taverns], or Chalk Farm [a tea-garden resort, with bowling alleys and a merry-go-round], they never would wash "theirselves"'[48] – an odd sentiment from a man whose house, according to Bronze, contained no soap for forty years.[49] Nollekens left her nineteen guineas in his will, but in his capriciousness made fourteen new wills, codicils and changes in which she was never again mentioned. 'As for the fate of poor Bronze', Smith added ominously, 'alas! a future page will declare it'.[50]

We can be sure that her end came in nothing like the comfort enjoyed by Sancho, Soubise or even Jack Beef, all of whom died well-fed and financially stable. By the last years of her life 'she was too old and feeble to do much; her hair had become grey in his service, and she was not altogether unlike the figure of the poor old soul so wretchedly employed in lighting the fire in the miser's room, represented by Hogarth in his first plate of the Rake's Progress'.[51]

Even into the nineteenth century, since West Indian and Bermudian slaves were not emancipated until 1833, the stories of black women treated badly abroad and in England show that gender was no assurance of humane treatment. The story of Mary Prince, born in Bermuda around 1783 and who arrived in England around 1828, was published by the British Anti-Slavery Society after it tried to help her return to Antigua as a free woman. As far as slave narratives go, it is a familiar story. She was lucky in knowing both of her parents, but they lived apart from each other because they had separate masters. She was sold away from them as a child and spent her life working for cruel masters.

The first time she left home she was hired out as a children's nurse, even though she was still a child herself. Her original mistress dying, Mary was ordered back with these words: 'Mary, you will have to go home directly; your master is going to be married, and he means to sell you and two of your sisters to raise money for the wedding.'[52] Mary's mother was forced to dress all her children in smocks and watch them being auctioned off, one by one. Mary went for the equivalent of £38 sterling, 'and our poor mammy went home with nothing'.[53]

In her new home Mary quickly learned that slavery perverted both white women and white men. Two slave boys in the house were continually beaten by the mistress, and to 'strip me naked – to hang me up by the wrists and lay my flesh open with the cow-skin, was an ordinary punishment for even a slight offence.

My mistress often robbed me too of the hours that belong to sleep. She used to sit up very late, frequently even until morning; and I had then to stand at a bench and wash during the greater part of the night, or pick wool and cotton; and often I have dropped down overcome by sleep and fatigue, till roused from a state of stupor by the whip, and forced to start up to my tasks.'[54] This was by no means unusual treatment for slaves, and Mary goes on to describe one female slave killed as a result of being whipped mercilessly when pregnant, and another who was thrown into poisonous thorny shrubbery and died two days later.

In an attempt to get away, she managed to be sold to the manager of a salt mine. The conditions there were much worse than she could have imagined. Up to their knees in brine all day, the slaves scorched in the sun and 'pickled' their legs so badly that in many cases the resulting boils ate all the way to the bone. Many died from the hard labour and the meagre diet of maize boiled in water. Again finding someone to buy her away for £67 Mary travelled with her new master, John Wood, and his wife to Antigua. Either constantly unlucky in her masters, or an example of how pervasive the abuse of slaves was, she again found herself mistreated and beaten. This time, however, she also found herself with stretches of free time while her master and his wife were away, when she was able to earn some money. She sold coffee and yams to ships' captains as well as taking in their washing, purchased a pig on a ship and sold it later for a profit, and in this way tried to save toward purchasing herself or finding someone willing to do it for her. About this time she began to attend the Moravian Church and discovered religion for the first time. To her master's displeasure she married a free black man, a carpenter. Marriages between free blacks and slaves were frowned upon, and sometimes banned, in case it gave slaves notions of freedom. Wood forbade her to let him on the property or to wash his clothes in the same tub she used for theirs.

After conferring with her husband, she decided to travel to England with Mr and Mrs Wood. She had developed a very bad rheumatism through the constant washing of clothes, and mistakenly believed the English climate might help cure her. More importantly, however, she and her husband hoped that she might

85

gain her freedom in England and return to him as a free woman. On landing in England her health grew immediately worse. 'I shewed my [swollen] flesh to my mistress', she said, 'but she took no notice of it. We were obliged to stop at the tavern till my master got a house; and a day or two after, my mistress sent me down into the wash-house to learn to wash in the English way.'[55] The English washerwomen recognized that Mary's poor health prevented her from doing such strenuous work and did her washing for her. Even the cook at the house the Woods took in Leigh Street, London, tried to convince Mrs Wood to hire someone to do this job, to no avail.

At this Mary broke down and railed against her master and mistress. They retaliated by showing her the door, but since she knew no one in London she remained with them. They did hire a washerwoman for a time, but treated her so badly she refused to return. Matters only grew worse until the fourth time they threatened to put Mary out. She 'knew [she] was free in England' (not in fact officially correct until 1834 when slavery was finally abolished), but 'did not know where to go, or how to get my living', but the continuing abuse and poor health were eventually too much for her. After a few months in Leigh Street she gathered her belongings and went to Moravian missionaries, who took her in. She eventually came to the attention of the Anti-Slavery Society where she met its editor Thomas Pringle and went to work for him. Pringle arranged for Mary to narrate her story and for it to be published. He also worked hard, but apparently unsuccessfully, to arrange for her return to Antigua as a free woman.

When all of the Society's letters to Wood were met with angry responses (he 'would not move a finger about her in this country, or grant her manumission on any terms whatever; and that if she went back to the West Indies, she must take the consequences'),[56] the Anti-Slavery Society drew up a petition and planned to present a bill to Parliament, guaranteeing the 'entire emancipation of all slaves brought to England with the owner's consent'.[57] John Wood however sailed back to Antigua, leaving Mary behind, '[e]very exertion for Mary's relief having thus failed'.[58]

In letters between Antiguans who knew of Mary's predicament and the Anti-Slavery group, more of the picture emerged. Wood

was a difficult man who tried to discredit her in every way possible. He said that her husband had been given a house on Wood's
property and shared it with a new wife. He claimed to have been
a kind and generous master, information which others who knew
him refuted. He said that she had brought considerable money
with her to England, and that the Society should therefore not
give her any financial assistance. Pringle knew better, for by now
she had worked for his family for several years. He allowed that
she had a temper and was much weakened by illness, but that
aside she was trustworthy, diligent and a caring and good worker.
He excused the information that she had before her marriage been
involved sexually with a white captain, on the grounds that a
society that forbids religious training and marriage to slaves can
expect no less. She felt 'deep, though unobtrusive, gratitude for
real kindness shown her. She possesses considerable natural sense,
and has much quickness of observation and discrimination of
character. She is remarkable for *decency* and *propriety* of conduct –
and her *delicacy*, even in trifling minutiæ, has been a trait of special
remark by the females of my family.'[59]

Pringle believed most of the particulars of Mary's narrative,
since some of them had been corroborated, but he had one reser-
vation: surely not all of the stories of atrocities she narrated could
be true? There 'surely must be *some* exaggeration; the facts are too
shocking to be credible.'[60] Even to an Anti-Slavery editor, used
to the horror stories of slaves' treatment, the naked truth seemed
unbelievable.

Most black women seem to have been far less well off than
their male counterparts, unable to get the kind of secure domestic
positions available to men. The latter were still seen as exotic
appendages or brute labour and had more appeal to employers
than black women who were in competition with white servants
for jobs. Positive accounts of their lives are rare, and they seem
to have lived in relative obscurity, popping up from time to time
in lawcourts, on slave ships, in brothels, or in the unenviable
positions of Mary Hylas, 'Black Mary' or 'Bronze'. Some were
brought to England by their white fathers, and not all biracial
children were raised as slaves or sold when their fathers died.
Some fared pretty well in England, for there race alone was not

87

an inherent deterrent to match-making. Some of them occupied an unspecified middle ground, not servants, nor completely family. In this respect they fell into that category often filled by poor relations, of the household but not quite of the parlour. An outstanding example is that of Dido Elizabeth Belle, the natural daughter of Sir John Lindsay, a captain of the Royal Navy.

Dido, also known as Elizabeth Lindsay, was born in England to a woman taken prisoner by Lindsay from a Spanish vessel. It is not entirely clear from the account by Thomas Hutchinson whether her mother was actually stolen by Lindsay or rescued by him from the Spanish, but in either case Lindsay acknowledged his paternity by providing generously for Dido in his will in 1788. She was raised and spent the first thirty years of her life in Kenwood, Hampstead, the home of her great-uncle William Murray. Kenwood was at that time sufficiently outside London to be considered the country, and boasted hayfields, a dairy and a poultry yard. These latter two became Dido's responsibility and apparently her pleasure. Murray and his wife had no children of their own and seem to have been delighted to raise both Dido and her cousin Lady Elizabeth Murray, the daughter of the English ambassador to Austria and Paris, whose wife had died when her child was still an infant. No word remains about Dido's mother and how her child came to be separated from her.

Her position in the family was undefined. She may have been, as one recent author asserts, partly 'a playmate and later a kind of personal attendant' to her cousin Elizabeth.[61] A portrait of the two as young women shows them walking happily arm-in-arm at Kenwood, and Thomas Hutchinson, Captain General and Governor-in-Chief of Massachusetts Bay, saw them in the same posture in the house, where Murray, to show his affection for her, 'called upon [her] . . . every minute for this and that, and shewed the greatest attention to everything she said.'[62] This was probably for the benefit of Hutchinson, an American living in London, who clearly did not approve of Dido's position in the family.

A Black came in after dinner and sat with the ladies and after coffee, walked with the company in the gardens, one of the young ladies having her arm within the other. She had a very high cap and her wool was much frizzled in her neck, but not enough to answer the large curls now in fashion. She is neither handsome nor genteel – pert enough. [They call] her Dido, which I suppose is all the name she has. He knows he has been reproached for showing fondness for her – I dare say not criminal.[63]

Dido would have been about fifteen at the time, and her appearance ten years later in the portrait by Zoffany proves her to have developed into a lovely young woman, both 'handsome' and 'genteel'.

Even so, at least on this occasion she evidently did not dine with the rest. Like a valued poor relation, she took down Murray's correspondence and cared for his poultry, but she also received a quarterly allowance, birthday and Christmas gifts. These were less than Lady Elizabeth, after all the legitimate daughter of an ambassador, received, but more than the servants were paid. When Lady Elizabeth married and left Kenwood in 1785, Dido remained behind with the now quite aged Murrays and continued to receive the same solicitous care even after their deaths. Her bed was hung with glazed chintz, she had ass's milk when she was ill, and a mahogany table made for her.[64]

At her father's death she received, together with a mysterious brother named John, one thousand pounds, and Lindsay's obituary in the *London Chronicle* referred to her 'amiable disposition and accomplishments [which] have gained her the highest respect.'[65] She received a further £500 plus £100 a year for life from her great-uncle in his will. He also made certain to confirm in the same document that she was free, in order to protect her future. Dido fades into obscurity after Murray's death, but surfaces long enough for us to assume she married: in 1794 her name changes to Dido Elizabeth Davinier and she leaves Kenwood. With her upbringing, family connections and income, she married well, probably to a clergyman.

All of this is extraordinary enough, but there is more. The great-uncle who so adored and protected her was none other than Lord Mansfield, the same justice whom Granville Sharp called upon to decide the fate of slaves in Britain in the 1772 Somerset court case and who wavered in the face of that momentous task.

CHAPTER FOUR

Sharp and Mansfield: Slavery in the Courts

Granville Sharp, who fought for the freedom of black people both privately and publicly, and Lord Mansfield, the Chief Justice presiding over most of the historic cases, could not have been more different in style, appearance or demeanour. Sharp was spare and religious, almost ascetic, with an unflinching moral sense. With the benefit of a formal education that ended by the time he was fourteen, he wrote numerous tracts and letters on slavery, religious history, social organization and even music. Rising no higher than a clerkship in the Ordnance Office, he was intensely religious; his greatest pleasure was in playing music with his brothers and sisters.

Mansfield, on the other hand, was robust, ambitious and wealthy, a supporter of commercial interests who knew well the value and strategies of political alliances. Raised in a Scottish castle and educated at Westminster and Christ Church, Oxford, he made a fortune through shrewd investments and owned homes in Bloomsbury Square and Hampstead. Famous for his prodigious memory, he rarely wrote things down, and his famous utterances and decisions come to us only through the agency of various court reporters and visitors.

They would hardly seem suitable or evenly matched adversaries, yet Sharp and Mansfield had certain similarities. Both were from large families and were younger sons. Both were painted by Zoffany and Reynolds. Neither had children of his own, although each was an affectionate uncle. Both knew the king and were friendly with Garrick (who seems to have had a vast circle of acquaintances, black and white, in Britain). Most importantly, however, both are mistakenly known for having freed Britain's slaves. While each man's work became connected with the fates of black people and was accompanied by questioning and soul-searching, as young men they would have been astonished to know that they would go down in history because of these associations.

Sharp was born on 10 November 1735, the youngest of five sons and one of eight surviving children in an ecclesiastical Durham family. Their paternal grandfather was the Archbishop of York, their father the Archdeacon of Northumberland. Their maternal grandfather was a prebendary of Durham. Except for Granville, by whose time the family's educational funds were exhausted, the Sharp sons all succeeded in professional careers. The oldest brother John followed the family career and was variously a curate in Bamburgh, vicar of Hartburn, prebendary of Durham, and archdeacon of Northumberland. 'Mr. Urban' of *The Gentleman's Magazine* claimed that as an honest clergyman, apparently a rare thing in his time, John Sharp was the model for Oliver Goldsmith's *Vicar of Wakefield*.[1] Thomas, who died young, was also a curate and rector. William, at whose surgery Granville met Jonathan Strong (see Chapter 1), was the King's surgeon. And James, who joined Granville in pursuing Strong's case, was a very successful engineer and ironmonger, 'the financial leader of the family'.[2] In the introductory chapter to his biography of Sharp, Prince Hoare allots the three sisters Eliza, Catherine and Frances a single sentence: 'Of Dr. Sharp's daughters, the virtues were domestic and exemplary.'[3]

Granville's share of the family money put aside to educate the brothers was used to send him to London as an apprentice, and accordingly he left Durham's public (i.e. grammar) school early in order to concentrate on the more useful subjects of arithmetic and writing at a smaller school.[4] When he was fourteen he left for London, where he commenced on a series of apprenticeships in 1750. The first was to a linen draper named Halsey at Great Tower Hill who died three years later; Sharp stayed on with Halsey's father-in-law, a justice of the peace. Two years later he went to work for Bourke and Company in Cheapside. In between he had received the Lord Mayor's permission to serve out his term with another of Halsey's companies but that judgement was later reversed. When his apprenticeship expired he went to work for another linen company, but because they were less successful than he had believed he left them. He was now in his twentieth year and, although he had worked for a number of different companies, was considered a reliable and serious employee.

One might expect that an intelligent young man in London who saw his brothers rising in their careers would have chafed at such mundane work, but Sharp seems to have used the time to develop his skills in argument and research. Each of his masters was of a different religion (Quaker, Presbyterian, Irish Catholic, and a non-practiser), and the apprentice taught himself Greek and Hebrew in order to argue persuasively with his employers and their colleagues. He later believed that '[T]his extraordinary experience has taught me to make a proper distinction between the OPINIONS of men and their PERSONS', a belief which was later tested when Mansfield had misgivings about a decision he made on the slave Thomas Lewis.[5] He learned to follow a paper trail so well that he succeeded in proving the right of one of his employers to a peerage and saw him seated in the House of 'Peers'.[6]

When in 1757–8 his parents died, he returned home to assist his brothers and sisters in closing up the house. He returned to London bringing his two unmarried sisters with him. The following year, when Sharp was twenty-two, he took up an appointment in the Ordnance Office and at that early age the pattern seemed set for his life: his work was unchallenging but regular, his brothers and sisters were close by, and he had time to continue his private studies. From these facts it is easy to picture him as a dry, studious young man, unaffected by the raucous pleasure palace that London was at that time. And much of that picture is true; from his portraits he resembled a thin and sober Tristram Shandy, with pointed features and a stern, unsmiling face. (Rather surprisingly, Sir Joshua Reynolds painted him more loosely and sumptuously, with relaxed limbs, satin vest and lace ruffles, and an enigmatic smile.) Sharp looked in his Bible for legal precedents as well as for spiritual sustenance. His income was never more than adequate, yet he regularly donated to charities. He was absolutely devoted to his brothers and sisters, and they to him, and for reasons unknown, he never married.

His sister Eliza, later Mrs Prowse, kept a diary and it is there that a fuller picture of the adult Sharp siblings emerges. For one thing they travelled regularly. At a time when travel was not only difficult but expensive and dangerous, the Sharps seemed to spend their weekends and longer holidays on jaunts more typical of the twentieth than the eighteenth century. His sister, according to Sharp's later biographer Lascelles, 'constantly insist[s] on the gregarious habits of the Sharps'. It was 'a rule of the family that they should attend all amusements and expeditions in a family party'.[7] They wrote circular letters to each other, in which each member added his or her news, describing such wide-ranging events as multiple-course meals or the Gordon Riots. Granville often signed his letters as 'G#'.

By far the most important family activity was the making of music. Granville played flute and hautboy, and the other brothers the cello, 'the jointed serpent' and the organ (known in the family by the joking sobriquet of 'Miss Morgan'). The three sisters played the piano and all sang 'at sight'. The family orchestra practised almost nightly, and even the unmusical spouses were expected to participate. They gave concerts on fortnightly Sundays at William's surgery in the Old Jewry, where Granville also kept rooms, attracting such figures as General Paoli, Lord North, Oliver Goldsmith and the ubiquitous David Garrick. The programme generally ended with a rousing version of Handel's Hallelujah Chorus and often included 'Granville's Song' about the Thames:

> Delightful Stream – That Life might pass
> Reflected from the Summer Glass!
>   Scenes of Innocence and Love
>   Thy flow'ry Meads might represent;
>   And the deep stillness of thy Wave
>   Should find its likeness in content,
> Whilst sooth'd alike by many a Song,
> The Kindred Streams should glide along.

These homely concerts were nothing compared to the Sharp family's later scheme of giving concerts on the Thames itself.

Since they already preferred to do their travelling by water, they built a floating barge on which they could perform. Designed by William, the *Apollo* was 'well equipped with bedrooms and dining-rooms below deck, and furnished with a movable awning above the deck to protect the orchestra from rain. Towed by a pair of horses, this remarkable craft, volleying Handel over the water, became a well-known sight on the rivers and waterways as far even as Norfolk.'[8] By 1770, five years after Granville's first meeting with Jonathan Strong and two years before the Somerset decision, the Sharps encountered the royal family several times. On the first occasion the Prince of Wales and his brothers came down to the water to request several songs, and later that year they met King George III himself, playing for him for one and a half hours. Seven years later the King noticed the barge moored for the night and unbeknownst to its occupants waited in the dark listening to the music. They received him properly the next day. Garrick too shared meals with them on the barge, as did foreign ambassadors.[9]

Granville Sharp was indefatigable. He worked full-time, spent evenings and weekends with his brothers and sisters, and yet once it began his political activity never seemed to flag. The energy and time that he put into his earlier theoretical research became focused after the meeting with Strong on the issue of black slavery. In this he had the complete approbation of his family, who not only adored him but who offered to support him financially for the rest of his life so that he might continue his unexpected mission.

Mansfield came from a larger family than Sharp, but he was considerably less close to them. The family home and his birth-place was Scone Palace in Perth, which began as an abbey and where all the Scottish kings from Robert the Bruce to Charles II were crowned from 1306 to 1651.[10] He was born William Murray into a Jacobite family, and it is probably for this reason that he seems to have increasingly, but not completely, divorced himself from them after he left home for school and university and began to advance in his career. 'Not a single letter has been discovered at Scone Palace or elsewhere from William to his parents', writes James Oldham in his exhaustive book on Mansfield's judicial judgements and career, however 'it is not reasonable to suppose

94

that he was never again in communication with either parent after he left Scotland in 1718 at age fourteen. Yet by all accounts, Murray never returned to Scotland, not even for a visit'.[11]

Vestiges of his Scottish upbringing remained with him. Known all his life for his stunning oratory and piercing gaze, he was nevertheless unable to completely rid himself of a Scottish accent and sometimes pronounced words oddly in a studied effort not to mispronounce them.[12] At school as well as in his career his intelligence and tenacious reasoning more than compensated for such potential defects. A prize winner at Westminster School, he also bested William Pitt in an Oxford Latin competition, winning with what was apparently a very bad poem indeed.[13] He embarked on the rather solitary study of law early, entering Lincoln's Inn while still an undergraduate. He was called to the bar in 1730, five years before Sharp was born. He married, happily, in 1738 and it was also around this time that his career took off.

It was also around this time that Murray learned two important things: how to use contacts and connections to further his career, and how to invest wisely. He presented a number of cases before Lord Chancellor Hardwicke, whose earlier opinion, as Sir Philip Yorke with Lord Talbot, on the legitimacy of slavery within Britain was later challenged by the Somerset case, and admired him greatly. He took a seat in the House of Commons in 1742 when the Duke of Newcastle arranged a vacancy for him. Oldham compares Murray's 'style of cool cerebration' to Pitt's 'fiery oratory', remarking that while the rowdier Commons appreciated Pitt's style, 'after elevation to the House of Lords, Mansfield's style was more appreciated'.[14]

He became Solicitor-General in 1742, working closely with the Attorney-General Dudley Ryder. When Ryder died and Murray was offered his position, he made another bold move and insisted 'that the appointment be accompanied by a peerage'.[15] 'Here, as always,' writes Oldham, 'Murray was clear about his goals and was supremely self-confident of achieving them.'[16] The obstacles to this, an alleged Jacobite link and his Scottish background, were overcome. Initially a Baron, he became the first Earl of Mansfield in 1776 and was well before that a powerful, respected and extremely wealthy man.

It is easy to imagine him on the bench, and transcripts of court cases give an idea of his lines of questioning and reasoning. What is harder to imagine is the private man who dined with friends and family at his Bloomsbury Square house and wandered the pastoral setting of Kenwood, his country seat. As a child he was known as Will, but this informal name does not suit the persona of the august judge. Even so he was not always serious, and enjoyed bringing together his political and artistic friends. Boswell reports that Mansfield 'sat with his tye wig, his coat buttoned, his legs pushed much before him, and his heels off the ground, and knocking frequently but not hard against each other, and he talked neatly and with vivacity'.[17] Richard Cumberland too found that he possessed 'that happy and engaging art . . . of putting the company present in good humour with themselves: I am convinced they naturally like him the more for his seeming to like them so well . . . He would take his share in the small talk of the ladies with all imaginable affability: he was, in fact, like most men, not in the least degree displeased . . . by their flattery. He was not a great starter of new topics, but easily led into anecdotes of past times; these he detailed with pleasure, but he told them correctly rather than amusingly'.[18] From this we get a picture of a man who was careful and correct, yet cheerful and friendly; persuasive and articulate yet not particularly imaginative.

There is no extant documentation by Mansfield of his personal feelings about Dido, his nephew's daughter by a black woman nor, aside from the circumstances of her birth, knowledge of the actual events which led to her being virtually adopted by Mansfield. His apparent affection for her was well-documented by visitors to Kenwood, as was her uncertain position in his household. One assumes Dido returned her great-uncle's affection and appreciated his care of her, despite her probably lonely early adult life. What is lost to us are their views on the larger political, and for Dido the necessarily personal, issue of knowing that the fates of thousands of black people rested in his hands. How far did Mansfield connect Dido with the black men who appeared before him in the courtroom? Did Dido herself feel a strong connection to them? Would she have read the newspaper reports on the cases brought by Sharp and felt any affiliation with those black people on trial, even though they were of a lower class? It is possible, albeit unlikely, that her great-uncle even discussed the cases in her presence. One wonders how as a judge he distinguished between the theoretical and the particular; whether he looked at Dido as she wrote his letters and saw a connection between her privileged and manumitted state and that of the young black men and women tied to masts on the Thames, dragged screaming from their English homes on to ships bound for Jamaica, or running errands in the streets of London, hoping not to be spied by their former masters.

This was the situation of Jonathan Strong, the slave Granville Sharp encountered at his brother William's surgery in 1765. Here in Mincing Lane was as pathetic an example of the brutalities of slavery as existed on the worst plantation in Jamaica or Mississippi. Strong, a young man perhaps still in his teens, was in terrible shape: his master David Lisle, who had brought him to England from Barbados, 'had beaten him so violently on the head with a pistol, which made his head swell very greatly, and, when the swelling abated, a disorder fell on his eyes, which nearly occasioned the loss of his sight. This was followed by an ague, fever, and lameness in both feet'.[19] (Sharp later wrote in a letter that Strong's last beating was so severe that the pistol's barrel and lock broke away from the stock.)[20] In this condition he was turned away as useless. Fortunately someone recommended that he go to Dr Sharp, who offered free medical aid to the poor every morning before seeing his regular, paying patients. Strong described his physical condition in court:

> I took his advice and went to Mr. Sharp. I could hardly walk, or see my way, where I was going. When I came to him, and he saw me in that condition, the gentleman take charity of me, and gave me some stoff [*sic*] to wash my eyes with, and some money to get myself a little necessaries till next day. The day after, I come to the gentleman, and he sent me into the hospital; and I was in there four months and a half. All the while I was in the hospital, the gentleman find me in clothes, shoes, and stockings, and when I come out, he paid for my lodging, and a money to find myself some necessaries, till he get me into a place.[21]

Granville and William Sharp feared that the affliction in Strong's eyes was 'so violent . . . that there appeared to be the utmost danger of his becoming totally blind'.[22] On first meeting him the Sharp brothers were more concerned about an individual in immediate need of help than with a more general political cause, and it was William, as physician, who necessarily took charge of the affair.

After he was released from St Bartholomew's Strong once again applied to William. As Granville later wrote, 'tho' he was cured of his Ague and Fever, yet the disorder of his Eyes continued for sometime longer as well as some degree of Lameness in his feet.'[23] It was Granville who found Strong a regular job running errands for a Mr Brown, an apothecary on Tower Street. Strong delivered medicines for him, sometimes accompanying Mrs Brown's carriage. Brown was pleased with Strong; after a time he put him in livery and they continued happily in this arrangement for nearly two years. Sometime during this period, according to Granville Sharp's notes, justices in Middlesex legally freed Strong from slavery. Over time the Sharp brothers forgot about their charitable intervention and apparently about Strong himself.

This comfortable situation changed abruptly on 5 September 1767. The now relatively healthy Strong was spied by his former master David Lisle, who, seeing an opportunity for financial gain, had him kidnapped and illegally imprisoned while he sought a buyer. Two city officers (there was as yet no police force) lured Strong to a public house by saying that someone wanted to speak to him there, and when he arrived seized him.

He was locked in the Poultney Compter (a prison and holding place for those accused of crimes) without a warrant, and although the apothecary Brown sent an emissary, William Poole, with money and food for Strong, 'the Door-Keeper of the Compter absolutely refused to let him be either seen or spoke with, though the said Poole went twice to the Compter to demand the same'.[24] When Brown himself arrived, a lawyer for Lisle 'violently threatened' him for having stolen his property, successfully scaring him off. Strong (who was baptized) sent for his godfathers John London and Stephen Nail, but they were not admitted either. At this point the terrified Strong managed to send a letter to Granville

98

Sharp. Forgetting at first who Strong was, Sharp sent back a messenger instead of going to see Strong in person. When the officers denied that anyone of that name was there, Sharp knew that something was wrong and immediately went himself to investigate.

This was Sharp's first encounter with the law yet he seemed to know exactly how to proceed. First ordering the prison master not to let Strong out under any circumstances, he went directly to Sir Robert Kite, the Lord Mayor, and stated the case. Kite agreed to look into the matter and duly summoned all involved to appear before him on 18 September. However when the hearing date arrived, it was not Lisle who appeared but two strangers to Strong named William McBean and David Laird, themselves representing a fourth man, James Kerr, who claimed to be Strong's new owner. Laird was the captain of the ship which was to carry Strong away. Strong was now completely terrified, 'put', as Sharp wrote, 'into extream Bodily Fear; they being both of them absolutely unknown to him, as well as the name of the Person for whom they acted'.[24] In Barbados Strong knew Lisle as John Lloyd but in England his former master assumed another name. As matters stood, although McBean, Laird and Kerr were unknown to him altogether, they were claiming the legal power to send him away to permanent and deadly plantation slavery for a mere £30 – the price on the bill of sale signed by Lisle.

The Lord Mayor heard the arguments and quickly decided that because 'the lad had not stolen any thing, and was not guilty of any offence, [he] was therefore at liberty to go away'.[26] At this pronouncement everyone leaped into action. Captain Laird attempted to seize Strong as the property of Kerr. At this the city coroner, who also attended the hearing, slipped behind Sharp and whispered, 'Charge him'. Sharp stepped forward and firmly announced that he would accuse the captain of assault if he attempted to touch Strong. Everyone left the hearing together, warily, but no one dared to lay a finger on Strong and he remained a free man.[27]

What had started as an act of charity by William now escalated into a larger family affair. James Sharp was also at the hearing, and both he and Granville were afterwards subjected to verbal and legal attacks. Kerr and two others went to see James and demanded that he deliver Strong to them. James replied that Strong was free and that no one had the 'Power or Authority whatsoever to deliver him up'.[28] Lisle himself, although he failed to appear at the hearing, challenged Granville to a duel, 'to which Granville Sharp replied that he should want no satisfaction which the Law would give him'.[29] Finally they tried legal action, bringing a suit against both Granville and James.

These seem disproportionate events for a matter of £30, and clearly far more was at stake than that sum. For Lisle, Kerr and their associates the rights of property had been challenged and defeated. In their view, blacks were chattel and the rules of private enterprise stated that a person's property could be bought and sold at will. The Sharps' actions were for them simple and intolerable theft, and accordingly they served the brothers with writs of trespass for denying them their property in Strong. That they would stoop to lay claim to a personal grievance after Strong had been so vilely treated was bad enough to Sharp, but that they would use the British legal system to support their grievance was nearly as bad.

The writs were a mess, full of errors and lies. For one thing, they were dated 8 July 1767, well before the theft of Strong took place. Kerr alleged a property right in Strong from that time, even though the bill of sale was dated the following September. The wording was so convoluted and erroneous as to make it appear that there were four slaves, not one, all named John Strong instead of Jonathan Strong. 'Thus James and Granville Sharp appear to be charged', wrote Granville, 'not with one Negro only, but with 4; and these as distinct from each other . . . as *one Person* may be said to be from "*one other*" Person; and yet not one of the four bears the *same Name* with that *Negro whom they really relieved*'.[30] Sharp was now fully awakened to the extent to which slavery and property governed moral behaviour, and to the lax way in which the legal system might be pressed into the service of such behaviour. If he and his brother had 'reason to complain of Mr. Kerr for litigiously and unjustly troubling them with a Law Suit', he wrote, 'they have much more reason to complain and be surprized at the scandalous abuse of our most excellent Laws in the proceedings of his Attorney'.[31] Less concerned about the damage to his reputation or person than that the two-edged sword of law could be taken advantage of by the unprincipled and used against those who most needed protection, Sharp threw himself immediately, wholly and methodically into challenging the legality of slavery in Britain. Without leaving his day job, he set out to train himself in law and to use the courts to prove that slavery was both morally and legally reprehensible.

His first publication was *A Representation of the Injustice and Dangerous Tendency of Tolerating Slavery; or of Admitting the Least Claim of Private Property in the Persons of Men, in England*, published in 1767 and 1769. He combined the authorities of Christianity and English law to refute the idea that slavery could be legal in Britain, citing both legal precedents and biblical authority. He quoted the famous 1706 opinion of Lord Chief Justice John Holt stating that 'as soon as a Negro comes into England, he becomes free: one may be a villain [a serf] in England, but not a Slave'.[32] He found that in the later case of Gallway v. Caddee the courts upheld this opinion and decided that slaves become free upon entering Britain. From this and other cases he deduced that English justices consistently upheld Holt's decision, despite the important 1726 pronouncement of Yorke and Talbot that slavery was indeed legal in Britain. Sharp argued that everyone entering England became a subject of the King and therefore his 'property' only; a slave was a subject of the King just as much as any other man. Slave owners bypassed this by in essence attempting to 'usurp as an absolute authority over these their *fellow men*, as if they thought them mere *things*, horses, dogs, &c'.[33]

From there Sharp launched straight into Strong's case, without mentioning him by name, expressing his strong indignation against Lisle, Kerr and their like.

> . . . I have too much reason to charge them with this inhumanity; for, in the case (wherein I am at present concerned) of a Negro being SOLD, during an unlawful confinement, without a warrant, in the Poultry-Compter, though he had been set at liberty from the insupportable tyranny of his master (THE SELLER) more than two years before, at a meeting of the Middlesex Justices, yet it has been alledged by the said *Seller* (even after the Negro had been a second time set at

101

liberty by the authority of the right honourable the Lord Mayor) that he, the said Negro, is *as much private property as a horse or a dog.*[34]

In the opinion of Sharp, the only way black people could be denied the same legal rights as other English people would be if their owners could prove, which naturally they could not, that they were not human.

The only reasons for them to attempt to do this were mercenary ones, and Sharp went on to deflate the financial argument as well. Here, however, his reasoning edged toward that of people who opposed British slavery for much less humanitarian reasons: 'It cannot be for the sake of a market, to make his money of him, because a stout young Negro, who can read and write, and is approved of in domestic service, is sold for no more than thirty pounds in England . . . he may be served, during his stay in England, full as well, and with as little expence, by free English servants'.[35] English servants needed the work. But lurking under this argument was a more complicated one.

> . . . some hardship should lie upon those selfish masters, who might be ungenerous enough *to think it a hardship,* than that a real and national inconvenience should be felt, by permitting every person (without any inconvenience to himself) to increase the present stock of black Servants in this kingdom, which is already much too numerous. Therefore, even if there should be really any inconvenience or hardship upon the master, contrary or different to what I have supposed, 'tis certainly not to be lamented, because the public good seems to require some restraint of this unnatural increase of black subjects.[36]

Furthermore,

> . . . there will not appear to be any great saving in the employing of Slaves; healthy and comely boys and girls, the children of our own free fellow-subjects may be procured out of any county in this or the neighbouring kingdoms, to serve as Apprentices . . .[37]

The real threat was that the colonial system of agricultural slavery – slaves bred like cattle and condemned to work on plantations – could be imported into Britain if legal steps were not taken to ensure that slavery on British soil was antithetical to its laws. If 'not only Negroes, but Mulattos, and even *American Indians*' could be condemned to slavery in the Americas, it was only a matter of time either before white people could be enslaved, or before 'mercenary and selfish men may take it into their heads' to use slaves in English agriculture, 'breed[ing] them like cattle on their estates . . . God forbid that this should ever be the case here!'[38] And, getting to the heart of the matter, 'If the present Negroes are once permitted to be retained as Slaves in England, their posterity . . . the mixed people or Mulattoes, produced by the unavoidable intercourse with their white neighbours, will be also subject to the like bondage with their unhappy parents'.[39]

Sorting out Sharp's concerns here is complicated. Clearly he believed slavery to be horrific, going against the laws of both God and man. Clearly too he believed black people were persecuted and treated with cruelty and inhumanity. There is no question of his genuine compassion for them, for he devoted much of his life to assuring their safety and freedom in both England and the Americas. Yet like the abolitionists in North America, he had worries about allowing them to remain in England. This was due, as he saw it, to the threat to their own well-being and to that of other English people. Among these perceived threats was that of intermarriage, and in this Sharp did not differ much from those who took a pro-slavery stance. He, like many others, seems to have believed in the purity of the English stock as well as the purity of English law.

During the time that Sharp's tract was circulating in manuscript form among various legal experts, the Strong case kept going around and around. Although Strong was free, his opponents, perhaps intimidated by the opposition, kept postponing the case they had begun against Granville and James. The law usually allowed three such postponements, but this one drifted on to eight, and they were finally forced to pay triple the costs as a penalty for not bringing the action forward. Kerr had to pay Strong's legal costs, a figure greater than the sum for which he wished to sell Strong in the first place. Sharp had not dispensed with the idea of pursuing a lawsuit on behalf of Strong however, and warned in his tract that he was willing to do so if Lisle, Laird and the others would 'acknowledge their error in writing . . . so that the same may be made public, in order to deter others from the like offences, and for the *vindication and right understanding of English liberty*' – and if they promised to behave themselves.⁴⁰ Although Strong was free there was no promising that he could not be kidnapped or 'trepanned' again and spirited away before anyone was aware of it.

This is in fact what happened in Sharp's next two excursions into the English legal system. The first of these, the case of John Hylas whose wife had been sold into West Indian slavery (see Chapter 3), came to trial in 1768 while the Strong case was still pending. While the decision was in favour of the black man, no judgement so far had determined incontrovertibly the illegality of slavery in Britain. Sharp wrote dozens of letters to English noblemen and those with West Indian interests, decrying slavery and injustice to all people, including East and West Indians, white servants and others, and distributing his tract. He collected advertisements for slaves and slavery-related products like iron muzzles and collars, and circulated copies of them. When he ran across an advertisement in the *Daily Advertiser* on 17 May 1768 'for the apprehending of a poor wretched Negroe Boy' to be returned to a Mr Beckford in Pall Mall, he fired off a letter to Beckford saying that as 'I have a very great esteem for the Name of Beckford on Account of your steady & independent Behaviour on all Publick Occasions and because I believe you to be a sincere well wisher to the true Interest, Constitution and Liberties of this kingdom', he hoped Beckford would reconsider his pro-slavery stance.⁴¹ He enclosed a copy of the tract. In 1772 to William Davy, who was representing the Somerset case at no charge to the slave, he sent an actual iron muzzle to be used as evidence of the horrors of slavery.

Mr. Granville Sharp presents his respectfull Compliments to Mr. Serjeant Davy and begs leave to lay before him a *further proof of the monstrous Wickedness of Tolerating Slavery*. It is, indeed *an Iron Argument*, which must at once convince all those whose Hearts are not of a *harder metal*, that Men are not to be entrusted with an absolute Authority over their Brethren. The Instrument is called a *Mouth Piece* and many wholesale Ironmongers in Town keep Quantities of them ready in order to supply the Merchants and Planters Orders for the West Indian Islands. They are used on various occasions, sometimes for Punishment, when Negroes are what they call *sulky* (and who would not be *Sulky* under arbitrary power), and sometimes to prevent the poor Wretches from gnawing the Sugar Canes . . .

And sometimes they are used to prevent the poor *despairing Wretches* in Slavery from *eating dirt* (as they call it) for human Nature is frequently so reduced and vilified in the poor miserable Slaves that they will lye down to mingle themselves as it were with their Parent *Earth* and endeavour to cram their Stomachs with it, in hopes of finding some *rest* in Death, which was denied them when *alive*. The Iron by the power of the Sun will be so heated as to excoriate their Nose, Mouth and Chin, which together with the torment and Confinement of the Flat Piece of Iron upon the Tongue and the suffocating Plate before the Mouth in so hot a Climate, must altogether be esteemed a diabolical Invention.[42]

The muzzle was probably similar to the iron bit, an instrument described as causing 'a wildness that shot up into the eye the moment the lips were yanked back. Days after it was taken out, goose fat was rubbed on the corners of the mouth but nothing to soothe the tongue or take the wildness out of the eye'.[43]

Sharp was also searching for a case which would force the determination of the slavery issue in court. At first the case of Lewis versus Stapylton seemed to be it. The cause of "Thomas Lewis (a Negroe) against Stapylton and others . . . for assault and Imprisonment . . . with Intent to transport and sell him as a slave' resembled the cause of Jonathan Strong except that Lewis had actually been forced on board ship and carried down the Thames.[44] Tried before Lord Mansfield and a jury of twelve on 20 February 1771, the case concerned Thomas Lewis, abducted, bound, gagged and dragged away screaming, in front of witnesses, the previous July. The situation seemed ready-made for Sharp to challenge the legality of slavery, but even so he tried to prevent its going to trial for several reasons.

First and foremost was the publicity and cost to Lewis's neighbour, rescuer and protector Mrs Banks, mother of the naturalist Joseph Banks, who would have to bear the expense of solicitors' fees. Lewis himself petitioned the court to avoid a trial, since he neither wanted to put himself through the ordeal nor, inexplicably, to ruin the men who had abused him. Rather, 'he only wishes that this Court may make them truly sensible of the heinousness of their offence, and obliged them to make public acknowledgment thereof, that others may be deterred from committing such unlawful and dangerous outrages'.[45] Sharp contacted Stapylton to say that a public apology would be sufficient. Stapylton refused all such overtures, insisting that the case go to court. Apparently he hoped not only to prove his right to Lewis as property, but also the larger issue of the right of Englishmen to own and sell slaves in England. At this Sharp offered to pay Lewis's expenses, but Mrs Banks appeared willing for the case to proceed and to take on the financial risk.

There were other concerns as well which concerned Lewis more immediately. For protection he had been placed in the home of another black man named John Thomas while awaiting trial. Thomas however accepted an offer to accompany a Captain Dampier to the East Indies as a servant, which left Lewis with neither lodgings nor protection. Under these conditions, Sharp was worried for Mrs Banks 'lest the poor ignorant lad's indiscretion should by any means frustrate your generous intention of establishing his liberty'.[46] In other words, he might become impatient and run off without a guardian to keep an eye on him. Furthermore, Mrs Banks feared that as Lewis was now without a job, he might 'contract an idle habit'. Her concern increased because, as she wrote to Sharp, 'he was for some time prevented *attending your kind bounty* by illness, but got quite strong and hearty some days ago, when I found he still neglected to *attend his schoolmaster*'.[47] These fears – insulting considering he was the victim and not the defendant – proved without foundation, and when the case came to trial seven months later, Lewis was in court and took the stand.

When the case came before Mansfield, the question upon which it hinged was whether or not Lewis had ever been free. There was already plenty of evidence that he had been abducted and Mansfield did not want to be in a position to decide whether or not he should *become* free. Time and again Mansfield stopped the

106

questioning of Lewis when his solicitors Dunning, Davenport and Lucas pushed this point. Dunning put this issue firmly in his opening argument, stating that 'Thomas Lewis the prosecutor has the misfortune as he finds it to be in point of Colour a Black and upon the Ground of that Discovery made by them, his having a Darker Complexion than the now defendants they have taken it into their heads to say he was not under the protection of the Laws of this Country'. Dunning stated unequivocally that 'I trust by your Verdict they will find themselves mistaken for by the Laws of this Country they have no such right'.[48]

Mansfield let this pass, but when Dunning attempted to establish the ongoing nature of the problem – there had been numerous attempts to remove Lewis so that he could not testify, and that as recently as the day before the trial began he had been seized but managed to escape – Mansfield quickly put an end to it. 'You can't go into that', he warned. 'I will not try anything but this indictment.' Dunning objected, saying that the jury should realize 'that whatever Idea they may have the prosecutor would be Safe in coming into this Court to give testimony' were false, and that as a black man attempting to prosecute his white offenders his life was in danger. 'That will make no difference now,' Mansfield said, 'it may come in another shape.'[49] In limiting the scope of this particular trial Mansfield, whether intentionally or not, left the door open for the question of slavery to be addressed in the future.

Lewis's history was a long, circuitous one, in many ways typical of those black men who found themselves living in England. Born on the Gold Coast of Africa, he went to live with his uncle after his father died. Both his father and his uncle, he said, were free men. Mansfield stated that Lewis could not prove himself free by his own word, but allowed that he would 'presume him free unless they [the defendants] prove the Contrary'.[50] After a year or so he went to work for an English general who asked him if he 'sho'd like to go abroad, if I did I sho'd learn the Language[.] I said I sho'd like it very well.'[51] Instead of being sent to England as might have been expected, he went by the first ship out to Santa Cruz. From then on he had a series of masters, including a nobleman, a clerk, an English merchant named Bob Smith, Captain Robert

Stapylton, and a hairdresser. He lived in New York, Boston, Santa Cruz, Havana, and one of the Carolinas. He worked as a personal servant, a waiter, a beer drawer at a pub, and in each place was given food, drink and some sort of wages. This last point was a crucial one, since unlike free men slaves received no wages. The fact that he had been consistently, although poorly, paid for his labour would, it was hoped by his supporters, establish his inherent and long-standing freedom.

During this succession of masters he was captured in a shipwreck by Spanish sailors, but some time later in Havana he saw Stapylton again and convinced him to help him get away. His former employer or master did not at once recognize him, but the next day informed the Spaniard who laid claim to Lewis that he in fact belonged to him and carried Lewis to Philadelphia and New York. There he began another series of masters which landed him in England twice, where he lived for some time with Stapylton as his servant before leaving him. Twice also during that time Stapylton kidnapped him when he left.

This second kidnapping was the occasion of the lawsuit. Stapylton, clearly not a trustworthy or even necessarily a law-abiding man, had called Lewis aside and told him that he was afraid a custom house officer had noticed the gin and tea Stapylton had stored on the wharf at Chelsea College, near the home of Mrs Banks. He asked Lewis to go at night and retrieve it, taking a particular back route so as not to be noticed by the officer. Lewis went, accompanied by one man but unaware of two others who were ahead of and behind him. In a dark passageway three men, John Maloney, Aaron Armstrong and Richard Coleman, jumped him.

> When I went there they seiz'd me directly then I began to call out for help[.] I call'd to Mrs Banks for help . . . then they began to fight with me and I would not go and I fought about a quarter of an hour with them in the way and at last they drag me about a hundred yards and dragg'd me upon my back upon the Ground and when I got to the Water side they shoved me into the Water instead of the Boat I would not go and then they put me into the Boat and then put a Cord round my leg.

Q. from Mr. Lucas[:] Did you cry out?

A. Yes Sir I cry out all the time, and then they put a stick across my mouth and Gagg me[.] I struggled and got it off then when I got past Chelsea Colledge then I hold my tongue then.

Q. Did any body give directions about tying or Gagging you[,] did you hear any body?

A. Yes I heard some people[.] I heard him cry out Gagg him says he.

Q. Who cry'd out Gagg him?

A. I thought it was Stapylton.

Q. You knew his Voice?

A. Yes Sir he was somewhere upon the Side of the shore crying out Gagg him.[52]

From the boat Lewis was put on board the *Snow* and carried down to Gravesend from where it was intended he be sent to the West Indies.

The three kidnappers clearly knew what it was they were hired to do. When Coleman took the stand he described how Stapylton approached him for a mysterious night-time errand which he guessed was 'to carry the Black down again'. He accordingly lay in ambush and when Lewis was attacked heard him cry out 'Mrs. Banks come help me for Gods sake they are going to trepanne me and take me on board the ship'.[53] When they finally wrestled him on board, said Coleman, Lewis declared that he would jump overboard and drown rather than be carried away, so they tied his legs and gagged him. He put up a prodigious fight and it took a great effort to subdue him and get him on board even though he was outnumbered three to one.

Fortunately for Lewis his neighbour Mrs Banks heard the outcry and sent her servants to help him. One of the kidnappers pulled a newspaper from his pocket saying that they had advertized for him there, hoping to prove thereby that he was legally their property. They also claimed to have a warrant for his arrest from the Lord Mayor. Seeing her servants rebuffed, Mrs Banks went to Granville Sharp the next morning, 3 July 1770, for help. Sharp lost no time in accompanying her to obtain a warrant for Lewis's return. The captain of the *Snow* however refused to surrender Lewis, declaring that he had a bill of sale from Stapylton which overrode the warrant, and he started to sail away. Sharp then went to the Lord Mayor himself and to various judges in order to receive a writ of habeas corpus which Mrs Banks sent off with her servant Peter.

Sir Thomas Clarkson, who was to become a fearless abolitionist, draws a more melodramatic but probably accurate picture of Lewis's predicament. 'The vessel had reached the Downs and had actually got under way for the West Indies', he wrote.

> In a few hours, it would have been out of sight. Just at this critical moment, the writ of *habeas corpus* was carried on board. The officer who served it saw the miserable captive chained to the mainmast, bathed in tears, and casting a last mournful look on the land of freedom. The Captain on receiving the writ became outrageous – but knowing the serious consequences of resisting the law of the land, he gave up his prisoner, whom the officer carried safe, but now weeping for joy to the shore.[54]

Not content with this, Sharp also obtained warrants for Stapylton and two of his accomplices, the watermen Maloney and Armstrong, to appear in court.[55]

In this story was not only the drama of Thomas Lewis's kidnapping and desperate struggle to remain free, but the involvement of so many white people in assisting him. Mrs Banks, her coachman and servants, Sharp, two judges and a baron all raised the alarm to prevent the man's unlawful capture and sale into slavery. More than that, Lewis apparently understood or at least hoped that he could count on these people to do so. Yet without Sharp's growing reputation as an opponent to slavery Mrs Banks would not have thought to approach him, and without the cooperation of bad winds which delayed the *Snow*'s departure, Lewis, like so many others in his position, would have been lost.

In his cross-examination, the lawyer for the defence, Mr Walker, attempted to prove ownership by Stapylton's care for Lewis in England. Stapylton was old and blind, 'incapable of carrying on any business'.[56] Further, Lewis had been ill in England and Stapylton had provided for him, sending him to St George's Hospital in Hyde Park Corner, paying his bills and for his food. The defence pressed this point, stating that 'All the time you was in England he took care of you', but Lewis answered, 'No Sir not always', adding that he left his employer 'when he used me ill'.[57]

The business of the hospital stay caused a dramatic moment later in the trial. A witness named William Watson explained that he had obtained a letter of permission allowing Lewis to enter St George's, and that there he had been asked for assurance that if Lewis survived 'you would give it under your hand that you will take him away if he does well'. Endeavouring to prove that the hospital officials would have asked for the same assurances even if Lewis were not black and a servant, Dunning observed, 'All this wo'd have happened if he had been your son'. Watson was beside himself. 'My Son a Negro!' he cried out. 'What! a negroe my Son[']' Dunning tried to calm him down: Don't be angry my friend[,] what is all this ferment about, it might have happened to you[;] they never had admitted people into the Hospital in any other way'.[58] To a supporter of a slave-owner, Dunning had unthinkingly made the one remark which could cause the most offence, and in front of the judge whose nephew was indeed the father of a Negro.

As the case proceeded, Mansfield acknowledged that its importance was greater than the freedom of a single man. 'I'll tell you what I think to do', he said, interrupting the interrogation. 'The central Question may be a very important one, and not in this Shape ever considered as I know of, If you have Title of property'. Reminding the court that Lewis's being black did not in itself prove him to be property, but that he had in the past granted a number of writs of habeas corpus for the return of slaves to their masters, Mansfield declared that 'whether they have this kind of property in England never has been Solemnly determined'.[59] He proposed that the question of Lewis's ownership be put to the jury; if there were evidence that Lewis was Stapylton's slave the kidnappers could be acquitted, since 'the fact in dispute is the kidnapping him and sending him away'.[60] If he were free the kidnappers could be indicted. In either case, the affair would remain specific and not address the larger issue of ownership of slaves in Britain. On this narrow territory the case moved forward, with Mansfield insisting more than once that 'the only point is, as to the property, which I shall leave to the Jury'.[61]

111

In his summation Dunning insisted on the larger question, 'that no such property can exist, which I will maintain in any place and in any Court in this Kingdom'.[62] Furthermore, was it to be 'made a question of, that . . . his colour being black makes him more his property than if he was white[?] is it be distinguishable only by Colour that such right is to exist?'[63] Mansfield however reminded the jury to stick to the specifics. Stapylton had taken Lewis from the hairdresser by force; in England he had also taken him by force. If the jury believed he was not a slave purchased by Stapylton, they would find the defendants guilty. If they found that Lewis was indeed Stapylton's slave they would find a Special Verdict 'and that will leave it for a more solemn discussion concerning the right of such property here in England'.[64] The jury found for Lewis, calling out 'Guilty, guilty'. At this Mansfield turned to Dunning and said, 'you will find more in the question than you see at present.' The judge went on:

> It is no matter mooting it now but if you look into it there is more than by accident you are acquainted with[.] [T]here are a great many opinions given upon it[.] I am aware of many of them but I know that . . . Lord Hardwick and Lord Talbot had several discussions concerning the right of property in Negroes . . . I dont know what the Consequences may be if they were to lose their property by accidentally bringing them into England . . . I hope it never will be finally discussed For I wou'd have all Masters think they were Free and all Negroes think they were not because then they wo'd both behave better.[65]

As Lewis prepared to leave the building, Dunning had a final request of the judge: a press gang was waiting in the hall outside to kidnap the young man. Could Mansfield issue a warning? Mansfield sternly ordered against any 'dar[ing] to touch the Boy', and for the officer to bring any such men before him. But turning back to Dunning, he went back to earlier legal opinions concerning black people: 'being Christians dont take away the right of property'. Lewis may have left the court a free man but nothing greater had been decided.

The case didn't end there, though. When Stapylton, Maloney

and Armstrong were called back to the King's Bench in June 1771 to receive judgement, Mansfield expressed surprise. He ruminated out loud at some length, saying that he had given the case a great deal of thought since the trial, and doubted whether 'the Negro could prove his own Freedom by his own Evidence'. Furthermore, he believed that Lewis had been improperly led into giving his evidence. The grounds upon which Lewis was proved free were not his own evidence, therefore, but the fact that his capture by the Spanish sailors had broken Stapylton's chain of ownership. He stated several times that he had many doubts upon the case and had reconsidered it since. It was something of a moot point: of the three times the men were called for judgement, they failed to show up twice and Mansfield himself once. None of them was ever sentenced.

What seems to have happened is that as the trial proceeded, Mansfield grew increasingly worried that it could set an important precedent, leading to all slaves entering Britain becoming automatically free. His concern was for property rights; he quoted the figure of 14,000 to 15,000 black people in Britain, all of whom could conceivably be set free at one fell swoop, observing that 'there being so great a number [of slaves] in the ports of this Kingdom, that many thousands of pounds would be lost to the owners, by setting them free'.[66] In his trial notes he refers explicitly to the break in ownership as determining that Lewis was not Stapylton's property. Oldham too finds that 'Mansfield's disinclination to resolve the property principle under English law was not surprising', and his requesting a special verdict, with its possibility that the larger question could be addressed, a shrewd but risky strategy. Others found Mansfield's refusal to give judgement against Stapylton a 'blatant refusal' to do what his office required.[67]

Granville Sharp was among them. Furious at Mansfield, Sharp wrote a scathing report of the case for his own use. Careful as always to distance Mansfield the man from Mansfield the judge, Sharp was nonetheless appalled at what he saw as a miscarriage of justice. On the last day that Stapylton was called for judgement, 28 November 1771, Mansfield expressed amazement that he was to be judged.

I am surprised, that Stapylton was brought up! I did not expect they would bring him up again! *I was in great doubt*, and so were my Brother Judges, & many of the Council, whether the Black could be a proper witness of his Freedom, he being the only Witness; and I wish any Body could satisfy me of that *Doubt*. But I did not think they would have brought him up; and I should advise *the Prosecutrix* [Mrs Banks] not to bring him up, as she has got the Black in her Possession.[68]

In other words, while he was quite willing that Lewis go free, he was equally unwilling for Stapylton to be punished for attempting to kidnap and sell him.

To Sharp this was nothing short of hypocrisy.

He seems to think the bare mention of '*a Doubt in his mind*' a sufficient excuse, without assigning any, the least, probable Grounds to justify *an Arrest of Judgment*. A *Practice this which must render all Trials at Law useless and trifling*; and must consequently reduce and annihilate the practice of Gentlemen, who profess the Law; because Men will be obliged to seek some other Determination (already too great) is increased: – for every reasonable person will carefull[y] shun the Expence of a Contest at Law when the issue depends, merely, on the *Will and pleasure of one man*.[69]

The courts were the natural arena for deciding momentous questions. If the questions were first deliberately limited and the guilty parties allowed to go free at the judge's whim, what recourse was there not only for slaves and their defenders, but for any citizen with a grievance?

Not only that, but why should Lewis have to prove himself free? Even men guilty of crimes were presumed innocent, and Lewis was a victim, not a criminal. The burden of proof was on Stapylton and his accomplices to show that he was their slave, not the other way round. Sharp also took exception to Mansfield's remarks during the trial that he had issued writs of habeas corpus to return slaves to their masters, a practice antithetical to the spirit of habeas corpus which was 'certainly *to relieve* from *false Imprisonment*, and not to *deliver up a poor wretch, against his Will*, into the Hands of a Tyrannical Master, who rates *him merely as a Chattel,*

114

or pecuniary property, and *not as a Man.*' Rather than an instrument of relief the writ became an instrument of oppression.[70]

Sharp now became determined in earnest to bring a test case which would force the courts to decide the issue of British slavery once and for all. The Yorke and Talbot decision which Mansfield referred to in the course of Lewis's case had stood as a precedent for forty-five years despite its being an unofficial opinion rather than an official decision. Mansfield himself admitted the informal and questionable conditions of the opinion which had prevented the freedom of black slaves on British soil for so many years.

After Thomas Lewis's case, Sharp became widely known as a defender of black freedom, and it may not have surprised him to hear the number of surreptitious knocks at his back door from slaves imploring his assistance. He gave aid, both financial and material, as he could but he was by no means well-off. He felt that the greatest gift he could bestow both for the maligned and abused slaves, but also for the honour of the British system of law and freedom, was once and for all to bring the issue of slavery to a real resolution. In the meantime, he went to work daily, studied at night, and even rescued a few more slaves, two men named John Thomas, and an East Indian.

This latter, listed in his accounting of rescued slaves, may be the same fourteen year old he discusses in a letter, advertised as 'Bob or Pompey', who disappeared wearing 'a Brass Collar round his Neck with a Direction upon it to a House in Charlotte Street, Bloomsbury Square'. 'Thus the *Black Indian Pompey*', wrote Sharp, 'was publickly treated with as little Ceremony as *a Black Dog* of the *same Name would be.*' He was appalled to discover that Pompey's master was esteemed '*a mighty good sort of Man*'.[71] This deliberate confusion of black men and dogs appeared in literature as well as in real life toward the end of the century. William Godwin, known for his radically liberal views as well as for his son-in-law Percy Shelley, repeatedly demeans black people in his 1799 novel *St. Leon: A Tale of the Sixteenth Century*, and draws a scene of a black servant weeping over the corpse of a black dog with whom he feels a racial kinship. Maria Edgeworth, in her 1802 novel *Belinda*, portrays a handsome young West Indian whose black manservant and black dog are both named Juba.

Sharp may have been confused about what caused differences in racial colour, but he knew well that this sort of entanglement of humans with animals was only made possible by chattel slavery which allowed certain kinds of people to be considered property. Until he could eradicate slavery on British soil, he believed, all of the abuses indicated by these advertisements and by the absence of positive law would legally continue. Individual cases appeared from time to time, but the judges confounded precedential decisions by keeping their judgements extremely narrow. He searched for a test case and one soon presented itself.

Mansfield too seemed by this time to want the issue settled, although when the time came he vacillated for months. Few court cases in Britain have been so fraught with irony, so discussed, and so misunderstood over such a long period of time as that of James Somerset. It is for this case and its repercussions that both Sharp and Mansfield are best known, but as for Somerset himself, whose name is permanently tied to the history of slavery and freedom in Britain, little is known.

His circumstances resemble those of Strong and Lewis. He was the servant of a Scotsman named Charles Stewart, a cashier and paymaster living in Boston, Massachusetts. Stewart returned to England on extended business on 10 November 1769, taking Somerset along to serve him 'in the parish of St. Mary-le-bow in the ward of Cheap'.[72] Somerset ran off after two years, but was recaptured on 26 November 1771 and put in irons on board the ship *Ann and Mary*. The captain, John Knowles, was to sell him into slavery when he reached Jamaica. Three people, Thomas Walkin, Elizabeth Cade and John Marlow, witnessed Somerset's capture and signed affidavits concerning it, and obtained a writ of habeas corpus from Lord Mansfield. Captain Knowles 'produced the body' of Somerset on 9 December, and Mansfield referred the matter to the Court of King's Bench, setting a trial date of 7 February 1772.[73]

Knowles' affidavit firmly stated that Somerset, without Stewart's consent and 'without any lawful authority whatsoever, departed and absented himself from the service of the said Charles Steuart, and absolutely refused to return into [his] service . . . during his stay and abiding in this kingdom'.[74] According to this

116

HEYDAY! is this my DAUGHTER ANNE.

1. A lady of fashion with her indispensable accessories: a huge wig, a lap dog, and an ornately-dressed young black page. An illustration of 1771 in *Drolleries*

KITCHIN STUFF.

2. A cook, kitchen maid and
footman relax below stairs.
Cartoon by Rowlandson, 1810

FLUNKEYS indulging themselves at the Drapers Door? A Fact

3. Two fashionably attired
footmen block the pavement.
Published in the
Looking Glass, 1830

4. A servants' card party, showing a drunken black servant waiting upon his crude colleagues. By Woodward after Cruikshank, 1799

5. The Duchess of Queensberry fencing with Soubise. Cartoon by William Austin, 1 May 1773

6. Francis Williams, known as the Negro Scholar of Jamaica, *c.* 1740, by an anonymous
artist

7. Francis Barber,
Johnson's servant and heir.
Portrait attributed to
James Northcote.

8. Ignatius Sancho, the London
grocer and correspondent of
Laurence Sterne. Portrait by
an unknown artist

FOOT PAD'S - OR MUCH ADO ABOUT NOTHING.

9. A lame highwayman and his black female accomplice go about their business. Cartoon by Isaac Cruikshank, 4 May 1795

10. One of the conspirators in the Cato Street plot to murder George IV's cabinet ministers was one 'W. Davidson, Cabinet Maker, a Man of Colour'. Cartoon by C. Williams, published in *Caricatures*, February 1820

The Sailor's description of a Chase & Capture. —

11. Many of the black men who came to England were sailors, treated as equals on board ship. Cartoon by Lieutenant John Sheringham, RN, January 1822

12. Olaudah Equiano, former slave, from the frontispiece to the original edition of his memoirs, 1789

13. Joseph Johnson, a famous London beggar, celebrated for his hat modelled after a ship.

14. Charles M'Gee, another renowned London beggar. Both cartoons by John Thomas Smith in *Vagabondia*, December 1815

15. The Sharp family aboard their barge, by Johann Zoffany, 1779–81. *Top row*: William Sharp and Anna Jemima Sharp. *Middle row*: Mrs James Sharp, Catherine Sharp (née Barwick) with Mary Sharp on her lap, Judith Sharp. *Bottom row*: cabin boy, bargemaster, James Sharp, Catherine Sharp, Granville Sharp, Elizabeth Prowse (née Sharp), Frances Sharp, John Sharp, Mary Sharp (née Dering)

16. William Murray, Lord Mansfield, 1783, by J.S.Copley

Pompey! by frequent use of the Cow-skin, I have made an Obedient good Servant of you, and have therefore remember'd you in my Will I have desired that when you die, you may have the Honor of being laid in the same Tomb with your Old Master.

Oh! tank you Massa! but radder not, Devil come, all dark you know! He no see at all, makes mistake and take Pompey instead of Massa!!

THE GENEROUS MASTER or African Sincerity. a WEST India caricatur

17. On the left wall hang cowskins, the whip used by West Indians to scourge their slaves, undermining the master's false generosity. Published in *Caricatures*, January 1819

18. The MP Jeremiah Dyson, caricatured as Soubise, the Duchess of Queensberry's black protégé. Cartoon by M. Darly, September 1772

A MUNGO MACARONI.

Publish'd according to Act, by MDarly, 39 Strand, Sept: 20. 1772

19. In the pro-slavery view, slaves were happy and well cared-for in West Indian bondage

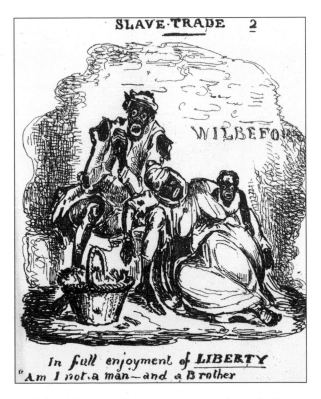

20. Another pro-slavery view was that of a free black family, starving on the streets of London

21. A virulent attack on the abolitionists using Gillray's *The Union Club* but showing blacks instead of Irish. Actual people represented include William Wilberforce, Zachary Macaulay and a black sailor named Billy Waters

22. Blacks were staple members of musical groups.
Cartoon by C.L.Smith, July 1794

wording it was Stewart whose rights had been trampled upon, and Somerset who had no legal right to absent himself from his master. Thus rather than being the injured party in whose name the suit was brought, it was implied that Somerset was the guilty party. At least this was how it seems to have impressed Mansfield. When he set the trial date, he placed Somerset under a stiff financial penalty should he fail to appear.

This infuriated Sharp. Somerset was the plaintiff in the case, 'yet he has been obliged to find Sureties for his Appearance'. Stewart, on the other hand, 'is nevertheless excused the trouble and expense of any such Recognizance . . . But at present he may laugh at the form and parade of the Court, in carrying on the appearance of so Solemn an Inquiry, and yet leaving him entirely at Liberty to *withdraw his Claim* and *himself* from the consequences of this enquiry; whenever matters are likely to go against him'.[75] In other words, the plaintiff was bound under heavy penalty to appear, but not only was the accused exempt from such penalty, he could cause the case to be withdrawn at any time merely by withdrawing his claim to Somerset's person. The legal roles were in this instance completely reversed. Somerset himself approached Sharp to complain and to ask for advice on 13 January 1772. The next day a Mr Cade of Cumberland Street, Drury Lane, possibly a relative of the witness, Elizabeth Cade, also appeared at Sharp's home to plead for the escaped slave.

Two weeks later Sharp had made up his mind. He paid £6. 6s to retain counsel, only a week before the trial was to take place.[76] He was as supremely fortunate in his choice of legal representation as the opposition was unfortunate. On 25 January he received a letter from a young barrister named Francis Hargrave, offering his legal services gratis on behalf of Somerset and against slavery. He apparently had contacted Sharp earlier during his and James's defence against Stapylton's charges, and now had some strong and fleshed-out arguments to use against slavery. Sharp not only gratefully accepted the offer but sent his reply to Lincoln's Inn via Somerset himself, who served both as courier and a visible and eloquent reminder of what the case was about.[77] It was through James Somerset too that Hargrave reported to Sharp that copies of the promised affidavits and writs which he needed for the hearing the next day had not arrived.[78] Both Sharp and Hargrave exchanged their arguments and tracts against slavery, often using James Somerset as a messenger, while he awaited not only his own fate but potentially that of all slaves in Britain.

Hargrave was joined by another barrister named James Mansfield (no relation to Lord Mansfield), and Serjeants William Davy and John Glynn. Mr Alleyne made the final summation. These were young men in the process of establishing their reputations. It made sense that they would choose a potentially precedent-setting and morally uplifting case for their debuts, but they did so also out of a genuine and strong conviction against slavery. All refused payment for their services.

Representation for the defence was amazingly enough taken by the same barrister, John Dunning, who had recently made his name in successfully prosecuting Stapylton, and by staunchly defending the right of Lewis and all black people to freedom on British soil. It was Dunning who had stood in front of Mansfield and the jury with his thumb in Sharp's tract against *Tolerating Slavery* and declared that 'our Laws admit of no such property'[79] and that it was nothing less than 'a Violent outrage done to the Laws of [our] Country'.[80] It was Dunning too who consistently endeavoured to make Lewis versus Stapylton a test case to condemn slavery in Britain, and Mansfield who consistently thwarted him. In a memorandum on the Somerset case, Sharp gleefully noted that Dunning had stood in the Lewis v. Stapylton trial and not only insisted that 'no such property can exist' in England, but that 'I will maintain [this] in any place and in any Court in this Kingdom reserving to myself a right to insist that our Laws admit of no such property'.[81]

Such ironies were lost upon no one. Even the defendant Charles Stewart wrote to James Murray of Boston on 15 June 1772 that in the later stages of the case 'some young counsel flourished away on the side of liberty, and acquired great honour. Dunning was dull and languid, and would have made a much better figure on that side also . . . I am very sorry for the load of abuse thrown on L–d M—— for hesitating to pronounce judgment in favour of freedom. Dunning has come in also for a pretty good share for taking the wrong side'.[82] Not only was Dunning labouring on the wrong side of a passionate and popular issue (though to be sure supported by the West Indian faction), but he was seen as a turncoat.

The issue circled primarily round the fact that there were conflicting rulings on slavery in England. Lord Chief Justice John Holt's, in 1706, was unequivocally anti-slavery, declaring that 'as soon as a Negro comes into England, he becomes free'. These fine and rousing words were often confusingly quoted in the context of Lord Mansfield's decision nearly seventy years later, but they were randomly trusted and erratically enforced. Such a view was at odds with the commercial facts of life. Edward Fiddes rightly noted in 1934 that eighteenth-century England 'had landed herself in a hopeless illogical position. She justly prided herself on the personal liberty which Englishmen enjoyed under the Common Law' and at the same time 'she sanctioned and even promoted a severe system of slavery in her colonies'. This contradiction 'was hardly to be solved by epigrams about the freedom-giving properties of English air or English soil'.[83]

It was the opinion of Attorney-General Sir Philip Yorke (later Lord Chancellor Hardwicke) and Solicitor-General Charles Talbot in 1729 that, for over forty years, carried greater weight despite the highly questionable circumstances surrounding its delivery. Accosted by representatives of West Indian planters and presented by them with a petition to decide the slavery issue, the two men delivered the opinion which stood as law for many: 'that a slave, by coming from the West Indies, doth not become free; and that his master's property or right in him is not thereby determined or varied'. Furthermore, baptism did not confer freedom, a point which Mansfield had pressured Dunning to confirm at the end of the Stapylton trial. Finally, 'the master may legally compel him to return to the plantations'.[84]

For a ruling that carried so much weight for so long, the circumstances and informality surrounding its delivery were highly unusual. Rather than a considered decision delivered in court, it was an 'opinion' delivered after a supper at Lincoln's Inn Fields. Even Mansfield drily noted the influences of food, wine and lateness of the hour when he stated at Somerset's trial that the Yorke–Talbot decision, 'might not, as he believes the contrary is not

119

usual at that hour, be taken with much accuracy'.[85] Even Hardwicke's biographer, apparently embarrassed by the inhumanit-
arian spirit of the opinion, hoped that if the matter had been a
more formally considered appeal, 'he might possibly have taken
a wider view, and one more consistent with justice and with the
general spirit of English laws and the constitution'.[86]

When the initial hearing on Somerset versus Stewart took place
on 24 January 1772, Davy requested that because of the importance
of the case, a later court date be set. Mansfield, however, refused
saying that 'if it should come fairly to the general question [i.e.
whether or not slavery in Britain was legal], *whatever the opinion
of the Court might be,* even if they were *all agreed on one side or the
other,* the subject was of so general and extensive concern, that,
from the nature of the question, he should certainly *take the opinion
of all the Judges* upon it'.[87] Even so Mansfield tried to get the case
dismissed by using a back door, and suggested to Elizabeth Cade,
'the poor Widow who had been at the Expense of the Writ', to
buy Somerset herself and set him free. She indignantly replied
that this 'would be an *acknowledgement that the Plaintiff had a right
to Assault and imprison a poor innocent man in this Kingdom,* and that
she would never be guilty of setting so bad an Example'.[88]

Since Hargrave wanted more time to prepare, it fell to Davy
to open the argument in front of Mansfield and Justices Aston,
Willis and Ashurst on 7 February. He followed the path recently
laid by Dunning in the Lewis versus Stapylton hearing, arguing
three main points: 1) that villenage, the feudal method of attaching
people to property and the only remotely applicable British precedent for slavery on her own soil, was long extinct; 2) that everyone
entering England automatically became a subject of the King, and
subject to English laws; 3) that if colonial laws on slavery could
be enforced in England, then *all* colonial laws could be enforced
in England. 'Where', he asked, 'will they draw the line?'[89] Mr
Serjeant Glynn followed Serjeant Davy, reasserting his arguments, and at the end of his speech Lord Mansfield announced that
since the case promised 'to go to great length, and it is the
end of the term', it should be held over until the next term,
9 May.

Somewhere in all this Somerset the man gets lost in Somerset the case. What little we know about him is set forth in the bare facts of the case, and he has existed since then as a symbol of how white Englishmen rallied to a cause. Of course the part of whites in the case is indisputable, and there would be no Somerset decision without them. Yet here was a black man enslaved in Africa, sold in America, and who took his own chance at freedom when he arrived in England. Knowles' assertion that Somerset 'absolutely refused' to return to Stewart parallels in many ways Thomas Lewis's furious fight against his three kidnappers: both men took assertive and active roles in opposing their own enslavement. In the eighteenth-century, however, the opponents of slavery had no language for this kind of positive and self-protecting black action. The sympathy generated by these and other cases often depended upon a characterization of blacks as helpless and innocent victims, each victim representing thousands of other victims.

This is the tack that Thomas Day took in his enormously popular 1773 poem 'The Dying Negro', based upon a true event.[90] The advertisement for it stated that '[t]he following poem was occasioned by an article of news which appeared last week in the London papers, intimating that "a Black, who a few days before, ran away from his master, and got himself christened, with intent to marry his fellow-servant, a white woman, being taken, and sent on board the Captain's ship, in the Thames; took an opportunity of shooting himself through the head"'. Unlike Lewis or Somerset, he was not rescued, but chose death over slavery. Day called directly upon the fact 'that in an age and country, in which we boast of philanthropy, and generous sentiments, few persons, (except West-Indians) can read the above paragraph, without emotions similar to those, which inspired the following lines'. Written in the first person as dedicated to his English wife, the dying Negro outlines his carefree childhood in Africa and the miseries of slavery. Now that he has been taken up once more, his only power is that of suicide:

> Blest with thy last sad gift – the power to dye,
> At length, thy shafts, stern fortune, I defy;
> Welcome, kind pass-port to an unknown shore! –
> The world and I are enemies no more.

> This weapon ev'n in chains the brave can wield,
> And vanquish'd, quit triumphantly the field.

Still, he knows that he leaves a mourning fiancée:

> How shall I soothe thy grief, my destin'd bride!
> O sad farewell, one last embrace denied?
> For oh! thy tender breast my pangs will share,
> Bleed for my wounds, and feel my deep despair.
> They tears alone will grace a wretch's grave,
> A wretch, whom only thou would'st wish to save.
> Take these last sighs – to thee my soul I breathe –
> Fond love in dying groans, is all I can bequeathe.

> Why did I, slave, beyond my lot aspire?
> Why didst thou fan, fair maid, the growing fire?
> Full dear, for each deluding smile of thine
> I pay, nor at thy fatal charms repine.
> For thee I bade my drooping soul revive;
> For thee alone I could have borne to live;
> And love, I said, shall make me large amends,
> For persecuting foes, and faithless friends;
> Fool that I was! enur'd so long to pain,
> To trust to hope, or dream of joy again.

The combination of betrayal, slavery, love and untimely death was irresistible to a sentimental public.

These were the same issues that a fascinated public recognized in the Somerset case, which with its arguments and the suspense of its delays became a media event. Between late May and late June, the newspapers were filled with letters and articles on the topics of Somerset and slavery, and the effects of England upon the black people who had lived there. One white creole (a native-born, white West Indian) argued that colonial slave rebellions were caused by 'those sensible slaves, who have been in England and carried back' because 'they learn here to despise the Whites'. In the West Indies, he argued, they were kept under control by the use of terror, 'but the negroe servants returning hence, with new and enlarged notions, take off that terror, and shew them all the weaknesses of the whites'.[91] Whites could only remain safely in

122

control in the West Indies if blacks were not exposed to life in Britain. The writer also believed that slaves in England were automatically free, and worried that the Somerset case could actually overturn that situation, creating havoc:

> . . . if that should happen, there will be numbers brought over, who will take the bread out of English servants and chairmens mouths; and a much more dangerous thing may happen, my fiery countrymen may possibly use them as the Portuguese do to assassinate their enemies, which they may do with safety; a slave can be no evidence. A black is more afraid of his master, whose whip he sees every day, than of the magistrate whom he seldom hears of. If he is taken, his confession is useless as a slave, and cannot be evidence against his master.

This hysterical vision of black assassins forced by their masters to commit murder presupposed that by allowing slavery on British soil, all the same conditions and laws that existed in the Americas to control slaves would be imported also. Like Granville Sharp's fears that plantation slavery could develop in England, this pro-slavery writer saw the evils of allowing English slavery but viewed English whites as dangerous.

Another writer used the opportunity to make facetious remarks about people of fashion, 'as some difficulties have lately occurred in determining who are and who are not to be deemed slaves'. He claimed that an order would soon be issued which would establish criteria of complexions. Since 'our Ministers have always been averse from employing slaves at home, and as no one can hesitate between the dark, clear complexion of Negroes, and the morning, unpainted one of persons of quality, and of many others in this metropolis, between the fact of Somerset and that of —— it will be enjoined all ships in the slave trade to take in their lading for the future from the port of London, and not from the coast of Guinea'.[92]

More serious writers proposed solutions to what they saw as the 'problem' of black people living in Britain. Their presence in England, wrote 'Benevolus' of Covent Garden, 'are not only irksome to themselves in general (as fish out of water) but disagreeable, if not oppressive and pernicious to society in general'. He proposed that those willing to depart England do so, and if unwilling either be transported at public expense and sold or remain in England as their masters' and mistresses' property, 'without any pretence to a benefit to our laws'.[93] While he saw this as a reasonable and humane solution, it proposed nothing less than that black people not be protected by English law.

Sometimes there were running arguments between the same anonymous writers in different newspapers at the same time. 'Negro' and 'No Party Man' battled it out on the pages of *The Craftsman* and *The Gazetteer*. 'Negro' was pro-Somerset, arguing that the 'difference, Sir, between you or any other Englishman, and a negro, is only in colour; and why that distinction should unfortunately exempt him from the blessings of liberty, I own I am at a loss to determine'. Whichever way the case would be determined, however, he knew that Mansfield could only decide it on the basis of English law.[94] 'No Party Man' made a virulent retort, referring to Somerset as 'your supposed *brother*' and accusing him of ignoring important parts of Mansfield's speeches.[95] He continued his attack on 15 June by publishing the same letter in *The Gazetteer*.[96] Perhaps in response to such letters, the editors of *Middlesex Journal* quietly stated that '[n]otwithstanding the many efforts even of a judicial nature to prevent the determination of the Negro cause, judgment will certainly be prayed for the very next Term'.[97]

When the case resumed in early May, James Mansfield defended Somerset, who for some reason does not appear to have taken the stand, by speaking in the first person as though he were Somerset himself, and as though Somerset were a generic black slave.

It is true, I was a slave; kept as a slave, in Africa. I was first put in chains on board a British ship, and carried from Africa to America: I there lived under a master, from whose tyranny I could not escape: if I had attempted it, I should have been exposed to the severest punishment: and never, from the first moment of my life to the present time, have I been in a country where I had a power to assert the common rights of mankind. I am now in a country where the laws of liberty are known and regarded; and can you tell me the reason

124

why I am not to be protected by those laws, but to be carried away
again to be sold?[98]

One can only wonder why Somerset, useful as a cause and as
a physical presence in the courtroom, useful too as an effective
messenger between the other actors on his behalf, was not deemed
particularly useful as a voice. Presumably, of course, this was
because his lawyers believed they could plead his case better than
he could.

More interesting though is that James Mansfield's argument
was the only one presented in the case which appealed directly to
the sympathies of the audience. The case was again deferred, this
time for a week, after Mansfield's speech, and when it resumed
Hargrave presented an eloquent, well-prepared, lucid but dis-
passionate argument. He made no bones about the fact that the
case was less about James Somerset than about larger issues: 'The
questions, arising in this case, do not merely concern the unfortunate person, who is the subject of it, and such as are or may be
under like unhappy circumstances', he said in a statement which
may indeed have startled Somerset himself. He was saying that
not only was the case not just about Somerset, it was not even
really about other slaves who were in or who might at some point
enter England. The questions it raised 'are highly interesting to
the whole community, and cannot be decided, without having
the most general and important consequences; without extensive
influence on private happiness and public security'.[99]

To some extent his remarks went over familiar territory. Villenage had gone out with Henry VI; foreign laws did not apply in
England; English law did not allow people to enslave themselves
by contract nor to introduce a new form of slavery; since slaves
were by their very state of enslavement unable to make contracts,
any contract they might enter upon to enslave themselves was
doubly invalid. He mentioned some of the precedential cases cited
in Lewis versus Stapylton, as well as others. He refuted the argument that although one could not be a slave in England, the state
might be temporarily suspended while one was in England and
resumed upon leaving. The result of all this was 'not merely that
negroes become free on being brought into this country, but that

the law of England confers the gift of liberty entire and unencumbered; not in name only, but really and substantially; and consequently that Mr. Steuart cannot have the least right over Sommersett the negro, either in the open character of a slave, or in the disguised one of an ordinary servant'.[100]

The defence was weaker, and played upon familiar fears. If slaves learn that they are free in England, 'they will flock over in vast numbers, over-run this country, and desolate the plantations', asserted Alleyne in his summation in terms more reminiscent of swarms of locusts than of impoverished and severely restricted American and West Indian slaves. (He did not address the fact that Canada, a haven for runaway slaves, had not been overrun in desolating numbers, despite its proximity to America.) Since there was no law in England prohibiting slavery it must be legal. He added, astoundingly, that since white slave owners needed to come to England, they also needed black slaves to get them there, 'for they cannot trust the whites, either with the stores or the navigating the vessel'.[101]

Here Lord Mansfield interrupted, wondering aloud about the possible financial disaster 'to proprietors, there being so great a number in the ports of this kingdom, that many thousands of pounds would be lost to the owners by setting them free'.[102] Told that in fact there were few slaves in these fleets, he nonetheless went on to reaffirm that far from being an assurance of release, habeas corpus was often used to force people to work abroad. 'A right of compulsion there must be, or the master will be under the ridiculous necessity of neglecting his proper business, by staying here to have their service, or must be quite deprived of those he has been obliged to bring over'.[103] On this note he adjourned the court for another week, leaving Somerset's fate unclear, and intimating that his sympathies were with the slave owners rather than with the slaves.

Dunning was clearly made utterly miserable by the unpopular and possibly discredited position in which he found himself. When the case resumed he kept repeating that he was there to defend Captain Knowles against the charge of false imprisonment, not to defend slavery. He was only doing his job, 'bound by duty to maintain those arguments which are most useful to Captain

Knowles, as far as is consistent with truth, and if his conduct has been agreeable to the laws throughout, I am under a farther indispensable duty to support it'.[104] Then he went on to make a string of incorrect and disconnected statements:

> About 14,000 slaves, from the most exact intelligence I am able to procure, are at present here, and some little time past, 166,914 in Jamaica. There are, besides, a number of wild negroes in the woods. The computed value of a negro in those parts £50 a head . . . Every family almost brings over a great number, and will, be the decision on which side it may. Most negroes who have money (and that description I believe will include nearly all) make interest with the common sailors to be carried hither . . . If it were necessary to the idea and the existence of James Sommersett, that his master, even here, might kill, nay, might eat him, might sell living or dead, might make him and his descendants property alienable, and thus transmissible to posterity: this how high soever my ideas may be of the duty of my profession, is what I should decline pretty much to defend or assert, for any purpose seriously. But this is what at present I am not at all concerned in, unless Captain Knowles, or Mr. Steuart, have killed or eat him.[105]

He ended his unconvincing argument by stating, pathetically, that he hoped 'I shall not suffer in the opinion of those whose honest passions are fired at the name of slavery. I hope I have not transgressed my duty to humanity, nor doubt I your lordship's discharge of yours to justice', then retreated.[106] Even the newspapers decided that Dunning 'advanced very little *materially* new',[107] and decided that Mansfield's later praise had been 'to the learning and ingenuity displayed by the young counsel, Mess. Hargrave and Allen'.[108] When Lord Mansfield at the end of that day expressed 'particular happiness in seeing young men, just called to the bar . . . able so much to profit by their reading', he surely did not refer to the miserable young Dunning.[109]

Throughout the months of the hearings Mansfield, who has gone down in history alongside Sharp as a saviour of black slaves in Britain, wavered so much in his stance that it was not at all clear what the outcome might be, although Sharp was encouraged that Mansfield seemed to be expressing himself '*More cautiously* upon the point than formerly and that he even went so far as to drop some hints of favourable wishes for the Cause of the Negro'.[110] Gentle and friendly in his personal relations, Mansfield could be strict and exacting in his legal interpretations. He was as likely to use writs of habeas corpus, Sharp's successful weapon against slave kidnappers, to return slaves into slavery as to free them. Time and again he warned juries not to let their feeling on behalf of slaves cloud their judgement of individual cases. It is not surprising therefore that he used a number of tactics to prevent Somerset's case from coming to a legal resolution, first by suggesting that Elizabeth Cade purchase and free him, then by repeatedly delaying the hearings. In large part this second ploy fuelled the public interest in the case. Suspense built as the months dragged on, the lawyers were able to build and publicize their positions, and the case became a topic of common conversation.

Mansfield's concerns encompassed more than the humanitarian one central to Somerset's, and all blacks', position. He worried publicly that 'the setting 14,000 or 15,000 at once loose by a solemn opinion, is very disagreeable in the effects it threatens'.[111] These 'disagreeable effects' primarily involved the loss of money to slave owners in England, which he estimated to be above £700,000 sterling. 'How would the law stand with respect to their settlement; their wages?' he wondered. 'How many actions for any slight coercion by the master?' Before setting the decision date, he again suggested that Stewart might still have time to free Somerset, avoiding the necessity for judgement. He also suggested that the merchants and planters potentially affected by the judgement should apply to Parliament directly to legitimize their rights to slaves, which they did in fact do. (Sharp was terrified that they might succeed, causing England to 'be not only . . . over ran with a vast multitude of poor wretched Slaves from the East and West Indies to engross the employment and subsistence of the free Labourers and industrious poor, but the latter . . . would be inevitably involved by degrees in the same horrid Slavery and oppression'.)[112] Mansfield insisted, as he had done all along, that whatever the outcome the judgement would apply to Somerset alone, and not stand as a general statement on slavery. None of these are the words or actions of a fiercely anti-slavery judge.

On Monday, 22 June 1772, Westminster Hall was packed. Black people crammed into the gallery, anxiously awaiting the words which would affect their lives and those of their children. Reporters from most of the major newspapers waited to take down Mansfield's words verbatim. Slave owners were there also in force. Even at the earlier hearings the courtroom had been so crowded that it was difficult to sit or even hear; among the throng at the 14 May session was John Baker, the late Jack Beef's owner, who had made a special expedition with friends to hear the case argued:

> Duke Douglas called early – chez lui; he and Brother John and I to Westminster Hall to hear Negro Cause – too early; all breakfasted Exchange Coho – there by little after 8, and Court not sit till near 11 – so Duke and I to Exhibition of Pictures – went back and Mrs. Sayer, once of Stᵉ Croix, joined us, but too late – one Hargrave speaking for the Negro but could hear nothing thro' the crowd . . .[113]

Inevitably the crowd was even greater when Mansfield delivered his decision.

The judge read a prepared speech, which was 'as guarded, cautious, and concise, as it could possibly be drawn up'.[114] First he dismissed the Yorke and Talbot opinion, the mistaken notion of baptism conferring freedom, and the precedent of villenage. But, he went on, the only question before the court was whether or not there existed sufficient cause to discharge Somerset. The only laws to be enforced were those of the country where the cause occurred. In England the implications of slavery were too great to be merely inferred by other existing laws; only positive law could approve it, and

> . . . the Power claimed by this Return was never in Use here; no Master ever was allowed here to take a Slave by force to be sold abroad, because he had deserted from his Service, or for any other Reason whatever; we cannot say the Cause set forth by this Return is allowed or approved of by the Laws of this Kingdom, therefore the Man must be discharged.[115]

Somerset was free.

The reaction was immediate. Transcripts of the decision appeared straight away in the *Public Advertiser*, the *Morning Chronicle and London Advertiser*, the *General Evening Post* of London, and the *London Evening Post*. It appeared later in *The Gentleman's Magazine*'s 'Historical Chronicle'. *The Craftsman*; or, *Say's Weekly Journal* did not reprint the speech, but did mention that 'the Court of King's Bench gave judgement in the case of Somerset the Negro, finding that his master had no power to compel him on board a ship, or to send him back to the plantations'.[116] This brief paraphrase of Mansfield's decision was accurate in its narrowness, recognizing that only Somerset was affected by the decision.

The newspapers took particular notice of the black people in the audience and their restrained delight at the decision. 'Several Negroes were in court yesterday, to hear the event of a cause so interesting to their tribe', said the *Morning Chronicle*.

> [A]fter the judgment of the court was known, [they] bowed with profound respect to the Judges, and shaking each other by the hand, congratulated themselves upon their recovery of the rights of human nature, and their happy lot that permitted them to breathe the free air of England. – No sight upon earth could be more pleasingly affecting to the feeling mind, than the joy which shone at that instant in these poor mens' sable countenances.[117]

Both *The Middlesex Journal* and *Bingley's Journal* reported that a 'great number of Blacks were in Westminster Hall yesterday, to hear the determination of the cause, and went away greatly pleased'.[118]

A number of journals and newspapers printed opposing views on slavery. *The Gentleman's Magazine* juxtaposed the pro-slavery argument of *A West Indian* with 'An Argument against Property in Slaves'.[119] The old enemies 'Negro' and 'No Party Man' continued to do battle on the pages of *The Gazetteer and New Daily Advertiser*.[120] Someone else regretted that 'the attention of the public is taken upon the affair of Somerset Negro', while little was paid to 'the poor apprentice boys and girls put out by the parishes in London . . . [who] are used with a brutish degree of rigour and cruelty, almost unknown to the regions of slavery'.[121]

Oddly enough Granville Sharp was not in the audience. A surprising note in his papers makes it clear that he learned of Mansfield's decision from none other than Somerset himself, and that in all likelihood he had never attended the hearings at all. The claims of his job were most likely the reason for this, although it is hard to recall that in this battle of masters and slaves Sharp himself was bound to his employer. Speaking of himself in the third person, he wrote that 'Thus ended G. Sharp's long contest with Lord Mansfield, on the 22d of June, 1772'.[122] With the decision, Somerset the man faded into obscurity, but Somerset the precedent took on a large life. Mansfield and Sharp became immortalized as friends of blacks, despite the fact that many then and now view the former as 'obviously slow, if not reluctant, to act' in the case, and that 'while posterity honors his memory, there is no occasion to forget that he followed, but did not lead, the revolution which abolished slavery in England'.[123] But it was the decision itself, even to those who never read or knew its exact wording, which had wide-ranging repercussions.

All over Britain and America, slaves, abolitionists, lawyers and judges cited the Somerset case as ending slavery in Britain, a precedent which many saw as applying to America as well: slaves who crossed into free states with their masters, even temporarily, tested the legality of slavery.[124] Despite Mansfield's many pains to reassert the deliberate narrowness of his decision, he seemed powerless to stem the tide of misinterpretation, demonstrating 'a legal world where things are not what they seem, a world of deceptive appearances and unforeseen consequences'.[125] One of the unforeseen circumstances was profiteering; the English abolitionist Thomas Clarkson discovered a plan whereby a West Indian slave dealer intended to sell slaves into British freedom by selling them to people who would subsequently set them free. Clarkson himself witnessed such a sale.[126] Despite the decision, slaves were still sold and sent out of the country for years afterward, often quite openly.

Subsequent cases, one presided over by Mansfield, referred explicitly to Somerset. Cay versus Chrichton in 1773 viewed Somerset as operating retroactively.[127] The more widely known Scottish case of Knight v. Wedderburn in 1778, the one that

Samuel Johnson so anxiously followed, cited Somerset, and reaffirmed that Scottish law not only did not permit a slave to be sent to the West Indies, but also denied the master a right to service in Scotland.[128] Thirteen years after the Somerset trial, Mansfield delivered a lecture on the narrowness of his earlier decision. The case of Thames Ditton involved a female slave brought to London, who having lived in two parishes, later sought parish relief. An exasperated Mansfield chastised the court, reminding them that the Somerset 'determination got no further than that the master cannot by force compel him to go out of the kingdom'.[129] The plaintiff was denied the funds.

In the end it didn't really matter what Mansfield had said, or what actually happened to James Somerset. The case became legend and to this day is still erroneously referred to as ending slavery in England. As long as everyone believed that slaves were free, it served as *de facto* freedom. Other slaves took their cue from Somerset, even in metaphoric ways. John Riddell of Bristol wrote to Charles Stewart on 10 July 1772, that one of his servants had run off after the decision.

> He told the servants that he had rec'd a letter from his Uncle Sommerset acquainting him that Lord Mansfield had given them their freedom & he was determined to leave me as soon as I returned from London which he did without even speaking to me. I don't find that he has gone off with anything of mine. Only carried off all his own cloths [*sic*] which I don't know whether he had any right so to do. I believe I shall not give my self any trouble to look after the ungrateful villain.[130]

In only three weeks the Somerset case had passed from the legal to the apocryphal. All over England, and sometimes in America, the 'nephews' of James Somerset left their masters and struck out on their own.

CHAPTER FIVE

The Black Poor

On both sides of the Atlantic the effects of Lord Mansfield's Somerset decision were felt almost immediately. In Britain, the common belief among slaves that the English air was now too pure to support slavery led to a number of slaves deserting their masters and seeking independent employment. Word of the decision reached American slaves almost as quickly and they too took flight. In the backwoods of Georgia a slave owner advertized that summer for his runaway man Bacchus, whom he feared would 'board a vessel for Great Britain . . . from the knowledge he has of the late Determination of Somerset's Case'.[1] When a couple absconded in 1773 their owner believed they would attempt to reach Britain 'where they imagine they will be free (a Notion now too prevalent among the Negroes, greatly to the vexation and Prejudice of their Masters)'.[2] American slave owners knew all too well that even though they might outlaw literacy and forbid them to congregate, slaves had developed such extraordinary methods of communication that, as John Adams noted in his diary, 'intelligence . . . will run several hundreds of miles in a week or fortnight'.[3]

The timing of the Somerset case affected both countries in ways that Sharp probably never anticipated. While he and others were fighting to resolve the issue of freedom for British slaves, the American colonists adopted similar rhetoric to agitate for white colonists' freedom from England. The hypocrisy of whites proclaiming themselves 'enslaved' by the British government and declaring a few years later the 'self-evident' truth 'that all men were created equal' was lost on neither American and British slaves. In Boston and elsewhere the Declaration of Independence in 1776 sparked a series of petitions, leaflets and newspaper announcements from free and enslaved blacks challenging those whites who demanded either liberty or death to free the real slaves. One fifth of the colonial population was black and the colonists, with some reason, began to fear a racial insurrection parallel to their own political one.

Realizing that trouble between Britain and its American colonies was inevitable, the British representatives in America were faced with two choices: either assume that few slaves would manage an escape to England – after all, an amazing feat – and ignore those who might arrive, or exploit a situation that could be turned to British advantage. In 1772, the same year as the Somerset decision, Lord Dunmore, the royal governor of Virginia, considered the thousands of runaway Negroes 'attached by no tye to their Master nor to the Country' and decided that it would make sense for the British to 'encourage them to revenge themselves, by which means a Conquest of this Country would inevitably be effected in a very short time'.[4] Three years later it was official: Lord Dunmore announced that he would 'arm my own Negroes & receive all others that come to me who I shall declare free' in order to advance the English cause. He solicited and promised freedom only to those slaves who would desert their rebel masters, not to those who belonged to loyal American Tories.

Within days of his proclamation five hundred black men reported to him, receiving guns 'as fast as they came in', three hundred of them forming Lord Dunmore's Ethiopian Regiment and wearing the words 'Liberty to Slaves' on their uniforms. Four years later General Sir Henry Clinton the elder made a similar offer, and despite bad treatment and poor conditions, 'tens of thousands of black men opted for the British side'.[5] With little reason to suppose that their own American masters would give it to them, they were willing to risk their lives for personal liberty. They served as foot soldiers, cavalry, guides and common labourers, but they were also 'pilots of coastal and river vessels, seamen, canoeists, miners, woodcutters, carpenters, blacksmiths, tailors, foragers, impressers of horses, nurses, servants to officers, servants to common soldiers, waiters, orderlies, drummers, fifers, and recruiters of yet more black men'.[6] Not all of them waited for the British call to arms. George Washington, the Marquis de Lafayette and Thaddeus Kósciuszko all had black servants who fought at their sides and were rewarded with liberty. As most American schoolchildren are now taught, one of the first to fall in the American Revolution was a black man named Crispus Attucks who died defending America in the Boston Massacre of 1770. Another black man was among the most ardent patriots to die in the battle of Bunker Hill.

The slaves' military exploits were colourful in a way that illustrates their passion for freedom but also the degrading and deadly predicaments in which they found themselves. A Hessian captain, John Ewald, wrote that each white mercenary was allowed a certain number of black men and women and horses according to his rank, and that in order to clothe themselves the 4,000 blacks had to forage from their former masters and mistresses with some speed: 'a completely naked Negro wore a pair of silk breeches, another a finely colored coat, a third a silk vest without sleeves, a fourth an elegant shirt, a fifth a fine churchman's hat, and a sixth a wig. – . . . one Negress wore a silk skirt, another a lounging robe with a long train . . . If one imagines all these variegated creatures on thousands of horses, then one has the complete picture . . .' At the end of the war the unthinking foreigners let them loose to face the revenge of their victorious masters, and it was not until after the war, when he ran across a starving group of blacks by the side of the road, that Ewald realized 'we should have thought more about their deliverance at this time'.[7] Their fate was shared by nearly all blacks who had fought alongside whites on either side.

Although a small number who had served the American side found their subsequent lives made easier for having served their fledgling country, those who had served the British often confounded the American judicial system. A slave named Billy was sentenced 'to be hanged by the neck until dead and his head to be severed from his body and stuck up at some public cross road on a pole' for aiding the enemy, but received a governor's reprieve because in the strict interpretation of law a slave was by definition incapable of treason.[8]

England too found itself in a bind. Not only had it lost the war and its important colonies, but the black men who had served now demanded fulfilment of Britain's promises. At the end of the war 14,000 blacks – a number equal to the entire black population of Britain – left with the British from Charleston, Savannah and New York, and went to Halifax, Jamaica, St Lucia, Nassau and England. Hundreds more were sent to Nova Scotia, expecting to receive allotments of land and funds from the British government, but found themselves continually put off and their claims denied. The number of those who left directly from New York for Great Britain was in the hundreds, not thousands – most were still penniless slaves, aware that the English government was reluctant to make good on earlier promises – and their colour, homelessness and destitution made them highly visible on English streets.

Up until 1783 Britain's black population consisted mainly of servants and former servants, musicians and seamen. Suddenly, with the end of the war with America, England felt itself 'overwhelmed' by an influx of black soldiers who had served the loyalist cause and who crossed the Atlantic for their promised freedom and compensation. Refugees from slavery shuttled between the West Indies, America, Canada, Europe and Africa looking for freedom, homes and work in a western world still financially dependent upon slavery and the slave trade. There was, it seemed, no safe harbour, no one to trust, no way to escape the effects of the African diaspora and 250 years of the triangular trade.

A government commission consisting of the lawyers John Eardley Wilmot, Daniel Parker Coke and others, worked their way through the claims of white and black loyalists. Few blacks appeared among the successful petitioners. Among the few were Benjamin Whitecuff, a former Long Island farmer and British spy who had saved 2,000 troops and had himself been rescued by the British cavalry a scant three minutes after his hanging had commenced, who now lived with his English wife Sarah on her £4 a year dowry and whatever else 'he could earn as a saddler and maker of chair bottoms'[10]; David King, who earned only 2 shillings a day as a shoemaker; and John Robinson, formerly a cook on a British warship, who had his own cookshop.[11] These three were poor but were fortunate to be employed at all.

One of the most successful of the black petitioners was also one of the most pitiful. The case of 'Shadrack Furman – a free Black' came before the commission in December of 1788. He had

[l]ived in Acamack County in Virginia when the Trouble commenced – he resided on a plantation which he leased – Joined the British Troops when Lord Cornwallis was in Virginia – the Americans on finding that he had assisted the British seized him, and treated him with great Cruelty, insomuch that he has totally lost his Eye Sight, and the Use of his right Leg – he resided at Shelburne since the peace – came to England in March last – he has a Wife with him – Lost property to the amount of more than 146£ – he has been able to support himself since he came to England by playing the Fiddle –[12]

The board found that 'this Man has suffered great Cruelties in America on Account of his attachment to Great Britain' and since he had lost the ability to earn his living as he used to it was 'with great propriety' that they awarded him £18 per annum, beginning immediately and retroactive by two months.[13]

The same record book reveals that 'Peters, George, a Black' was awarded £10 in 1786. He was an independent miller from Pennsylvania who had served as a waggoner and labourer in the war, and had been instrumental in guiding the British army through the fords in the River Schuylkill. He arrived in London when the British army was evacuated from New York. There he worked as a servant 'in a gentleman's house' but was only able to earn eighteen pence per week. His official compensation was low because as a single man he 'may probably get into some employ,'[14] but whether he could ever find a more generous employer was doubtful.

These two cases at first seem to indicate Britain's relative colour-blindness but in fact the opposite was the case. Like many of their white counterparts, both Furman and Peters presented Certificates of Loyalty from those under whom they had served in America and as required presented their petitions in writing. Testimonials and literacy as requirements for such petitions excluded many of the black poor. For the 5,000 white petitioners compensation began at £25, making Furman's £18 seem slight; and there were only twenty successful black petitioners out of forty-seven who attempted to receive compensation for their efforts and losses.[15]

Even with their meagre incomes, Furman and Peters were in better shape than most of the poor black people now living in Britain, many of whom were forced into beggary to stay alive. Even when they were not beggars, their race caused them to be treated as though they were. The *Daily Universal Register* of 26 January 1785 reported the tragic case of a 'poor black [who] fell down in a fit nearly opposite the Mansion-house. The churchwardens of a neighbouring parish were sent for to take care of him, but instead of doing it, they ordered him to the Compter; while they were disputing about the unfortunate man, he died.'[16]

Long before the American War there were black people among the professional beggars, a number of whom were colourful additions to English streets. John Thomas Smith, who wrote about Bronze and Sancho, collected his drawings and recollections of late eighteenth-century beggars into a volume called *Vagabondia, Or, Anecdotes of Mendicant Wanderers through the Streets of London*. Among the *Portraits of the Most Remarkable Drawn from the Life* were drawings of Joseph Johnson and Charles M'Gee, two black men well known on London's streets. Johnson was denied a seaman's pension because he had worked in the merchants' service; 'his wounds rendering him incapable of doing further duty on the ocean, and having no claim to relief in any parish', he began singing on Tower Hill before moving on to the streets.[17] Johnson's subsequent success as a beggar resulted from a flash of brilliance, when he built a model of the ship *Nelson* which, 'when placed on his cap, he can, by a bow of thanks, or a supplicating inclination to a drawing-room window, give the appearance of sea-motion'. Nor did he confine himself to the streets of London:

> Johnson is as frequently to be seen in the rural village as in great cities; and when he takes a journey, the kind-hearted waggoner will often enable him in a few hours to visit the market-places of Staines, Rumford, or St. Albans, where he never fails to gain the farmer's penny, either by singing 'The British Seaman's Praise,' or Green's more popular song of 'The Wooden Walls of Old England.'[18]

Charles M'Gee, born in Jamaica in 1744, had a 'stand' at the foot of Ludgate Hill which was 'certainly above all others the most popular, many thousands of persons crossing it in the course of the day'.[19] His portrait shows him wearing a natty coat given him by a pastry cook, in which he was known to attend a Rowland Hill meeting house on Sundays. No doubt the fact that he had lost an eye contributed to his popular appeal. The English liked characters and, as Smith pointed out, 'Black people, as well as those destitute of sight, seldom fail to excite compassion'.[20] (It may well be that Shadrack Furman received compensation because he was both black and blind.) Their race may have contributed to Johnson's and M'Gee's success at their trade, but their eccentricities assured it. The majority of black beggars, those who like Shadrack Furman played their fiddles on the street and asked for handouts near St Paul's, excited sympathy of a less amused sort.

It was Jonas Hanway, elderly benefactor of the down-and-out and abused of London – chimney sweeps, fallen women, foundlings – who in 1786 first noticed the plight of the black poor and commenced the concerted effort to aid them. Unofficially aided by Granville Sharp who had been overwhelmed by the number of poor black people desiring his financial help, he launched an appeal to assist the 'Black Poor'. His initial concern had been for the East Indian seamen who were as destitute as the American and West Indian blacks, but it quickly became clear that the latter far outnumbered the former. Hanway gathered several of his colleagues in banking, business and philanthropy each week at Batson's Coffee House to assess the special problems the black poor encountered and to organize a solution. Among the group was Samuel Hoare, the banker whose Fleet Street establishment was (and still is) only a short stroll around the corner from Dr Johnson's Gough Square house. It was Samuel's son Prince who wrote the first biography of Granville Sharp. There were also Sir Joseph Andrews and James Peter Andrews, Montague Burgoyne, George Drake, John Cornwall, Thomas Boddington, General Melville, George Peters, William Ward, Richard Shaw and John Julius Angerstein whose portrait hangs at Kenwood, Lord Mansfield's country home. The influential world of eighteenth-century London was a small one.

With the £800 they collected, what now became known as the Committee for the Relief of the Black Poor (later shortened to the Committee for the Black Poor) distributed food each day at two public houses – the White Raven at Mile End and the Yorkshire Stingo at Lisson Green – and opened a 'hospital' to care for the sick among them. The more seriously ill, like Jonathan Strong in 1765, were sent to St Bartholomew's Hospital. The Committee also helped those who wished to return to sea or to other countries if not born in Britain.

The lure of a handout was a strong one. The Committee's agents began distributing six pence per person on 20 April 1786, when they gave money to seventy-five black people. The next day they paid 119 people. On the following two days there were 166, the next two 196, the next two 224, and so on, until by 15 May, less than a month later, they had given money to 1,943 destitute black people in London. They ran out of money for several days but when they resumed, with the government's assistance, began also paying such expenses as hospital bills and coach hire for the ill, rent for the meeting room at Batson's and passages for one man who decided to rejoin his master in Holland and another who had opted to try his luck in Antigua.[21]

It is difficult to gauge the exact number of black people living in London from these figures. Since no names are attached to these numbers it is impossible to know if any received more than their weekly share, or how many were not in need of financial assistance. Even so, the bare figures far exceed the strictest accounting of former soldiers carried to Britain after the war, and indicate that those already residing there formed the majority of the destitute.

The Committee advertized its services, printing and dispensing hand bills 'to Collect the Poor'.[22] Given the low level of literacy among the black poor, it is likely that word of mouth was its most effective advertisement. Most of the recipients were not only in desperate and immediate need but were hoping to find a more permanent solution to their poverty. There was barely any work for them in Britain if they were unattached to white people or, unlike Sancho or Barber, they had no independent income to use in setting up a business.

There seemed to be one possible solution to black poverty in

England, and oddly enough it was one on which the government, the philanthropists and the poor themselves agreed. They could leave Britain, individually or *en masse*, and try to make a go of it somewhere else. The government, delighted to help them leave, contributed enormous sums of money to sustain them before, during and after their departure. It believed that such an investment would be more than paid back by ridding the country of such a visible problem. The Committee for the Black Poor had truly charitable concerns and wanted to keep them from literally living and dying on the streets. Black people themselves wanted to find a place where they could establish a working community and support themselves independently.

It seems now an astounding marriage of goals and interests where the underlying motives were quite opposed. There is no doubt that racism and a certain amount of xenophobia motivated government, which did not want Somerset's legacy so obviously displayed while it refused to alter its policy on slavery and the slave trade. Certainly many of the blacks involved recognized this but at the same time welcomed any opportunity to achieve the basics of food, shelter and work. Except for slavery, anything was better than starvation and the opportunity to found a colony seemed a heaven-sent solution. On this the Committee agreed.

It was a situation ripe for exploitation. When the Committee's and government's original idea of sending the people to Halifax fell through, in 1786 a man named Henry Smeathman stepped into the picture like a Pied Piper of oppressed humanity. He was a businessman and botanist, which pleased the government; he offered a vision of a self-sufficient and lucrative African colony, which delighted the Committee; he had lived on the west coast of Africa and claimed it was entirely habitable, which was of prime importance to those blacks who read his proposal when it was distributed later that year in the form of a handbill. In short, he told everyone what they most wanted to hear. Styling himself a 'Gentleman', he sent a memorandum or 'memorial' to the Lords Commissioners of His Majesty's Treasury couched in language which indicated that he had been called and was willing to serve: '. . . being informed that a great number of Blacks and People of Colour, many of them Refugees from America and others who have by land or sea been in His Majesty's service, were from the severity of the season in great distress; and that certain benevolent Gentlemen nominated a Committee, to receive and distribute money for their relief, were deliberating on some plan of sending them abroad', Smeathman wrote, 'your Memorialist did, about the beginning of February last, wait on the said Committee, with Proposals for removing such a burthen from the Public for ever; and of putting them in a condition of repaying this Country the expense thereof, by opening a new and beneficial channel of trade and commerce . . .'[23]

Neatly avoiding the fact that most of the proposed black settlers had earned the right to government assistance through their military service, Smeathman's offer to rid his country of a dreadful infestation used terms quite similar to those later used by Hanway's biographer in 1940. According to him, Hanway 'opened a subscription for the benefit of Negroes cast adrift in London. To prevent the assimilation of coloured persons the Treasury supplied Hanway's committee with money in order that the blacks might be settled in other lands. Perhaps many servants such as those employed by Samuel Johnson and Lady Mary Wortley Montagu were transported to more happy environments.'[24] The government's war-ravaged pockets apparently went deep enough when it came to avoiding racial 'assimilation', and 'transportation', that word associated with criminality, was here assumed to lead black people to greater happiness.

Smeathman's proposal was this: for about £14 each, the black poor would be carried to Sierra Leone, given three months of provisions, 'cloathing', bedding, tools and medicine. Once there they would build housing and become self-sufficient, and quickly begin to supply Britain with various raw materials. He worked out the plan in enormous detail, tabulating how much bread, beef and pork, 'pease' and 'melapes', oatmeal, flour, hot barley, suet, raisins, and 'rum for grog' each person would need for the voyage and subsequent three months. He estimated that each man would need both a striped and a blue flannel jacket, a pair each of canvas and flannel 'trowsers', a pair of shoes, four shirts, two knives, a razor and a hat. Women's clothes would be 'in proportion'. He itemized which and how many tools each group of twelve people would need after landing. He provided the names of the outfitters and agents who would assist him. And, in an addition which the Committee later admitted should have alerted them, he meticulously and anxiously listed the medicines he considered absolutely indispensable, spending far more space itemizing them than any other necessities.

His four years in Sierra Leone, he said, revealed a benign climate, fertile soil, and compatible neighbours. It would be necessary to come to an arrangement with their new African neighbours in order to acquire land, but England had a long and comfortable history of contracts with the local chiefs. He would remain among them to assist the fledgling colony. He urged government to move quickly so that 'His Majesty's Subjects may [no longer] be exposed, to any further inconveniences on account of the calamitous situation, to which the said Blacks, Descendants of Africans, and People of Colour are now daily exposed'.[25] To the Committee and the Treasury, Smeathman with his knowledge and his exhaustive lists seemed nothing less than a godsend. His plan was presented scientifically and humanely, and the fact that he and his investors expected to make money on the enterprise appeared only just and appropriate. The Committee's only concern, and one upon which they spent considerable time, was that an appropriate clergyman be appointed to accompany the colonists. Granville Sharp pressed this concern, and the Committee convinced the Archbishop of Canterbury to send someone. Smeathman concurred in this request, perhaps because of Christian feeling, perhaps because he wanted to assure his critics that the settlers would stay under control.

In their haste to accept such a relatively straightforward solution to the 'problem' of the black poor, neither the Committee nor the government did much investigating. Had they done so they would have discovered two important facts: first, that Smeathman himself had testified to a government commission only one year earlier that the climate of Sierra Leone was so deadly that if a convict station were set up there one hundred would die each month; and second, that he and his associates intended to establish a profit-making estate there by using slave labour. The black poor were being ushered into a deadly trap, yet on 24 May Hanway and the others commended him for having 'spoken and behaved with a Propriety entirely to the Satisfaction of this Committee'.[26] Sharp too referred to him as an honourable man.

In the meantime, the numbers of black poor flooding the distribution points continued to increase, 'but whether from the Country or by Shipping, I cannot ascertain,' wrote the payment agent at Lisson Grove. Between 22 May and 1 June he paid out £365 even though he had received only £350 from the Committee. At this point too he began to keep more detailed records about the recipients. Charles York, for instance, was given £1.2s for clothing when he went back to sea. John Ramsey sailed for the West Indies in the *Sir Sam Hood* and was given £1.1s for his fare. On 20 June Richard Cooper had to be carried to the hospital at a cost of 4s.6d. Probably more than any other documents, the Committee's minutes and accounts, along with Treasury and Admiralty Office records, shed profound light on the late eighteenth century's black population. In them we find the names of hundreds of black people, only a rare few of whom are called 'Pompey' or 'Caesar'. We learn that they were a sickly lot, and discover not only their ailments but what it cost to treat them. We learn their trades, skills and abilities, and find out who among them were literate. When they attend occasional Committee meetings we learn what they themselves had to say about their plight and their preferences. For the first time names and voices can be given on a large scale to these previously nameless and silent people.

One of the reasons the Committee began to keep such careful records was that they needed to begin rounding up and organizing the hundreds of people they proposed sending to Sierra Leone – or, as they trustingly put it, those whom they 'intended to be happily settled on the Grain Coast of Africa'. They decided to use printed lists with the headings of name, marital status, age, whether Negro, Mulatto or East Indian, whether or not they had had smallpox, whether or not born in England and, if not, how long they had resided there. Among the potential settlers were twenty-three East Indians, many of whom had lived in England for many years, and who 'seem disposed to mix with the Blacks and to accompany them to Africa'.[27] From these lists they wanted

to choose group leaders, or corporals, who were skilled and prefer-
ably literate, and who could be placed successfully in supervisory
positions among their peers.

By 7 June 1786 eight men had been selected, though Hanway
hoped for a dozen or two by the end. James Johnson, 31, was
born in New Jersey, knew husbandry, and had been steward of a
ship. He could read but not write. William Ramsay, a 24-year-old
domestic servant, was born in New York and had also been a
ship's steward. Aaron Brooks, 25, knew husbandry, could read
and write, and had been captain and cook of a Royal Navy vessel,
as had John Lemon, a 29-year-old Bengali hairdresser and cook
who could read. John Cambridge, a 40-year-old netmaker from
Africa who could read, was a domestic servant. John Williams
was a 25-year-old seaman from Charles Town in Massachusetts.
William Green, a 40-year-old domestic from Barbados, could both
read and write. And Charles Stoddard, a 28-year-old cooper who
arrived in England from Africa as a domestic, could also read.
None of these men was born in England, and they may well have
been chosen partly for that reason. Four of the eight were seamen,
accustomed to travel, and expressed a willingness both to depart
and to lead others on the way.[28]

This was a major qualification, for despite the Committee's
good intentions they encountered a difficulty that they had not
anticipated: black people themselves began to question the Committee's and government's motives and their own safety. When
Hanway visited the Yorkshire Stingo on Saturday, 3 June he found
a distrustful group of black people who refused to agree to embark
unless the government could ensure their continued liberty in the
colony. They had not fought England's war and fled slavery, they
argued, only to jeopardize their freedom in Africa surrounded by
slave traders. They wanted official documentation, with government seals and signatures, of their status as free colonists. Frus-
trated and angry, the elderly Hanway 'formed them into a Ring
and harangued them, appealing to God and the Common Sense
of Mankind for the pure and benevolent Intentions of Government, as represented by the Right Honble. the Lords Commissioners of the Treasury, and no less for the Charity and
Benevolence of the good People of Britain exprest by the Commit-

tee for the Black Poor, and that for himself, as an old man on the Confines of Eternity, who had no wordly [*sic*] Interest to serve, he must be the worst of the wicked on Earth to deceive them.'[29]

A ninth selected leader 'said to be a Person of weight among the Blacks, left the Room saying he would consider of it', but the other eight 'declared they were satisfied, and that they considered it as the fairest and most just Agreement that ever was made between White and Black People'.[30] Still, of the 156 men and 52 women offered their regular 6 pence payments on Monday, 5 June, thirty refused the money which obligated them to leave and wanted more time to think about it, while others declared they preferred to take their chances in America and the West Indies. Discontentment grew, and two days later, when Hanway repeated his speech to a crowd at the White Raven at Mile End, he was only partially successful in convincing them that the government's and Committee's intentions were honourable.

He brought this disconcerting news back to the Committee, who first responded by thanking him 'with the highest Approbation of his Zeal and Attention to the Object'.[31] This unsuspected assertiveness of the black people rattled them, for after discussing the form such documentation could take (they proposed affixing a 'Sixpenny Stamp as a Pauper's Indenture' to the settlers' contracts) they expressed a strong desire to get all of the people documented as soon as possible so that they could be located 'and shipped off without Delay'. In fact, they finally expressed their fear that the paupers would take charity money but, when the time came, refuse to leave Britain. Some of the homeless poor had already been rounded up by parish beadles and charged with vagrancy.

Accordingly the Committee wrote a week later to the Treasury Office asking that Smeathman's deputy be appointed immediately so that the plan could move forward. They had already arranged for 500 of Smeathman's proposals and 750 contracts to be printed. Most telling of the Committee's concerns, however, was a short note Hanway sent to the Treasury Office on 16 June, absolving the Committee from 'any loss of what kind soever' should a ship be contracted for but not enough black people 'be found so as to embark'.[32] Poor and hungry though they were, the recipients of his charity had minds and reasonable concerns of their own.

Smeathman's *Plan of a Settlement to be Made Near Sierra Leona, on the Grain Coast of Africa* was 'Intended more particularly for the service and happy establishment of Blacks and People of Colour, to be shipped as freemen under the direction of the Committee for Relieving the Black Poor, and under the protection of the British Government'.[33] While the title page clearly stated the intended races of the settlers, the first paragraph was addressed to 'Any person desirous of a permanent and comfortable establishment, in a most pleasant fertile climate . . . where land may be purchased at small expence', leaving an ambiguity which later inspired several white skilled workers to join the settlers. Even so, the end of the document reiterated the racial composition of the proposed colony: 'whereas many black persons and people of Colour, Refugees from America, disbanded from his Majesty's Service by sea or land, or otherwise distinguished objects of British humanity, are at this time in the greatest distress, they are invited to avail themselves of the advantages of the plan proposed'.[34]

Smeathman delineated the fare, the clothing, the intention to purchase land cheaply upon arrival. Those who had money, however, could be accommodated as 'steerage, steward-room, or cabin passengers', a clear indication that the term 'black poor' was a generic rather than exclusive one, and that they intended to cast their nets more widely than previously expressed by the Committee. In glowing and optimistic terms he described how 'within a few days after their arrival, a township will be marked out; and houses run up by the joint labour of the whole' – a whole town to be created, like the earth, within a week, with each Sabbath to be a day of rest.[35] Nature too would co-operate; livestock in Sierra Leone reproduced 'with a rapidity unknown in these colder climates', fish were abundant and easily caught, the forests were full of game, cultivation was simple, and the natural resources of Africa would allow a lucrative trade with Britain.[36] Settlers were not to be put off by reports of disease and famine, for those who had perished were white people who had 'led the most intemperate lives', chosen unhealthy and close quarters to live in, and ignored proper diets or medications. None of these problems would exist in this new and well-ordered society. There would be school-teachers, a clergyman and a surgeon. Appended to it was the Committee's handbill, authorizing Smeathman and making it clear that an earlier plan 'to send Blacks to Nova Scotia . . . was laid aside, as that country is unfit and improper for said Blacks'.[37] Sierra Leone was made to sound like heaven on earth, in the hope that it would prove irresistible to the hungry and homeless.[38]

Meanwhile, the expenses and the number of people receiving a variety of aid grew. In only two days 328 people were helped. William Johnson, confined to Bridewell Prison for assault, asked the Committee to help release him from jail so that he could sail with the rest of his family. John Lemon, one of the appointed group leaders, was ill, as were Edward Jackson, George Brown, Ann Stirling and John Lawrence. Some of them needed clothes, and Ann Stirling had to be conveyed to the Committee's hospital.[39] The list of patients in the hospital stretched out: John Ramsay, George Brown, George Hill, John Davis, Sarah Brown and Rachel Thomson had fevers. John Stevens had an inflammation of the breast. Joseph Brown had 'very bad ulcerated legs'. Benjamin York, Francis Williams and Phillis Franklin suffered from rheumatism. Peter Dickson had a 'very bad fever & foul disease'. Lewis Morris, 'surfeit & ulcerated all over'. Charles Morris had a 'very bad Itch', Thomas Neal a 'large Abcess on the back', John Lamplay a 'foul foot, very bad'. Frances William had a 'foul and white swelling'.[40] Things were so bad among them that the Committee wondered not only how many would choose to go, but how many would be alive and well enough to go if they wished to. These illnesses worried the planners, who conducted an investigation into whether everyone in the hospital needed to be there. The most unexpected illness was the fever of Henry Smeathman himself, who suddenly took ill and died on 1 July.[41]

Although the Committee met immediately to sort out expenses and receive the balance of Smeathman's account from his widow, the whole Sierra Leone scheme was thrown into disarray. Smeathman had inspired and arranged the plan, and without him there was no one who seemed sufficiently knowledgeable and willing to go in his place. They acted quickly to search for a new leader or a new destination – the Bahamas was a suggestion – but even so a number of blacks, probably as panicked as their sponsors, began applying for passages elsewhere: Mary Ann Davidson decided to go to Jamaica, Elizabeth White and her son to New York, William and James Freeman to Montserrat.[42] All such requests were approved, provided they fell within the £14 limit and the petitioners could prove they were definitely going as planned.

It was the black leaders or 'corporals' who finally decided the matter. Unaware of Smeathman's ulterior motives, they knew only that he and his assistant Joseph Irwin seemed to have treated them well, that he had convinced them of the workability of the scheme in glowing terms, and that the government approved of it. They were alarmed at the possibility of being sent to the Bahamas, where slavery would surround them and they would have little protection from American predators, and the group of corporals, now fifteen in all, including one Sarah Brooks, drafted a petition which they presented to the Committee on 15 July. In it they praised Smeathman's 'humane Plan' and asserted that no one but Irwin could execute it. Irwin, they believed, had 'conducted this Business from the Beginning with so much humanity and justice and so much to the satisfaction of your Petitioners' that they wanted not only to continue the Sierra Leone arrangement but to have Irwin conduct them there. In addition they complained that since Smeathman's death they had received none of the 6 pence payments promised to them, and were suffering greatly without it.[43]

On 26 July, five of the corporals attended the Committee meeting at Batson's Coffee House to present their argument in person. The Bahamian plan was doomed to fail, they told the Committee, because the majority of the black people willing to leave Britain 'were not inclined to go there'. Not only did they fear slavery, but feared they would be unable to support themselves. Only in Sierra Leone, they were convinced, could they earn their bread in comfort, information they had obtained not only from Smeathman but from an unnamed 'Person now residing in London who is a native of that country and gives them assurance that all the natives are fond of the English & would receive them joyfully'.[44]

In response, the Committee fired off a series of letters to the Treasury, expressing and concurring with the concerns the corporals had raised, and trying to abort the government plans for Nova Scotia or the Bahamas (revived after Smeathman's death) which by now had progressed quite far. 'The Blacks', Hanway wrote, 'are afraid of putting themselves in any situation where Traffick in slaves is carried on, and so far we cannot but approve their caution.'[45] When Patrick Fraser (the Archbishop's choice of clergyman to accompany the colonists), representatives of the Treasury, and several of the black corporals met the Committee on 31 July, the government continued to press the Canadian and Bahamian plans and the black people continued to balk. They agreed in the end to discuss the proposals one more time with the other colonists and to attend the next meeting in a few days' time.[46] Immediately after the meeting George Peters, who often chaired the Committee in the place of the ageing Hanway, wrote to Thomas Steele at the Treasury that 'The Committee approves the [Bahamas] Plan; but the Blacks are very averse to it, and I am afraid will hardly be prevailed upon to go to any other place than Sierra Leona'.[47] Only two days later, however, he received an answer from Steele detailing the supplies and ship needed for a settlement of black people in the Bahamas, blatantly ignoring the expressed preferences of the settlers.

Hanway, now in the last month of his life, was profoundly disturbed to discover that Smeathman had been little more than an opportunist into whose hands the fates of hundreds of black people might have passed. He understood their concerns about the government's North American proposals, but now had many reservations of his own about their safety on the slaving coast of Africa. Acknowledging the government's right to judge for itself the best course of action, he nevertheless counselled it to weigh the arguments extremely carefully. The western African coast was full of slavers of various nations, and even if armed the settlers would find themselves in a hostile environment requiring constant vigilance and defence. And how could they trust what little they knew about Sierra Leone, since most of the information came from Smeathman himself?

[H]e had the art of telling his Story very well and represented things in the most favourable light; but in the latter days of his life he avowed his Intention of *trafficking in Men*, so far that he would though he would not sell. The Committee thought that his Judgment misled him, if not his heart; and if he had not changed his mind or said that he would acquiesce in the Sentiments of the Committee, the Committee would have certainly dropped any further connection with him. What his real Designs were when he should have landed in that Country and had nothing further to hope or fear from the Committee, will be a subject for strong suspicion in the Breast of every Man concerned as long as they live.

. . . There is another great ambiguity respecting the Coast of Africa. The various accounts given leave many doubts. Mr. Smeathman himself brought from thence a Constitution which lasted him but a little while, and always seemed to be more anxious about his medical Knowledge and Medicine Chest than his Tools for husbandry.[48]

It seemed to Hanway that New Brunswick in Canada offered the greatest chances for safety, liberty and economic survival, despite the expressed objections of the black poor. This letter was read to the black people attending the 4 August meeting and, while they accepted the arguments it set forth, only sixty-seven of the hundreds of potential settlers agreed to consider New Brunswick, and five of those later changed their minds. Sierra Leone it was to be. Accepting this decision the Treasury approved the plan and turned matters over to the Navy Board by 25 August.[49] On 5 September Jonas Hanway died.

The plans now moved ahead quickly. The Navy Board wrote to the Committee to say that two ships would be ready at Gravesend on 31 October, to receive 500 settlers whose names they asked the Committee to provide. Irwin gave the names of 617 settlers who had signed the contract, and since he expected at least 750, the Board revised its plans to include three instead of two ships. The Committee had two concerns: 'considering the disposition of the Blacks and their want of discipline', it wrote to George Rose of the Navy Board, 'it may be proper that they should embark in the River near Blackwall'. Secondly, there were still twenty-five people in the hospital whose assistance needed to be continued until the last moment since 'many . . . in all probability will not be fit to embark in the first Ships, if at all'.[50] George Peters added a postscript to this letter, reminding the Board to consider the settlers' requests for firearms and 'some kind of certificate, bearing his Majesty's Arms, or some conspicuous Mark of Authority, to shew that they are Freemen, going of their own accord; and to protect them from insults'.[51] In the Board's haste to round up and send away the black poor, they had not prepared for their safety once they arrived in Africa. A sample certificate was drawn up stating that the holder and his or her 'Heirs, Executors and Administration' were to 'have hold and enjoy all the Emoluments, Liberties & Priviledges' of free people. Each certificate was 'to be printed on parchment & given to each person in a small Tin Box' which, like precious manumission papers in the Americas, would be kept on each settler's person and protected from theft and the elements.[52]

With both Smeathman and Hanway dead, neither the Committee nor the settlers had a representative other than Joseph Irwin. Then the Navy Board made an ostensibly brilliant but ultimately unsuccessful move: it appointed a black man, Olaudah Equiano, known in England as Gustavus Vassa, to act as Commissary for the expedition. His job was to supervise the preparations as well as act as an intermediary between the settlers, Committee and government. He willingly took on the job, unaware of the enormous frustrations and dangers that accompanied it. Some of Equiano's most notable characteristics were his honesty and trust, coupled with an indefatigable desire for freedom and self-improvement. His appointment as Commissary did not suddenly materialize out of anonymity: he had been publicly known for some time for his letters to various newspapers and applications for African posts. He had, for example, tried for ordination in 1779 in order to return to Africa as a missionary. In many ways, despite the horrors and injustices of slavery that he witnessed and experienced throughout his life, Equiano had the life for which Francis Barber had longed. His was an active life; unlike the sedentary and rather self-centred course that Barber seems to have followed, Equiano became a relentless activist for abolition and racial justice. He published his autobiography in 1789, and while other such accounts told of the capture of black people and their subsequent life, his was the most detailed, realistic and literate narrative of a black person's life that the world had yet seen. By his death in 1797 it had run through nine editions. It is readily available even today.

Perhaps one of the reasons for the success of Equiano's story is its method. Beginning with his African life before his capture, it reflects the world as seen through a child's eyes and sensibilities. As his knowledge of the world grows, so does the language he uses to describe it. Lacking the effusive rhetoric so popular in eighteenth-century fiction and abolitionist works, his book is more convincing and accessible. A skilful and fluent writer, he needed no corrective editing – a charge justifiably levelled against his friend Ottobah Cugoano whose *Thoughts and Sentiments on the Evil of Slavery* appeared in 1787. Like Sancho's letters, Equiano's work provides as much insight into eighteenth-century life in general as it does into slavery. But unlike Sancho, Equiano had seen the world, travelling from Africa to America, the West Indies, England and Europe, and even to the Arctic, so that his autobiography also becomes a fascinating and unusual travelogue.

An Ibo from Nigeria, he was born around 1745 and was stolen from Africa as a child. Taken first to Jamaica, then almost immediately to Virginia, in 1757 he was taken to Britain. In this brief period he carried four different names: in Africa his name was Olaudah Equiano and when first enslaved he was called Jacob. His next owner gave him the name Michael and finally, over his objections, his new master renamed him Gustavus Vassa (or Vasa), after the early Swedish leader. It was this last name that he used for the rest of his life in all his official dealings.

One remarkable aspect of Equiano's early life was that while he loathed the white people involved with slavery, most of his closest and most formative relationships were with whites. This ability to work with them was his greatest asset in Britain. On the ship to Britain he was befriended by a fifteen-year-old white boy named Richard Baker who was not only his friend but became his first tutor. He stayed in Falmouth and Guernsey, where he was lodged by his master with a white family and played happily with their young daughter before being moved to London. Most of the next two or three years of his youth were spent in England and at sea. Back in England and friendly with two sisters named Guerin and their brother, he was baptized in St Margaret's

Church, Westminster, in February 1759, with one of the Miss Guerins acting as his godmother – no small favour at a time when baptism was widely believed to confer freedom on slaves. The two Miss Guerins sent him to school while his master was away, and much of his time was spent studying and playing with white friends. He was educated both on land and sea, for many ships had tutors for their numerous boy sailors, and he spent a long stretch of time on the Isle of Wight when he was not required at sea.

It was here that Equiano had an experience which illustrated the isolation of many black boys and men in Britain. One day when walking in a field he was seen by a black boy of his own age who had been looking out of his master's window. Overcome with excitement the boy flew from the house and 'caught hold of me in his arms as if I had been his brother, though we had never seen each other before. After we had talked together for some time he took me to his master's house, where I was treated very kindly. This benevolent boy and I were very happy in frequently seeing each other till about the month of March 1761, when our ship had orders to fit out again for another expedition.'[53] Outside of London, where black servants were common, the loneliness of African slaves must have been overwhelming no matter how well they were treated.

A less happy period followed in the West Indies and the American south, where for the first time he experienced unremitting racial prejudice and the atrocities and double-dealings associated with slavery. Later in life he relentlessly attacked apologists for slavery like James Tobin and Gordon Turnbull who, in their respective works *Cursory Remarks & Rejoinders upon the Reverend Mr. Ramsay's Essay on the Treatment and Conversion of African Slaves in the Sugar Colonies* (1785) and *Apology for Negro Slavery: The West-India Planters Vindicated from the Charge of Inhumanity* (1786), tried to convince the public that slavery was a benign institution. Referring in the *Public Advertiser* to their 'warped minds',[54] Equiano not only lashed out against the blatant falsehoods they promoted but suggested it would 'be more honour to us to have a few darker visages than perhaps yours among us, than inundation of such evils'.[55] In attacking the sexual violence that slavery bred, he asked 'why not establish intermarriages at home, and in our Colonies? and encourage open, free, and generous loves upon Nature's own wide and extensive plain, subservient only to moral rectitude, without distinction of the colour of a skin?'[56]

In America and the West Indies he became involved with a black community on a steady basis and found himself standing up to their white oppressors, sometimes putting his own life and liberty in jeopardy. It was also in the Americas that he developed his skills as an entrepreneur, using his many voyages to turn a profit on goods he loaded and re-sold. Such financial dealings eventually enabled him able to purchase his own freedom, and when he returned to England he used his accumulated wealth to hire tutors and add new skills, such as hairdressing, mathematics and playing the French horn, to his accomplishments. Whenever his money ran short he shipped out again or hired himself in England. In 1758 he worked, for example, for a Dr Charles Irving in Pall Mall who successfully desalinated sea water to make it drinkable. He also travelled to Turkey, Italy, Portugal and Greenland.

When Equiano arrived in London after a trip to Philadelphia in August of 1786, he learned of Smeathman's plan. Far from seeing it as an opportunity to rid Britain of unwanted aliens, he pronounced himself 'agreeably surprised that the benevolence of government had adopted the plan of some philanthropic individuals'.[57] With his combination of fierce abolitionism and enthusiastic mercantilism, he believed the plan offered independence to the settlers and the possibility for England to develop commerce with Africa in goods rather than people. He was acquainted with some members of the Committee, and they approached him to take on the role of superintendent. At their recommendation, and after several interviews, the Navy Board appointed him Commissary and put him in charge of making sure all supplies were provided and loaded as ordered.

Thrilled not only by the government's recognition but by the opportunity to assist fellow former slaves, he outfitted himself at his own expense and threw himself into the execution of his duties. These included making sure that all goods granted to the settlers be provided or accounted for. In October, before Equiano was made Commissary, over 675 'Men Women and Children whose

Names are undersigned being Seamen Labourers and of various other descriptions' – in other words the black poor – had been presented with a contract by Joseph Irwin in which they acknowledged the government's charity and promised to go on board by 20 October, and help with the running of the ship and other necessary work. In return they would be provided with 'the necessary Cloathing Goods Provisions and all other reasonable Necessaries for and during the said intended passage and voyage' and for four months afterwards.[58] The settlers also asked for 'the indulgence of a little Tea and Sugar for their Women and Children . . . and some other Articles' and this was granted to them.[59] A request for cannons to protect the colony was less favourably received.[60]

There were other issues to sort out as well. The Committee asked that the City of London Lying In Hospital admit two white students to be trained in midwifery for the voyage and settlement, yet while they admitted them the Hospital doubted they could become proficient in so short a time. An unsigned petition from some of the settlers apparently demanded the release of a Mr Clarke, who perhaps was in prison, 'and threatening not to go if he did not accompany them', but the settlers attending the meeting denied any knowledge of the affair. There were, however, five men and one woman who remained in prison, as well as six men who 'keep out of the way' in order to avoid being forced to leave.[61] The problems Equiano faced were three-fold: despite the large numbers who needed aid (715 were paid on 20 September and 736 on 2 October), enough of the settlers now understood the government's keenness for them to leave and therefore made demands and conditions about leaving; secondly, quite a number of the settlers, now that the time was approaching to board the ships, were having serious second thoughts and had gone into hiding; and finally, there was enough money to be made on the voyage by potentially unscrupulous outfitters and suppliers that Equiano not only had to double-check all the accounting but had to pray that race would play little or no part in any resulting confrontations.

This was too much to hope for. Scrupulously honest and quick to defend himself and his African charges against mistreatment, it became almost inevitable that Equiano would run into trouble.

It wasn't long before he started to notice discrepancies between what was ordered and what actually appeared on board ship. For example, supplies were ordered for 750 passengers, and when there were only 426 on the passenger list he was ordered to send the remainder back to the King's stores at Portsmouth. Apparently Irwin, though given money for the full amount, had only ordered the smaller amount and pocketed the money for the rest.[62] Once the settlers went on board, beds and clothing were missing and 'their accommodations were most wretched'.[63] Equiano tried to reason with Irwin and when that failed twice brought the captain of the ships' convoy, Thomas Thompson, as a witness. The black poor themselves sent a letter to the *Morning Herald*, published on 4 January 1787 and signed by twenty of their leaders, complaining of their shabby treatment.

While Equiano was trying to keep order on ship and shore, the black poor began to board the ships. By 22 November there were 105 on board the *Belisarius* and 154 on board the *Atlantic*. There they sat, for a total of 259 people was far below the plans of the Committee, Navy Board and Admiralty Office. Patrick Fraser, the chaplain, embarked at Gravesend. A white engineer and his wife requested to join the settlers, as did a doctor, but despite encouragement and a sailing date now delayed to the beginning of December, no more potential black settlers appeared. In frustration the Committee suggested that a proclamation be drawn up, 'enjoining all those who have been relieved by the humanity of the British Government to go on board the Ships which are now ready for their reception; and that Ten Days after the Date thereof all Persons of that description who are found begging or lurking about the Streets will be taken up on the Vagrancy Act'.[64] In other words, if they did not board the ships they would be arrested.

By 1 January 1787 they had still not sailed. Some had now been on the ships for five weeks without being allowed to disembark. Their provisions were running as low as their spirits and they, along with Equiano, again complained about their treatment. The master of the two transports wrote to the Navy Board criticizing the 'irregular behaviour of the Black Poor' who were guilty of such things as 'burning Fires and Candles all night and wasting the Water'. He considered it prudent to sail as quickly as possible and let the third ship follow later.[65] Some of the 'irregular' behaviour may have stemmed from the fact that everyone on board, including children and the ill, was given regularly an equal quantity of rum. The Committee asked that this practice cease since 'some disorderly behaviour and irregularity have arisen therefrom'. The children were to have no more, but the sick people's portions would be set aside for them until they were well.[66] The Committee also recommended that no more white people be allowed to board, an unexplained decision that months later would be countermanded by an astonishing development.[67]

By 16 January there were 242 people on the *Atlantic* and 184 on the *Belisarius*, and the Admiralty Office finally allowed them to proceed as far as Spithead and place themselves under the command of Captain Thompson, the same man whom Equiano asked to witness Irwin's deficiencies and the blacks' living conditions. From the letters between the Navy Board, the Committee and the Admiralty Office, it is clear that they were not yet fully supplied or ready to sail, and by mid-January the officials were still wondering how much canvas would be needed for temporary shelters in Sierra Leone, and loading the gunpowder for the settlers' weapons. They were nowhere near ready to depart, and the black poor were still incarcerated on the ships.

By this time, however, the project had become a matter of public interest and something of a showpiece for the government. The *Public Advertiser* reported on Wednesday, 17 January 1787, that on 'Saturday Samuel Hoare, Esq; Chairman of the Committee for relieving and providing a settlement for the Black Poor, had an interview with Mr. Pitt, when he laid before him the proceeding of the Committee from their establishment; at which the Minister expressed his satisfaction. The two ships, having on board as many of those people as could be collected, sailed from Gravesend on Thursday last, with a fair wind, for Sierra Leona, on the coast of Africa, where they are to be landed, in order to form the intended new settlement.[68] In fact they had sailed, but only as far as Plymouth where they were to remain until more settlers could be collected, but in the public's eyes the Committee and the government had achieved a laudable goal. 'To every humane mind it must afford a peculiar pleasure, by reflecting on your beneficent plan, adopted for the relief of the poor unhappy Blacks, whom you have released from a state of poverty and distress to a prospect of comfort and happiness', wrote a man who signed himself *Humanus*.[69]

In reality the situation was very bad. The black settlers had been cooped up for months, supplies were dwindling without being replenished, and it was bitterly cold. Some of them managed to get to shore at Plymouth, perhaps in search of food and warm clothing, but once in town their deplorable condition became an object of public concern. 'Some Blacks that arrived here, in order to embark on board the ships going to Africa,' one person wrote to the *Public Advertiser*, 'the vessel not being ready to sail, rambled about the streets, when by the severity of the cold, two of them dropt down dead; and the rest, had it not been for the humanity of the inhabitants, who gave them cloaths and necessaries, would have shared the like unhappy fate.'[70] Three months later the magistrates of Plymouth wrote to the Admiralty Office that more blacks had come on shore, causing concern that they might remain behind 'to the great nuisance of the country'.[71]

While race almost certainly played a part in this concern, the visibly miserable state of the settlers alarmed the local citizens for the same reason they alarmed the Londoners who had sent them away: at this time the care of the destitute fell upon the parish they came from. All over England strangers, especially those without obvious means of support, had to register with the local parish authorities, and could be returned to their home parishes if it appeared they could not provide for themselves. (Documents exist of just such an interview for Francis and Elizabeth Barber when they moved outside London.) If there were no home parish, their care might devolve upon local coffers and authorities. With nearly three hundred black men, women and children anchored offshore under impoverished circumstances, the Plymouth magistrates feared an influx of black dependants.

Meanwhile, the fears of the settlers increased. In late January it was announced that they would be conducted to Sierra Leone by a Commodore Philips, who was *en route* to Botany Bay with convicts, causing many of the black people to believe they too were being transported as criminals.[72] Late in February an 'epidemical fever' broke out among them, but was quickly diffused by ventilating the hold which housed them.[73] The best thing would be for the ships to sail, and on 27 February lists of those on board the three ships (by now the *Vernon* had been added) were submitted to the Commissioner of the Navy by Equiano. The lists contained 643 names, and some surprises. For instance, there were sixty-eight black men, ten black women and two black children on board the *Vernon*, along with thirteen white men, four white women married to white men and four white children, but there were also seven white women married to black men and 'two White Women more to be married'.[74] There were sixteen white women married to black men on the *Belisarius*, and forty white women married to black men on the *Atlantic*.

In the government's desperation to fill the ships and have them sail, not only had a number of probably unwilling blacks been rounded up and forced on board, but a number of white prostitutes had been made drunk and taken on board. Anna Maria Falconbridge, who later accompanied her husband to Sierra Leone to assist the new settlement, encountered a number of these women living in distressed circumstances in the African colony. They told her how they had awakened on board ship to discover that they had been married to black men the night before and were now to be transported to Africa with their new husbands.[75] Certainly the London authorities had been given *carte blanche* to rid the city of 'undesirables' such as poor blacks and prostitutes.

This swelling group had to be fed and clothed, and most importantly kept under control as they sat without any appearance of leaving England. Equiano found himself in an impossible situation. Unable to remedy the problems, persuading various people to visit the ships to see how bad the situation was, he opened himself to the charge of fomenting trouble among the settlers. Unbeknownst to him his supposed ally, Captain Thompson, wrote to the Commissioners of the Navy to complain 'of the conduct of Mr. Gustavus Vasa, which has been, since he held the situation of Commissary, turbulent, & discontented, taking every means to actuate the minds of the Blacks to discord'. Thompson feared that 'unless some means are taken to quell his spirit of sedition, it will be fatal to the peace of the settlement, & dangerous to those intrusted with the guiding it'. Joseph Irwin fell equally under Thompson's censure as being 'not the least calculated to conduct this business: as I have never observed any wish of his to facilitate the sailing of the Ships, or any steps taken by him which might indicate that he had the welfare of the people the least at heart'.[76]

At first the Navy Office was sympathetic to Equiano, and was not at all surprised that conflicts had arisen between him and the less scrupulous Irwin. They found that Equiano had acted with propriety all along, and had alerted them to his suspicions about Irwin's trustworthiness early on. Their main concern seemed at first to prevent the settlers from going ashore, but within a day or so had decided to dismiss him. Before he was notified of this decision, however, Equiano, desperate to help the settlers but finding himself thwarted at every turn, sent the following letter, addressed to his friend John Stewart (Ottobah Cugoano), and published in the *Public Advertiser* on 4 April:

I am sorry you and some more are not here with us. I am sure Irwin, and Fraser the Parson, are great villains, and Dr. Currie. I am exceeding much aggrieved at the conduct of those who call themselves gentlemen. They now mean to serve (or use) the blacks the same as they do in the West Indies. For the good of the settlement I have borne every affront that could be given, believe me, without giving the least occasion, or ever yet resenting any.

By Sir Charles Middleton's letter to me, I now find Irwin and Fraser have wrote to the Committee and the Treasury, that I use the white people with arrogance, and the blacks with civility, and stir them up to mutiny: which is not true, for I am the greatest peace-maker that goes out. The reason for the lie is, that in the presence of these two I acquainted Captain Thompson of the Nautilus sloop, our convoy, that I would go to London and tell of their roguery; and further insisted on Captain Thompson to come board of the ships, and see the wrongs done to me and the people; so Captain Thompson came and saw it, and ordered the things to be given according to contract – which is not yet done in many things – and many of the black people have died for want of their due. I am grieved in every respect. Irwin never meant well to the people, but self-interest has ever been his end: twice this week [the Black Poor] have taken him, bodily, to the Captain, to complain of him, and I have done it four times.

I do not know how this undertaking will end; I wish I had never been involved in it; but at times I think the Lord will make me very useful at last.[77]

It became very quickly clear how the undertaking would end, for news that Equiano was sacked came immediately after his letter was printed. 'He came up from Plymouth to complain', said one London newspaper account on 6 April, 'and is now gone back again to take his effects on shore.'[78]

With Equiano's dismissal the settlers became alarmed for their future, since he had been their only ally in what looked like a dangerous fiasco. They began to fear a conspiracy which had dragged them from relatively safe poverty in England to return them to slavery in Africa or the West Indies. The newspaper noted that 'many of them served under Lord Dunmore, and other officers in America, in the British army – Also on board the British Fleet in the West-Indies – That the contract, on Mr. Smeathman's plan to settle them in Africa, has not been fulfilled in their favour, but a Mr. Irwin has contrived to monopolize the benefit to himself.'[79] Furthermore,

they fear the design of some in sending them away, is only to get rid of them at all events, come of them afterward what will. – In that perilous situation they see themselves surrounded with difficulties and danger; and what gives them the most dreadful presage of their fate is, that the white men set over them have shewn them no humanity or good-will, but have conspired to use them unjustly before they quitted the English coast – And that they had better swim to shore, if they can, to preserve their lives and liberties in Britain, than to hazard themselves at Sea with such enemies to their welfare, and the peril of settling at Sierra Leona under their government.[80]

Response was quick, but it was not from the government. Irwin himself was recognized as a troublemaker whose own job was in jeopardy. It seems likely that a letter to the *Public Advertiser* on 11 April, which referred to the 'improbable tales propagated concern-

162

ing the Blacks, especially as the cloven foot of the author of those reports [Equiano] is perfectly manifest', was by him or his friends.[81] Not willing to drop the analogy, another letter a few days later refers to 'falsehoods as deeply black as [Equiano's] jetty face' and to disparage 'those *black* reports which have been so industriously propagated; for if they are continued, it is rather more than probable that most of the *dark* transactions of a *Black* will be brought to *light*'.[82] The writer placed final blame on the Committee for the Relief of the Black Poor whose 'over-care' and 'delicacy' in wishing 'to avoid the most distant idea of compulsion, did not even subject the Blacks to *any* government, except such as they might chuse for themselves'.[83]

Neither Equiano nor Irwin was destined to sail for Sierra Leone. Equiano was crushed by his personal and public humiliation which was also a public humiliation for his race. Expressing 'great grief and astonishment' over his treatment, he applied for reimbursement for his expenses and attempted to vindicate himself. In attempting to fulfil his commission and serve both government and the black settlers, he feared he had 'created a number of enemies, whose misrepresentations, he has too much reason to believe, laid the foundation of his dismission'.[84] He was awarded £50 in reimbursement, which heartened him with the thought that they thought well enough of his service to pay him more than the £32.4s he had requested.[85] He threw himself then into working within Britain for the abolitionist cause, pausing only briefly from his mission to marry a Miss Cullen of Ely. Their marriage was noted in *The Gentleman's Magazine*'s list of 'Marriages and Deaths of considerable Persons' for April 1792.

After these disasters, the government finally stepped up the pace of the resettlement. Captain Thompson was ordered to purchase food and six months of supplies for the settlers, including three oxen for their later use. On 22 April 1787 he wrote to the Commissioners from the island of Teneriffe (*sic*) that 'I have the satisfaction to acquaint you that I arrived here yesterday at noon, with the three transports after a very quick passage of thirteen days from Plymouth, and that the Blacks have hitherto conducted themselves remarkably well, but I am sorry to say that fourteen have died since our departure from England'.[86] With the eventual departure of the three transport ships many believed that the unwanted black people of Britain had finally sailed away.

CHAPTER SIX

The End of English Slavery

A great deal of energy had gone into getting the black poor on board ships and out of England, but very little had gone into arranging a sustainable life for them once they arrived in Africa. The Committee for the Black Poor, including Granville Sharp himself, believed enough of Smeathman's description of Sierra Leone to imagine a fertile land where settlement would be quick and simple, the weather agreeable, the native population cooperative, and that the settlers – largely sailors and servants – would exhibit a natural talent for agriculture. No one, including the settlers, had counted on the potential destructiveness of climate, poverty and human nature. Of those who set sail from Plymouth, only two-thirds survived the first three months.

When the settlers finally sailed, the Committee succumbed to a wishful naïvety. Sharp outlined an ambitious system for the settlers which included tithings, church-building and laid-out streets – all to be accomplished within weeks of their arrival. From his London vantage point, the tropical world seemed an ideal place for an orderly experiment in civilization, what Christopher Fyfe calls Sharp's dream 'of the primitive simplicity of pastoral life'.[1] He wrote to his brother on 23 June 1787, that

> I had the pleasure of hearing this day of the safe arrival of the African Settlers at the Madeira islands; and that all the jealousies and animosities between the Whites and Blacks had subsided, and that they had been very orderly ever since Mr. Vasa and two or three other discontented persons had been left on shore at Plymouth. Schools are established on board each ship, as I had proposed; and they have daily prayers. The account is from the chaplain, Mr. Fraser.[2]

It was easy to blame Equiano for the difficulties that occurred in England, and to pin his hopes upon Irwin and Thompson, whom Equiano maligned.

It was a costly and perhaps even arrogant mistake. The Committee had in effect killed the messenger and ignored the message. By the end of October Sharp 'had but melancholy accounts of my poor little ill-thriven swarthy daughter, the unfortunate colony of Sierra Leone'.[3] This child of their benevolence proved unruly, but as much blame fell on the haste with which England acted on its desire 'to rid the nation of what they regarded as a pestilent influence. Throughout its planning for the colony, the committee worried more about speed than about anything else . . . and the wishes of the blacks were ascertained only when it was absolutely necessary'.[4]

Thompson, Irwin and Fraser were charged with getting things up and running quickly. It was Thompson's job to negotiate a land settlement from the African chiefs once they landed, and accordingly he met almost immediately with King Tom (possibly named thus by the English), a lesser king under King Naimbanna (or, in the *Nautilus* log, 'Annamboyna'). All seemed well; on 11 June Thompson signed an agreement with King Tom and two other sub-chiefs, but not with Naimbanna himself, exchanging £59 of trade goods for about 200 square miles of land. They named the settlement Granville Town, after their benefactor Sharp, put up temporary tents and marked lots. It was a promising enough start but within four days the rainy season began, the worst the area had seen in years, and the long delay in Plymouth and Deptford started to take its toll in Africa.

The white men fared much better than the black settlers, mainly because of their orders to sleep on board and do no manual labour. They were given Canary wine, a supposed restorative. The settlers on the other hand had salt food and rum, slept in soggy tents, and many fell ill and died. As they became more and more discouraged – not the least for being blamed by Thompson for being 'vicious, drunken and lawless, unfit to colonize' – they were less and less agreeable to the orders of the better-off whites. Even the gardener and the seeds sent along to assist them died, and when they tried to cultivate at the end of the rains they found nothing would grow. They moved to better ground but had to barter the government-sent stores for rice to prevent starvation, and were blamed for this also.[5] By 16 September three white leaders were gone: Irwin returned to the *Vernon* after the settlers refused to obey him, and died soon after, Fraser left for Bance Island when the settlers refused to build him a church, and Thompson absconded last.[6] Many settlers also began to leave, 'drifting away to work on passing ships or for neighbouring slave-traders'.[7] One of these was Henry Demane, only the year before rescued by one of Sharp's habeas corpus writs from a slave ship sailing away from Portsmouth.[8] By March 1788 only 130 black settlers were left; the rest had either died or run off.[9]

Back in England there seemed only two alternatives. One was to abandon the colony and let the survivors fend for themselves. The other was to fortify it with more settlers and supplies. Sharp, worried about the health and safety of the current settlers, chose the latter, and with a great deal of his own hard-earned money, £200 from the government for livestock, and £100 from a friend, he outfitted the brig *Myro* and sent thirty-seven more settlers and two white doctors to Sierra Leone. Of these, twelve died on the journey and four left before arrival. But with fresh supplies, the ability to trade, and a crop planted, the colony finally seemed to steady itself.

As the internal health of the colony improved, danger appeared from another direction. When he signed the agreement with King Tom, Thompson failed to anticipate others' claims to the same land and to the common local practice of demanding a share of the revenue of passing ships. Granville Town's neighbours, the Temne people, confronted the unprotected settlers, and King Tom sold two of them to a French ship. In retaliation five of the settlers robbed the nearby Bance Island store. They too were caught and sold to the French. When King Tom died it became clear that Naimbanna himself had never signed the treaty, and he now ordered them to leave. The arrival of the *Myro* reopened negotiations (its captain used the occasion to sell such useless supplies as satin waistcoats and a fake diamond ring), and a new treaty was signed on 22 August 1788.[10]

This was not yet the beginning of a settled peace, however.

Slave ships did not like having this independent black community in their slaving territory, and their captains and crews sometimes captured settlers. The settlers retaliated by tracking down and punishing the kidnappers, infuriating the captains and leading them to encourage another local leader, known as King Jimmy, to oppose them. When Americans kidnapped some of King Jimmy's people, he killed three Americans and sold the boat. The settlers, far from living in the safe and hospitable environment described by Smeathman, were in a near war zone full of local arguments and battles for power, with nearly everyone resenting their presence. An English ship, the HMS *Pomona*, was sent to protect them, but its captain, Henry Savage, watched from the deck as the settlement was attacked, going ashore only to bury the dead. He refused the settlers' pleas to carry them to safety, and sailed away on 3 December. Three days later Granville Town was burned down.[11] Relief did not arrive for nearly a year, until January 1791, when Britain sent another ship, the *Lapwing*. Like the previous ones it was full of useless supplies, but shortly afterward, at the beginning of 1791, the Directors of the St George's Bay Company, set up by Granville Sharp to aid the colony, sent as agent Alexander Falconbridge, a passionate abolitionist, known as much for his drinking habits as for his humanist sentiments. His wife Anna accompanied him and recorded in bitter detail the condition of the settlers. Written unashamedly for publication, her journal gives an extraordinary view of the African life.

Anna indicated early on that she did not necessarily share her husband's political beliefs, nor did she have much respect for him. Stating that 'the gentlemen whom Mr. Falconbridge is employed by are for abolishing the slave trade: the owners of this vessel are of that trade, and consequently the Captain and Mr. Falconbridge must be very opposite in their sentiments'; she goes on to say that they are always arguing, 'and both are warm in their tempers, which makes me uneasy . . .'.[12] Alexander Falconbridge died in Sierra Leone during their second visit, and she immediately married another white man in Africa and defended herself in print for doing so.

When she first arrived at Bance Island, a slave depot on the outskirts of the settlement, Anna Falconbridge was, like Aphra

Behn in Surinam over one hundred years earlier, an object of curiosity: 'The people on the island crowded to see me; they gazed with apparent astonishment – I suppose at my dress, for white women could not be a novelty to them, as there were several among the unhappy people sent out here by government, one of whom is now upon the island'.[13] The presence of other white women was expected, but on 13 May she encountered in Granville Town a wholly unexpected group of white women: the prostitute wives of the black poor, forced by the English authorities in London to marry settlers and leave the country.

I never did, and God grant I never may again, witness so much misery as I was forced to be a spectator of here. Among the outcasts were seven of our country women, decrepid with disease, and so disguised with filth and dirt, that I should never have supposed they were born white; add to this, almost naked from head to foot; in short, their appearance was such as I think would extort compassion from the most callous heart; but I declare they seem insensible to shame, or the wretchedness of their situation themselves; I begged they would get washed, and gave them what cloaths I could conveniently spare: Falconbridge had a hut appropriated as a hospital, where they were kept separate from the other settlers, and by his attention and care, they recovered in a few weeks.

I always supposed these people had been transported as convicts, but some conversation I lately had with one of the women, has partly undeceived me: She said, the women were mostly of that description of persons who walk the streets of London, and support themselves by the earnings of prostitution; that men were employed to collect and conduct them to Wapping, where they were intoxicated with liquor, then inveigled on board of ship, and married to *Black men*, whom they had never seen before; that the morning after she was married, she really did not remember a syllable of what had happened over night, and when informed, was obliged to inquire *who was her husband*? After this, to the time of their sailing, they were amused and buoyed up by a prodigality of fair promises, and great expectations which awaited them in the country they were going to: 'Thus', in her own words, 'to the disgrace of my mother country, upwards of one hundred unfortunate women, were seduced from England to practice their iniquities more brutishly in this horrid country'.

Good heaven! how the relation of this tale made me shudder; – I questioned its veracity, and enquired of the other women who exactly corroborated what I had heard; nevertheless, I cannot altogether reconcile myself to believe it; for it is scarcely possible that the British Government, at this advanced and enlightened age, envied and admired as it is by the universe, could be capable of exercising or countenancing such a Gothic infringement on human Liberty.[14]

Her anger was with the British government, and her disgust was at the marrying of white women to black men. Prostitution sank rather low on her list of malfeasances, far below the lack of personal hygiene, and she makes no mention at all of the black men who were forced to marry prostitutes as they were held on board the stalled ships in England.

From beginning to end, even with the most altruistic and charitable of motives, England's involvement with the Sierra Leone colony had involved intrigue, greed and poor planning. Anna recorded with disgust that the Board of Directors of the newly formed St George's Bay Company, in charge of the colony, listened with 'too much credulity, to a pack of designing, puritanical parasites, whom they employ to transact business; I cannot help thinking so, nay, am convinced of it, from the cargoes they have sent out, composed of goods, no better adapted for an infant Colony than a cargo of slaves would be for the London market'.[15] Little had changed in the five years since Equiano had been dismissed for blowing the whistle on disreputable captains and suppliers.

From various records it becomes clear that the colony was publicly recognized as being in deep trouble. *The Gentleman's Magazine*'s report on Parliamentary Proceedings for 1791 showed that in both houses the colony's history caused great concern: 'Mr. Grenville Sharpe [*sic*], that philanthropic genius, had furnished them with a code of laws. What was the consequence? They fell out amongst themselves – the code was torn – numbers died – and desolation daily marked the scene.'[16] A later issue of *The Gentleman's Magazine* referred to a letter from Africa containing 'a most moving account of the mortality among our people in that country',[17] and a report in May 1791 on a 'very unlucky circumstance [which] attended a well-meant attempt to reconcile

170

a difference which had taken place a few months ago between the Black Sovereign, and the settlement at Sierra Leone in Africa': in firing a shot into the thatch of one of the settlers' cabins, an English sailor inadvertently caused a fire which destroyed the town and set off a deadly gun battle.

Sharp, contrary to his original expectations, continued very busy with the affairs of the Sierra Leone settlers. Drained of his own money, he sought a government contribution to the colony and decided that a commercial corporation stressing trade and profits rather than straightforward humanitarian aims would be most successful in raising the necessary funds. With the assistance of people like William Wilberforce, later known as the Great Emancipator for his unflagging effort to end the slave trade, he drew up plans for the St George's Bay Company, which first met in February of 1790, and chose the banker and MP Henry Thornton to be its chairman. Not only had he been a member of the Committee for the Black Poor, but like Wilberforce and Sharp he was on the Committee for the Abolition of the African Slave Trade, formed the same year that the settlers left England.

The colony still needed more money and more settlers if it were to succeed. Sharp could with difficulty arrange for funding from various sources, even though he remained disheartened by the number of settlers who capitulated by joining slave traders or who perished. Fortunately, however, a new source of settlers appeared, one previously overlooked by the English. After the American Revolutionary War, when black loyalists made their way to England, over three thousand others took refuge in Nova Scotia, Canada. There they awaited from the British government their promised allotments of land and grants, few of which ever materialized. Unable to compete with the demands of white loyalists, the black refugees fell victim to a thwarting racism. By 1790, after waiting for restitution for six fruitless years, Thomas Peters, a former sergeant in the Black Pioneers, a group of Canadian settlers, obtained power of attorney from over 200 black families in Canada and went to England to deliver a petition demanding their land to Secretary of State William Grenville.[18] In London he became friendly with poor blacks, who told him about Sierra Leone and introduced him to Granville Sharp.

171

Peters' stay in London is poorly documented, but some believe that though he was poor he was lionized in England. This is fairly unlikely, but it is not clear whether he approached the newly formed Sierra Leone Company expressly with the desire to remove the black people in Nova Scotia to Sierra Leone, or whether the Company suggested this plan to him when he presented his petitions. It is clear that the Company preferred black settlers to whites for a number of reasons. Because of the earlier difficulties in the colony, the settlers had lost, in Sharp's words, the 'privileges of granting land by the free vote of their own Common Council', a condition of the Sierra Leone Company's taking them over, a change which Sharp found 'humiliating' and 'disagreeable'.[19] Secondly, although a party of 119 white skilled workers, including ten with families, was chosen to go in 1791, black families were seen as essential to the black colony's future. Finally, since part of the Company's function was missionary, black settlers were seen as a better conduit to African conversion.[21]

By 1794 there were enough problems between the Nova Scotian settlers and the Company for the latter to prefer that this migration appear to have been the new settlers' idea.[21] When thirteen years later the Company's directors wished to make the British government responsible for the Nova Scotian black settlers, Wilberforce went even further and asserted that the government had insisted the Company accept these settlers. But, as one historian notes, 'the truth probably lies' somewhere in between those conflicting statements. The black poor told Peters about Sharp and the Company and gave him the idea of resettling in Sierra Leone. Simply because the Nova Scotians' petition said they were willing 'to settle anywhere in the British Empire need not imply that his original intention was to apply for land in Africa'.[22]

However the idea of African migration was planted, it resulted in an exodus that dwarfed the sailing from England: on 15 January 1792, under the leadership of a harried abolitionist named John Clarkson (brother to Thomas Clarkson who worked for the Society for the Abolition of the Slave Trade), 1,196 black loyalists sailed from Halifax in a fleet of fifteen ships, arriving in St George's Bay, Sierra Leone, in early March.[23] *The Gentleman's Magazine* reported happily, six months later, of the mission's success:

'Accounts of the most flattering nature have been received from this place. The Colonists were on the happiest terms of friendship with the natives, and making every possible progress in completing their buildings, and laying out their lots of land for cultivation. Only one death had happened among the Whites since the date of the last dispatches . . . In addition to this good news, their excellent Governor, Mr. Clarkson, was in the most perfect state of health.'[24] No specific mention was made of the black settlers at this time, but an article in January 1793 reported that '35 men, 18 women, 7 boys, and 5 girls: total, 65' died on the passage over, and 'Since their arrival, 28 men, 28 women, 21 boys, and 22 girls: total, 99. General total, 164.'[25] Despite this death rate the survival of the vast majority was the true beginning of the colony and of the country which exists today, founded by the combined efforts of British humanitarians and black leaders.

If John Clarkson, who finally left the colony because of his ill-health, and Granville Sharp thought that distance would shield them from having much to do with the colonists, they were wrong. Over the next several years they received numerous letters and petitions and appeals for help, ranging from requests for soap ('Since I hav bin to this plais I hav bin Sick and I want to git Som Sope verry much to wash my family Clos for we ar not fit to be Sean for dirt', wrote Susana Smith),[26] to divorce ('Mr Clarkson Sir if it please to Grant Rose morral her request She have no peace with her husband Sir if it please your eccellent honnah as to part us or bound him over to the peace Before your honnah go home to London in so doing your honnah will oblig your humble Servent Rose morral').[27]

Other letters concerned less personal matters, for the colonists desired guidance and protection in the making of their laws, and negotiations among themselves and their neighbours. Recognizing that 'we have not the Education which White Men have yet we have feeling the same as other Human Beings and would wish to do every thing we can for to make our Children free and happy', colonists wrote to Clarkson to complain of blatant extortion practised upon them by representatives of the St George's Bay Company after his departure.[28] On 28 November 1792 they presented him with a petition asking him to return as their agent:

. . . from the time he met with us in novascotia he ever did behave
to us as a gentilmon in everey rescpt he provided every thing for our
parshige as wors in his pour to make us comfortable till we arrived
at Sierraleon and his behaveor heath benge with such a regard to us
his advice his Concil his patience his love in general to us all both
men and wemen and Children . . . and thearfour we wold Bee under
stud by the gentilmon that our ardent desier is that the Same John
Clarkeson Shold returen Back to bee our goverener our had Com-
ander in Chef for the time to com and we will obay him as our
governer and will hold to the laws of England as far as lys in our
pour . . .[29]

Black people were not only shunted between North America
and England but also travelled under different circumstances
between Africa and England. At the end of the Falconbridges'
first stay in Sierra Leone, King Naimbanna asked them to carry
his twenty-nine-year-old son, Prince John Frederic, back to England to be educated. Another of his sons had been sent to France,
the King thus shrewdly dividing his offspring between two of the
countries desiring to trade with him, making sure that through
them he learned their languages and business practices. Despite
his troubled early dealings with the English colony, Falconbridge
was able to win him over so thoroughly that by 1791 Naimbanna
was able to write to Sharp through his English-educated African
secretary that 'I ever was partial to the people of Great Britain,
for which cause I have put up with a great deal of insults from
them, more than I should from any other country. My son, I
hope, you will take care of, and let him have his own way in
nothing but what you think right yourself.'[30] With his father seemingly unconcerned at his departure and his mother weeping, the
prince stepped on board ship wearing a blue cloak decorated with
gold lace, a black velvet coat, and white satin breeches. Anna
Maria Falconbridge described him as being short and stout, and
very dark skinned, with teeth filed to points as was his country's
custom.

She found him quick and intelligent (shortly after she taught
him the English alphabet he learned to 'read any common point
surprisingly well') with a useful ability to read people as well. He
was 'easy, manly' in his deportment, but in 'his disposition he is

surly, but has cunning enough to smother it where he thinks his interest is concerned; he is pettish and implacable, but I think grateful and attached to those he considers his friends; nature has been bountiful in giving him sound intellects, very capable of improvement, and he also possesses a great thirst for knowledge'.[31]

Sharp felt greatly honoured at being entrusted with the King's son, writing to Naimbanna that even without the gratitude he owed the King for his 'kind and very friendly conduct toward the poor Black Settlers at Sierra Leone, whose interest I have had so much at heart', the 'natural good disposition, modesty, behaviour, and great diligence and application to learning, would alone be sufficient to ensure my esteem and regard' for the prince.[32] Sharp also promised to work for the recovery of three of the King's relatives, Corpro, Banna and Morbour, stolen away by the captain of a Danish ship. Sharp and Thornton placed the twenty-nine-year-old prince under the tutelage of the Revd Gambier in Kent, although apparently two other clergymen actually saw to his education. The young man had already received the praise of two English bishops, and was soon baptized 'Henry Granville' after his English benefactors.[33]

By and large John Frederic's tutors concurred with Anna Maria Falconbridge's earlier assessment of his character and intelligence. In a report they remarked that

A desire of knowledge was the predominant feature in his character: he would continually urge his instructors to prolong the time of their reading together. He was forward in declaring his obligations to every one who would assist him in the acquisition of useful learning: he would express regret if he had been led into any company where the time had passed away without improvement; and when it happened that he was left entirely to himself, he would employ not less than eight or ten hours of the day in reading.

At the same time he showed 'much natural courtesy and even delicacy of manners' and was 'of a kind and affectionate disposition'.

He was quick in all his feelings, and his temper was occasionally warm; some degree of jealousy also entering into his character: in particular, he was indisposed to answer questions put to him by strangers concerning the state of his own country; for he was apt to suspect that they meant to draw comparisons unfavourable to its character; and he would therefore, on such occasions, often turn the conversation, by remarking, that a country so unfavourably circumstanced as Sierra Leone had hitherto been, was not to be supposed capable of having made any attainments worthy of being the subject of conversation in Great Britain.[34]

This clever way of deflecting criticism from his country was only one of the things for which he was known.

As was expected the prince was made much of in England during his stay, but it is for another reason that he was to be remembered: on his way back to Africa after his father's unexpected death in 1793, just before arrival in Sierra Leone, he became mysteriously and suddenly ill, and died. In his farewell letter to Sharp the prince had promised 'to write to you again on my arrival in Sierra Leone' and assured him 'that I feel sensibly your great attention to me'. He signed himself 'H.G. Naimbanna', a name which combined his African heritage and English education and religious conversion.

By this time African princes were stock characters in English literature and, like Aphra Behn's Oroonoko, the wrongly enslaved African prince or the noble savage was of literary use on a number of fronts. The anti-slavery movement used him as a plea for abolition. Novelists and poets used him for sentimental value, both as a main character or as a tale within a tale. And the moralists, mainly writing didactic literature for children, used him as a religious and behavioural exemplum. Hannah More recounted Prince Naimbanna's story in 'The Black Prince', one of her *Cheap Repository Tracts; Entertaining, Moral and Religious*, 'Consisting of a great variety of separate performances, written in a neat, yet simple style, and eminently calculated for the amusement and instruction of the youth of both sexes'.[35] Her tale begins '[i]n Africa, the country where the negroes live, and from which slaves are taken'.[36]

Although based upon fact and recounted at times nearly ver-

176

batim from the tutors' report, More's retelling of the Naimbanna
story centres on the prince's studious conversion to Christianity
and his premature death. The obstacles to his learning Christian
forgiveness and understanding are greater than those facing any
English child, she says. She explains how during his two years in
London Naimbanna not only had to learn to read and write in
English, but to forgive the pro-slavery debaters he heard in Parliament, a man on the street who cruelly beat his horse, and the rude
and drunken sailors on board the ship carrying him home to
Africa. When he realized that Christian law required him to give
up one of his two wives waiting for him in Africa, he chose the
one who bore his only child. When his father died he rushed home,
and when he was taken ill himself he made a will, stipulating that
his brother oppose the slave trade and that his people become
Christians. His devotion to God allowed him a peaceful death,
from which point More launches into the lessons to be drawn
from his story.

> May we not conclude, from the above story, that God has given to
> the most rude and savage people, minds capable of knowing, loving,
> and serving him. And may we not learn hence, to cherish sentiments
> of kindness and affection towards all men, whatever be their colour,
> or however low they may stand in the scale of human beings. Those,
> especially, who know to estimate the blessings of religion, and who
> have a regard for the everlasting happiness of their fellow creatures,
> will be encouraged by it, to promote with zeal every plan which tends
> to introduce Christianity among the savage nations of the earth, or
> to remove the hindrances to its introduction. Happy, if through their
> instrumentality, those who now sit in darkness shall be brought, like
> Naimbanna, to know God and themselves, and to rejoice in hope of
> his glory.[37]

The tale required a particular kind of African who was both
reinforced and contradicted by those one read of in the newspapers
and journals. The report of the Sierra Leone Company on 27
March 1794 depicted his death in moving terms, also mentioning
how he furnished 'a memorable instance of the effect of education
on the mind of Africans, and a most encouraging and happy omen
in favour of his benighted countrymen'.[38] The Naimbanna story

as told by both More and the Company report had all the hall-marks of Christian abolitionism, a movement which had by now been in full force in England for some time.

To understand fully the momentum of the English abolitionist movement, we must go back to 6 September 1781, when the English ship *Zong* set sail from Africa with a cargo of African men, women and children. It was to become the most notorious slave ship in English history, forcing even those who believed strongly in the economic and ethical beneficence of the slave trade to re-examine their positions. Well into the journey, the *Zong*'s captain and crew discovered that they were running low on water and other supplies. With a number of the slaves very ill and sixty-seven slaves and crew already dead, the master of the vessel, Luke Collingwood, made the decision to throw 133 living slaves over-board, in batches, over a three-day period and over the objections of some of the crew, including the mate James Kelsal. Colling-wood himself selected the doomed Africans, telling Kelsal that 'it would not be so cruel to throw the poor sick wretches into the sea, as to suffer them to linger out a few days under the disorders with which they were afflicted'. Because they fought back, the last batch of thirty-six, on the third day of the genocide, were shackled before being thrown over. One survived by pulling him-self back up by a rope; ten others threw themselves overboard on the last day.[39]

Inhuman as the captain's decision was, the reasoning behind it was just as shocking. Insurance covered slavers' losses, except for loss through illness and subsequent death of slave 'property'. However in this case the insurance company refused to pay in full and the ship's owners sued. A public uproar followed as more information about the *Zong* massacre, as it came to be known, surfaced. Not only had there been sufficient water, if rationed, to last the trip, but a heavy rain had fallen during the voyage and there was a surplus of 420 gallons when the ship arrived in Jamaica on 22 December.[40] In their suit the ship's owners wanted to recover their loss of £3,960. They were represented in court by the solicitor-general John Lee who argued that '[t]his is a case of chattels or goods. It is really so; it is the case of throwing over goods; for to this purpose, and the purpose of the insurance, they are goods and property: whether right or wrong, we have nothing to do with.'[41] The callousness of this statement shocked the British public. Accustomed to the romantic anti–slavery arguments of the abolitionists, this was a hard–hitting reminder that somehow they had arrived at a point where the unabashed murder of black people was seen as making economic sense.

It was Olaudah Equiano who brought the *Zong* massacre to Granville Sharp's attention after reading an anonymous letter about it in the *Morning Chronicle*. Sharp attended the trial, arranged for a shorthand writer to transcribe the proceedings, and sent copies both to the Admiralty Office and the Duke of Portland, a Whig peer and 'principal minister of state' who opposed abolition. They refused to act. Sharp then published accounts of the massacre in the press, spurring public indignation and rousing other writers to join the abolitionist cause. Correspondence between Americans and British on the subject of slavery, particularly among Quakers like the Philadelphian Anthony Benezet and abolitionists like Sharp, were also growing.

Thomas Day, already known for his poem 'The Dying Negro', published in 1784 a copy of a letter sent eight years earlier to an American slave owner who sought his advice on slavery. His uncompromising opinions reflected what many English men and women were beginning to feel. 'Robbers invade the property and murderers the life of human beings', he wrote, 'but he that holds another man in bondage, subjects the whole sum of his existence to oppression, bereaves him of every hope, and is, therefore, more detestable than robber and assassin combined'. This controlled tone soon gave way to outright anger: 'Who, sir, gave you a title to their labour, or a right to confine them to loathsome drudgery? And if you have no right to this, what are the punishments you pretend to inflict but so many additional outrages? Has a robber a claim upon your life because you withhold your property; or a ravisher a right to a woman's blood because she defends her chastity?' Calling slavery 'the greatest of all corruptions', he declared the natural equality of all men.[42]

This was not a universal opinion however. Perhaps more than ever before, a pitiless racism against black people appeared in England, growing rapidly over a twenty–year period between the

1770s and the 1790s. The worry about white employment covered a thinly disguised fear of miscegenation. In 1773, less than a year after the Somerset decision, a letter to the *London Chronicle* begged the government to rid England of its African population.

> It is therefore humbly hoped the Parliament will provide such remedies as may be adequate to the occasion, by expelling the Negroes now here, who are not made free by their owners, and by prohibiting the introduction of them in this kingdom for the future; and save the natural beauty of the Britons from the Morisco tint; and remove the envy of the native servants, who have some reason to complain that the Negroes enjoy all the happiness of ease in domestic life, while many of those starve for want of places.[43]

A 1786 writer to the *Morning Post* invoked solicitor Dunning of Somerset fame, in arguing against racial mixing:

> When the late Mr. Dunning was some years ago reasoning against making this country a refuge for all the blacks who chose to come here, he observed, 'That the numerous dingy-coloured faces which crowded our streets, must have their origin in our wives being terrified when pregnant, by the numerous Africans who were to be seen in all parts of the town, and if the legislature did not take some method to prevent the introduction of any more, he would venture to prophecy, that London would, in another century have the appearance of an Ethiopian colony['].[44]

A week later, a writer to the same paper lauded a proposed bill to keep blacks from being brought into Great Britain, stating that '[w]hen so many of our own young men and women are out of employment, and, literally speaking, are starving in the streets, it is abominable that aliens, and more particularly Black aliens, should be suffered to eat the bread of idleness in Gentlemen's houses, &c.'[45]

These were the same arguments against black people that had been expressed for years, but now the anti-slavery movement emerged alongside the desire to keep Britain white. The last twenty years of the eighteenth century saw a steady increase in tortured public and parliamentary discussions on the abolition of the slave trade and the emancipation of slaves. It would be early in the next century before the first could be achieved, and well into it before slavery in all of Britain's colonies was ended.

In 1783, six Quakers formed themselves into a group dedicated to fighting slavery through continual anti-slavery publications and letter writing. These men, William Dillwyn, George Harrison, Samuel Hoare, Thomas Knowles, John Lloyd and Joseph Woods, were joined later by Sharp and others. Some of this group had sat on the Committee for the Black Poor, but others belonged to a group known as the 'Clapham Sect', after the district of London where most of them lived. All were known for their extremely high moral and religious stands. They included James Ramsay, a clergyman who returned from nineteen years on St Kitts violently opposed to slavery; William Wilberforce, who spent twenty years of his life pushing anti-slavery legislation through Parliament; William Pitt, who became Prime Minister in 1783 and not only was Wilberforce's great friend, but encouraged him to bring up the anti-slave trade question; Henry Thornton the banker and MP for Southwark; Charles Grant, Thornton's next door neighbour and Anglo-Indian who later also sat in Parliament; another Anglo-Indian named John Shore; James Stephen, also a former resident of St Kitts who published accounts of slavery there; Zachary Macaulay, who later became Governor of Sierra Leone; William Smith and Thomas Gisborne, both Members of Parliament; and Hannah More, the moralist and writer. The ages of the members varied widely, and because their mission took so long to accomplish, they were later joined by a younger group of men.[46]

The year 1787 saw the departure of the Sierra Leone colonists and, with this accomplished, on 22 May Sharp and some of his colleagues formed themselves into the Society for the Abolition of the Slave Trade. While Sharp chaired the Society, perhaps its most important and courageous member was Thomas Clarkson, who risked his life in order to gather crucial evidence against the trade in England. His 'conversion' to abolitionism started as an academic exercise, but eventually took the form of an epiphany. While at St John's College, Cambridge, Clarkson wrote an exhaustive essay in Latin for a contest which asked entrants to argue for or against slavery. His essay against slavery won, but in the course of his research and writing, Clarkson remained surprisingly unaffected by the subject matter. One day it occurred to him that if he fully believed in his position, it followed that he ought to support the anti-slavery movement in real ways. He sent the essay to Sharp, who promptly had it published in translation and widely disseminated.

Clarkson still hesitated to devote himself to a cause which would necessitate total devotion. Stopping while on the road to ponder this dilemma, he sat under a tree to decide his future. Like other successful young men, Clarkson was ambitious with 'a thirst after worldly interest and honours, and I could not extinguish it at once'.

> I was more than two hours in solitude under this painful conflict. At length I yielded, not because I saw any reasonable prospect of success in my new undertaking (for all cool headed and cool hearted men would have pronounced against it), but in obedience, I believe, to a higher Power. And this I can say, that both on the moment of the resolution, and for some time afterwards, I had more sublime and happy feelings than at any former period of my life.[47]

With that he gave up a promising career as a clergyman, and embarked on an unprecedented journey. Like a detective for humanitarianism, he visited all of England's slave-trading centres, including Bristol and Liverpool, tracking down hard evidence of the iniquities of the trade and exposing himself to tremendous danger from its supporters.

He was supported by a number of influential people in his opposition to both slavery and the slave trade. In his memoirs he describes a dinner party consisting of Wilberforce, Reynolds and Boswell, among others, in which he displayed some of the artefacts – stories of the horrors inflicted not only on slaves, but on sailors in the trade, and samples of African cloth to encourage other kinds of trade – with which the men 'seemed to be greatly impressed . . . Sir Joshua Reynolds gave his unqualified approbation of the abolition of this cruel traffic.' He and others were dismayed therefore when a year later Boswell and William Windham, a Whig MP, inexplicably changed their minds after several years of supporting the cause and strongly opposed it.[48]

It was a dangerous undertaking for Clarkson to visit slave-trade cities by himself. Liverpool, and to a lesser extent Bristol, built their wealth on the slave trade and were in no mood to give up their booming economies. Half of all the ships involved in the trade sailed from Liverpool, but Bristol was deeply involved as well, transporting more than half a million slaves between 1698 and 1807.[49] It seemed that everyone from the most prosperous banker to the lowliest clerk had an investment in some aspect of it, whether it be in the products created by black labour or in black people themselves. Another tier of commerce thrived on supporting the slave trade, from ships' chandlers to insurance agents. No one was ready to give up a trade which 'had flooded Liverpool with wealth, which invigorated every industry, provided the capital for docks, enriched and employed the mills of Lancashire, and afforded the means for opening out new and ever new lines of trade.'[50]

Some of the stories Clarkson collected concerned the seamen in the trade, both black and white, whose abysmal treatment sometimes rivalled that of the slaves themselves, and who seemed to die in nearly equal proportions to them. One, a free black man named John Dean committed 'a trifling circumstance, for which he was in nowise to blame'. The Captain 'had fastened him with his belly to the deck, and . . . poured hot pitch upon his back, and made incisions in it with hot tongs'.[51] Historian Peter Fryer reports the case of a black cook on the slaver *Little Pearl* who in 1786 was repeatedly abused by his commander, Joseph Williams, who 'appeared to enjoy a particular Pleasure in flogging and tormenting' him, and 'he often amused himself with making the Man swallow Cockroaches alive, on pain of being most severely flogged, and having Beef Brine rubbed into his Wounds.'

> The black cook, who sometimes opted for a flogging rather than swallow 'the nauseous Vermin', was chained by the neck night and day to the copper in which he prepared food for the slaves and crew; and 'the Body of this poor Wretch, from the Crown of his Head to the Soles of his Feet, was covered with Scars and Lacerations, intersecting each other in all Directions, so that he was a most miserable Object to behold'. The ship's surgeon said afterwards that not a man on board had escaped the captain's fury.[52]

Most of the seamen, however, were white and while Dean's and the cook's punishments may have been exacerbated by their race, such things were by no means exclusive to black seamen. A white man named Peter Green was killed on a ship from a beating with a knotted rope so severe that a sailor was able to fit three fingers into the wound in his head.[53]

Clarkson learned that John Dean's ship, *Brothers*, had such a reputation for cruelty that it 'could not get her seamen, and that a party which had been put on board, becoming terrified by the prospect of their situation, had left her on Sunday morning'. Thirty-two hands had died on her last voyage, all 'so dreadfully used by the captain, that he could not get hands for the present'.[54] There were stories, all of which Clarkson managed to corroborate, of slaves knifed, shot, starved, thrown overboard, blistered by having 'scalding water mixed with fat' poured on them, all in addition to the general atrocities committed as a rule in the passage across the Atlantic.[55] The trade was barbaric for both blacks and whites, and Clarkson believed that by revealing this he could influence law makers and private citizens who might otherwise support the trade.

Gathering this information took cunning, for the seamen were afraid of repercussions if they told the truth, and the slaves themselves were in the Americas. Among his informants was the same Alexander Falconbridge who later led the Sierra Leone colony and died there. Falconbridge at one point proposed to speak to a man who was afraid to confide in Clarkson, so the men met in a public house with Clarkson stationed in the dark by the window, witnessing the exchange.[56] At other times he received death threats from supporters of the trade, once barely escaping an attempt on his life.

What Clarkson presented was of inestimable value to the Society (also known as the Abolition Committee). In Liverpool, where 'horrible facts concerning [the slave trade] were in every body's mouth', he discovered instruments of slave torture sold openly. Among these were iron handcuffs used to fasten the right wrist of one slave to the left of another, secured with bolts and padlocks; thumbscrews which not only induced painful pressure but eventually caused blood to spurt from the ends of the thumbs; and a 'speculum oris' used to wrench open the jaws of slaves who refused to eat. Starvation was a common form of slave suicide, and the seller of these implements informed Clarkson that 'slaves were frequently so sulky as to shut their mouths against all sustenance, and this with a determination to die; and that it was necessary their mouth should be forced open to throw in nutriment, that they who had purchased them might incur no loss by their death'.[57] Clarkson also found a detailed diagram of a slave ship, showing how tightly the slaves were packed on the various decks, far more so than suspected by those outside the trade. All these he purchased and sent back to London along with drawings he made of them, where they became effective staples of anti-slavery lectures and literature.

Soon, newspaper items like the following notice in *The Times* of 12 May 1791 became common:

A very important question upon the Slave Trade, adjourned from Thursday last – At Coachmakers-Hall, Society, Foster Lane, Cheapside: This evening will be debated the following adjourned question: 'Would the abolition or continuance of the Slave Trade, be more likely to promote the commercial interests and dignity of Great Britain?' – So interesting to the feelings of humanity, so important to the honour and character of this country, to its trade, commerce and political security is this question considered, that this Society on Thursday last was visited by several Members of the House of Commons, Gentlemen at the Bar, and a great number of the most respectable trading and commercial men in the kingdom, all these and many more distinguished characters are expected to be present this evening. The question being adjourned by the unanimous desire of the audience, in order to afford opportunity for many Gentlemen to deliver their opinions. The *African*, who was kidnapped, taken to the West Indies, and by an extraordinary exertion of genius obtained his freedom, will be heard with due attention – Chair taken at a quarter past eight o'clock – admittance sixpence each person.

The following January, the same society debated a similar question: 'Is it not the duty of the people of Great Britain, from a principle of moral obligation and regard to their national character, to abstain from the consumption of West India produce till the

Slave Trade is abolished and measures are taken for the abolition of Slavery.' At their previous meeting 'a gentleman produced what the late Serjeant Davy called an iron argument; he exhibited to the audience the same iron mask that was produced in court upon the memorable trial respecting Somerset the negro, and explained the manner in which it was used as an instrument to punish the unfortunate African slave'.[58] By the 1790s the British anti-slavery movement had gained widespread and dramatic popular support. In a case similar to Somerset's, a black woman in Jamaica sued her master for her freedom. Not only did she win, but *The Times* reported that 'every Gentleman on the Jury made her a present'.[59]

In each place that Clarkson visited he suggested local people set up their own anti-slavery committees, and in some he also suggested they draw up petitions, but because he rarely read the newspapers while travelling, he had no idea how successfully these ideas had caught on. Stating on 12 March 1792 that 'the Slave Trade is now the topic of general conversation,' *The Times* began publishing lists of places from which petitions to Parliament for its abolition had been received. Week by week the list grew. Between 9 February and 5 March there were 73 petitions; by 14 March there were 154; by 20 March there were 242; by 26 March there were 272, and an additional 86 had been delivered 'but we have not yet got their names'. From Yarmouth to Penrith, from Newcastle to Leeds to Cardiff, from cities to small villages, British citizens signed petitions and implored their government to stop trading in human lives. In the midst of these petition drives William Wilberforce gave notice to Parliament 'that on Thursday the 29th of March he should make a motion for the Abolition of the Slave Trade'.[60]

It was not long before opposition to slavery and the slave trade became positively fashionable. The poet William Cowper, already known for his anti-slavery poem 'The Task', composed a poem called 'The Negro's Complaint' ('What are England's rights, I ask, / Me from my delights to sever, / Me to torture, me to task?') which his abolitionist friends in London 'ordered . . . on the finest hot-pressed paper, and folded it up in a small and neat form, [and] gave it the printed title of "A Subject for Conversation at the

Tea-table"'. Like Clarkson's essay and, in 1788, Falconbridge's book on his years in the slave trade, thousands of copies were sent around the country. Eventually it was even set to music 'and then it found its way into the streets, both of the metropolis and of the country, where it was sung as a ballad'.[61] It was also during these years that William Blake's poem 'The Black Boy' was written.

Similarly, the sentimental but effective Wedgwood-designed medallion of a kneeling black man, holding up his shackled wrists and pleading 'Am I not a man and a brother?' appeared everywhere. Originally designed by the Abolition Committee, Josiah Wedgwood copied it as a cameo in black on white and distributed it throughout Britain. Clarkson himself had no fewer than five hundred. They were an immediate hit, and some men had them 'inlaid in gold on the lid of their snuff-boxes. Of the ladies several wore them in bracelets, and others had them fitted up in an ornamental manner as pins for the hair. At length, the taste for wearing them became general; and thus fashion, which usually confines itself to worthless things, was seen for once in the honourable office of promoting the cause of justice, humanity, and freedom.'[62] Women took the lead in the campaign to refuse buying or using sugar or rum, the two major products of slave labour.

To the novelists of this decade at least a nodding expression of opposition to slavery became *de rigueur* and it was now quite common for novels whose subject had little or nothing to do with the issue of blacks or enslavement to include such gestures. Dozens of novels appeared during the abolitionist decade of the 1790s which contained black characters.[63] Particularly amongst women writers, abolition and fiction seemed to go hand in hand, even when the works did not preach equality. By the end of the century black characters appeared in both West Indian and English settings. No longer was it sufficient merely to place them in exotic settings; now they also could be used to point out the hypocrisies of class at home. Like Shirna Cambo, the fictional character based on Ignatius Sancho, they could be presented as a new type of Englishman, people who began life elsewhere, endured kidnap and enforced labour, but eventually found a certain simple nobility and repose in England.

Still, with the growing pressures against the slave trade, the most popular image of the black person was the highly sentimental one of the stolen African who never made it to the 'free air' of England but died miserable and alone in the West Indies. The subject of fiction, but more often of poetry, this kind of black character was constantly before the British reading public by the end of the century; even ordinary people were trying their hands at such literary portraits. The following poem, 'The Dying African', from *The Gentleman's Magazine* of November 1791, begins:

> Stretch'd on the ground the panting Slave was laid,
> Around his temples stifling breezes play'd;
> Faint mov'd his pulse; his glistening eyes were dim;
> Wither'd and feeble was each toil-worn limb:
> While thus unheeded sinking to the grave,
> No heart to mourn him, and no hand to save,
> Amid his frequent sighs and lab'ring throes,
> These faltering accents from his lips arose . . .

And so it goes on for several pages, describing the horrors of West Indian plantation slavery.[64]

An important factor in this huge upswelling of public feeling in the last decade of the eighteenth century was of course the revolution in France. Before news of widespread atrocities reached England, many celebrated what they saw as the birth of equality and the rights of the common man in Europe. The abolition of slavery seemed to go hand in hand with these ideals, indeed it was abolished in the French colony of St Domingo (now Haiti) during this time. But even as the English shied away in horror from the Reign of Terror, many continued and even strengthened their opposition to slavery.

As the abolitionist movement heated up, the pro-slavers naturally tried to counter their assertions. The 'no sugar, no rum' campaign was mocked, and on both sides exaggeration and mis-statement abounded. A letter of 21 March 1792 to *The Times* purported to be from a child disillusioned by abolitionist assertions. Claiming to have spoken to those who know better, the 'child' has learned from '[s]ome of the gentlemen [who] had been in the country where the Negroes make sugar' that 'they are never so well nor so happy as when they are making it, for they eat and drink as much as they will, and they love it as much as we do. They say likewise, that these poor Negroes don't work near so hard as the men who dig your papa's hop grounds, and live much better.' Furthermore, '[d]oes it not, Lady L——, seem as if people were hypocrites who make fortunes by using cotton and other things provided by the Negroes labour, and at the same time tell us it is wicked to make use of Sugar?' These familiar pro-slavery arguments were called upon more and more frequently as public agitation against the slave trade increased.

From Clarkson's account it would seem that black people themselves had little to do with the English emancipation movement. He apparently talked to few, if any, black people during his travels throughout England, although he does refer to an enormously successful but rare sermon he preached against the slave trade, at which 'a great crowd of black people [were] standing round the pulpit. There might be forty or fifty of them.'[65] During an extended visit to France, however, he met and talked to a number of black people from the insurrectionist St Domingo.

Clarkson went to Paris in 1789 to get support from Lafayette and others who also opposed the slave trade. As in England, a strong pro-slavery contingent felt threatened by the anti-slavery societies and he, along with the French 'Friends of the Negroes' received threatening letters and were vilified in the press. They were accused of sending weapons to black insurrectionists in St Domingo and their committee rooms were searched by soldiers. Clarkson's address was published in the press and for safety's sake he had to move and print a public rebuttal to the accusations.

While in Paris he met a number of times with a contingent of six 'people of colour' from St Domingo. Their position differed profoundly from that of African slaves, for not only were they mulatto or mixed race ('of a sallow or swarthy complexion', Clarkson remarked, 'not darker than that of some of the natives of the south of France'), but they were free, taxpaying landowners who outnumbered the whites on the island.[66] They came to France wearing the uniform of the Parisian National Guard and seeking a voice in their island's legislature for the thirty thousand they

189

represented, who had no vote or position in government because they were the descendants of African slaves.

These men confirmed to him that the slave trade itself 'was the parent of all the miseries in St Domingo, not only on account of the cruel treatment it occasioned to the slaves, but on account of the discord which it constantly kept up between the whites and people of colour, in consequence of the hateful distinctions it introduced. These distinctions could never be obliterated while it lasted.'[67] The first item on their agenda, should they gain access to their Assembly, was the immediate abolition of the slave trade, with slaves to be emancipated in fifteen years. In this they made a clear distinction between themselves as free men of mixed race, and the black slaves. In fact many of this class in St Domingo were themselves slave owners, and even though they favoured amelioration of slavery as it existed they were unwilling to fight for immediate and total emancipation.

Their mission in France proved frustrating. While the president of the National Assembly welcomed them in the egalitarian mood beginning to sweep France, Paris like London was full of West Indian colonists who 'openly insulted them' and set up a series of barriers to their success.[68] Clarkson counselled patience and forbearance, especially when they began to speak in more revolutionary terms, but finally their patience came to an end and they sailed home. One of them, Ogé, furious at the treatment he saw of the people of colour by whites at home, armed his slaves, was cornered and defeated, 'and his enemies, to strike terror into the people of colour, broke him upon the wheel'.[69]

In England there were by now black people in all social strata. Francis Williams was a noted Latin poet who studied at Cambridge University, but like the black American slave poet Phillis Wheatley was dismissed out of hand by some who had never met him, although admired by those who had. The philosopher, David Hume, for instance, remarked offhandedly that 'tis likely [Williams] is admired for very slender accomplishments, like a parrot who speaks a few words plainly'.[70] While the black residents and citizens of England were aware of and grateful for the abolitionists' work, they too were involved in the movement to end the slave trade and slavery.

Foremost among leading black activists was Olaudah Equiano, who spent the years following his embarrassing dismissal from the Sierra Leone project touring and lecturing. In early 1788 he published his response to James Tobin's 1785 *Cursory Remarks upon the Reverend Mr. Ramsay's Essay on the Treatment and Conversion of African Slaves in the British Sugar Colonies* in the *Public Advertiser*,[71] kept up a ceaseless correspondence about slavery with private people and in newspapers, and published his *Narrative* in 1789. He took a break only to marry his English wife in 1792 and then went immediately back to work, leaving for Scotland a little over a week after his wedding to sell copies of the *Narrative* and 'Trust that my going has been of much use to the Cause of Abolition'. He spent eight and a half months in Ireland in 1791–2, where he sold 1,900 copies of his book, and went to Durham, Hull and Stockton in 1792, and Bath and Devizes in 1793.[72] While he gained considerable support for the cause, everywhere he went Equiano also encountered hostility. Some tried to discredit his writing, others asserted that he was not really born in Africa. But it is a measure of his success that Sharp, who seemingly abandoned him during the Sierra Leone fiasco, visited him on his deathbed in 1797, and later said that he 'was a sober, honest man'.[73]

Paralleling the Abolition Committee was a group of black men who called themselves the 'Sons of Africa'. Their number varied, but they included in addition to Equiano, Ottobah Cugoano (often signing himself John Stuart or Stewart), George Mandeville, William Stevens, Joseph Almze, Boughwa Gegansmel, Jasper Goree, James Bailey, Thomas Oxford, John Adams, George Wallace, John Christopher, and Thomas Jones. Like the white Abolition Committee, they too embarked on letter-writing and public-speaking campaigns. They were always immensely grateful to Sharp and others in the Society for the Abolition of Slavery for their unflagging energy in the battle. Calling Sharp 'our constant and generous friend', they wrote to him that '[w]e are those who were considered as slaves, even in England itself, till your aid and exertion set us free'.[74] They requested him to collect his writings 'for the benefit and good of all men, and for an enduring memorial of the great learning, piety, and vigilance of our good friend'.[75]

They also made public appeals. Writing to the MP Sir William

Dolben in the *Morning Chronicle and London Advertiser*, they discussed their position in England and elsewhere:

> Our simple testimony is not much, yet you will not be displeased to learn, that a few persons of colour, existing here, providentially released from the common calamity, and feeling for their kind, are daily pouring forth their prayers for you, Sir, and other noble and generous persons who will not (as we understand) longer suffer the rights of humanity to be confounded with ordinary commodities, and passed from hand to hand, as an article of trade.
>
> We are not ignorant, however, Sir, that the best return we can make, is, to behave with sobriety, fidelity, and diligence in our different stations whether remaining here under the protection of the laws, or colonizing our native soil, as most of us wish to do, under the dominion of this country; or as free labourers and artizans in the West India islands, which, under equal laws, might become to men of colour places of voluntary and very general resort.
>
> But in whatever station, Sir, having lived here, as we hope, without reproach, so we trust that we and our whole race shall endeavour to merit, by dutiful behaviour, those mercies, which, humane and benevolent minds seem to be preparing for us.[76]

Dolben's answer was couched in gracious but abrupt terms. Thanking them and hoping their behaviour would recommend them to the British government, 'he must earnestly desire to decline any particular address upon the occasion'.[77] Yet he had been so upset by what he saw on a slave ship anchored in the Thames in 1788 that he immediately proposed a bill limiting the horrifically cramped shelving of slaves being transported.[78]

When Thomas Clarkson was at the beginning of his conversion, William Wilberforce was already involved with several people who opposed the slave trade. He was tremendously influenced by John Newton, the former participant in the slave trade who became an adamant opponent of it, and is probably best remembered as the composer of the hymn 'Amazing Grace'. Wilberforce was also close to the Revd James Ramsay, author of a famous anti-slavery pamphlet, and Sir Charles Middleton, an MP opposed to slavery. But by far his greatest influence and the person upon whom he pinned his abolitionist hopes was William Pitt, who had the most potential power to end the trade.

Wilberforce and Pitt were close friends during their Cambridge days, and were now influential young men of around thirty, Wilberforce as an MP and Pitt as Prime Minister. Wilberforce had gathered a substantial amount of information about the trade, but in 1787 had not yet committed himself to an all-out battle against it. Like Clarkson, he felt nervous about the giving up of more worldly pleasures and rewards that devotion to the cause would surely require, and Pitt was somewhat reticent about asking him to do so. The turning point came on a day in 1787 when they sat 'at the root of an old tree just above the steep descent into the vale of Keston' and Pitt said, 'Why don't you, Wilberforce, give notice of a motion on the subject of the Slave Trade? . . . Do not lose time, or the ground may be occupied by another.'[79] Thus supported by Pitt, Wilberforce began the long battle in Parliament which would occupy both of them for the rest of their lives. Unlike Pitt, Wilberforce remained loyal to the cause, unencumbered by the concerns of partisan politics and war with France that the Prime Minister had to face. Like Clarkson and Sharp, Wilberforce worked himself into grave illness in its service, nearly dying in 1788 before his public attack could begin.

Agreeing with the Abolition Committee, Wilberforce planned to wage one battle at a time and threw himself first into abolition of the trade rather than wholesale emancipation. He gave his first speech in the House of Commons on the subject on 12 May 1789. He stressed the barbarism of the wars slavery promoted in Africa, the wretchedness of the slave ships' conditions, and the amelioration of slaves' conditions in the West Indies that would necessarily result if they were not so easily replaced. He called upon Parliament and the merchants of Bristol and Liverpool to 'put an end at once to this infamous traffic! Let us stop this effusion of human blood! The true way to virtue is by withdrawing from temptation. Let us then withdraw from these wretched Africans those temptations to fraud, violence, cruelty, and injustice, which the Slave Trade furnishes! Where the sun shines, let us go round the world with him, diffusing our beneficence.'[80]

Supporting speeches by Pitt and Charles James Fox followed

his, but Wilberforce's twelve proposals were no competition for the money and influence wielded by the trade. As his biographer noted, '[w]hen negroes were suffering in London, the legal mind had concentrated – after some hesitation – on the slave's right to freedom; but when negroes were suffering on the Guinea Coast or in mid-Atlantic, the legal mind was more concerned with the owner's right of property. Were numbers of Englishmen to be suddenly deprived of what the law allowed them to possess, of a livelihood, which, unpleasant though it might be, they had so long been permitted to pursue by public opinion and with at least the tacit authority of Parliament?'[81]

Against the torrent of humanitarian evidence presented by the Abolition Committee and others, supporters of slavery and the trade presented calm and indeed cheerful assessments of slaves' lives and conditions. Robert Bisset published *The History of the Negro Slave Trade, in Its Connection with the Commerce and Prosperity of the West Indies* in 1805, including chapters on the necessity of blacks to the plantation system, 'Negro capacity, ascertained by experience', 'Frequency of famine in Africa', 'Cheerfulness of Negroes during the crop season', and 'Joy of West India Negroes at the arrival of African Negroes'.[82] Such works were intended to counter the alarming information on the slave trade and slavery now widely available through speeches and pamphlets.

For instance, everyone knew that slaves were captured in wars and sold to traders by Africans, but it had always been contended that such sales kept them from certain death. Now it became clear that the traders themselves encouraged such wars by offering material incentives to the victors. Where slavers spoke of the middle passage (the voyage from Africa to the Americas) as conducive to health since slaves danced on deck every day, ate a nourishing diet and were allowed to wash, it was revealed that to keep their muscles from atrophying in the barbarically crowded shelves of the hold, they were forced to shuffle while still in shackles. They were given horse beans to eat, breathed permanently fetid air, and died in their hundreds. Planters asserted that they were responsible for saving Africans from idolatry and barbarism; abolitionists proved that slaves were in fact denied the opportunity to learn about or to practise religion on plantations.

Even when finally everyone acknowledged the truth of the abolitionists' assertions, such conditions were conceded to be the necessary price of such a lucrative business.

Wilberforce's first speech on abolition was the beginning of a long and difficult saga. He put forward an 'annual motion to abolish the trade' – the very words used by the press to describe his efforts – his famous speeches were reported in their entirety by *Parliamentary History* and in part by *The Gentleman's Magazine* and others, and yet although each year he amassed more and more material to support his position, each year he failed to rally enough votes. The supporters of the trade tried to call a premature vote on Wilberforce's motion in early 1790 after only its side of the evidence had been heard, and in 1792 it passed the House of Commons but failed in the House of Lords. World events also conspired against Wilberforce. Slave uprisings in Dominica in 1791 and in St Domingo in 1792, among others, terrified even those previously supportive of abolition. Surely, they believed, total emancipation would eventually succeed abolition of the trade, making the slaughter of whites and the end of whites' plantations inevitable. Events in France, where revolution developed into the Terror and in turn gave rise to the Napoleonic Wars, occupied Pitt and nearly everyone else, adding to the fear of insurrection elsewhere.

In the press, in Parliament, and in court Wilberforce became completely associated with abolition and, by extension, black people. Sir James Johnstone claimed to quote Grenadian slaves when he declared in debate, 'Mr. Wilberforce for negro. Mr. Fox for negro. The Parliament for negro. God Almighty for negro.'[83] *The Times* reported a highly unlikely and probably facetious scenario: that the 'name of Wilberforce is in such high estimation among the negroes in the French colonies, that in the island of San Domingo, after they have finished their daily labours, they carry about his effigy, and afterwards dance round it; making bonfires that every one may see the object of their joy and adoration.'[84] Such a scene was more likely to be found in a sentimental novel of the period. Pitt called Wilberforce's indefatigable cadre of workers 'Wilberforce's white negroes'.[85] George III referred to slaves as Wilberforce's 'black clients', and Wilberforce was 'truly humiliated to see, in the House of Lords, four of the Royal Family come down to vote against the poor, helpless, friendless slaves'.[86] Even though he was unmarried, Wilberforce was rumoured to have a Negro wife.[87]

Former slaves living in England attempted to console him and his colleagues for the lack of progress with letters of appreciation. 'We will not presume to trouble you with many words', six of them wrote to Pitt in 1788. 'We are persons of colour, happily released from the common calamity, and desirous of leaving at your door, in behalf of our Brethren, on the Coast of Africa, this simple, but grateful acknowledgment of your goodness and benevolence towards our unhappy race.' To Fox they wrote a similar letter on the same day, explaining that 'feeling very sensibly for their kind' who were still bound by slavery, 'we have thereupon assumed the liberty (we hope, without offence) of leaving this simple, but honest token of our joy and thankfulness at your door'. To both letters they signed their names, adding 'For ourselves and Brethren'.[88] Even in a time of extreme politeness, the tentativeness of such letters is striking. Writing to thank and encourage their benefactors, they nevertheless recognized that their letters might be an imposition on men who, while they worked hard to improve the slaves' lot, did not necessarily seek personal connections with slaves and former slaves.

Nowhere was this made clearer than in the case of Granville Sharp himself. He was a great man; like Clarkson and Wilberforce he devoted his career, his time and his money to attacking slavery and the slave trade. To the former slaves living in Britain he was a god. The modern mistake is assuming that such compassion and devotion to a just cause naturally equated to an egalitarian view, especially in a world where egalitarianism led to wars in France and America. Yet, like abolitionists in northern America, such selflessness had little to do with personal relations. Indeed, in a society changing rapidly on many fronts, it was natural that Sharp's unflagging dedication to humanitarian causes would coincide with a religious and scientific enquiry.

One of the biggest questions facing Europeans in contact with other peoples was exactly how race and colour worked. Did it have to do with climate and geography? Were perceived racial differences a result of ancestral actions? All over Europe thinkers attempted to establish racial hierarchies, with whites at the top of the human scale, a great Chain of Being with animals at the bottom and angels at the top, and where '[m]any commentators treated the Negro's blackness as a degeneration from original colour'.[89] David Hume's comment that 'I am apt to suspect the negroes, and in general all the other species of men (for there are four or five different kinds) to be naturally inferior to the whites' was fairly typical of his time.[90]

The most common theory, and Sharp apparently subscribed to it, was that black people were descended from Ham, the dark son of Noah, who was punished along with all his descendants to be 'hewers of wood and drawers of water' for seeing his father naked. The assumption here and elsewhere was that 'the original color of man was white . . . which gave special sharpness to the question why the Negro was black. It was not so much a matter of why the Negro was black as why the Negro had become the very negation of white.'[91]

For many others like Sharp, the question was one of religion, since biblical history and science could be equally and compatibly called on to answer such questions of origins. Thus as far back as 1772, shortly after the Somerset decision, Sharp wrote to the author Jacob Bryant, for whom he had 'conceived a high opinion of your abilities by perusing your learned account of Egypt and the Shepherd Kings', and asked,

> I had always supposed that Black Men in general were descended from Cush because a distinction in colour from the rest of Mankind seems to have been particularly attributed to his Descendants, the Cushim, even to a Proverb: 'Can the Cushi change his Skin &c.' (Jeremh. 13.3) and therefore I concluded that all Negroes, as well East Indian as African, are entitled to the general name of Cushim, as being, probably, descended from different Branches of the same Stock, because the Proverb is equally applicable to both with respect to their complexion, though in many other respects they are very different. But in C. 254 of your learned Work, where you are speaking of the Cuseans in general you say 'that they are to be found within the Tropics almost as low as the Gold Coast' &c. – as if you apprehen-

ded that the Negroes on the Gold Coast and below it were not descended from Cush.[92]

In trying to clarify this matter, Sharp had the highest of aims: to support the anti-slavery cause by refuting all arguments against the humanity and descent of black people. But the most telling line of the letter to Bryant followed his request for information. 'I am far from having any particular esteem for the Negroes', he wrote, 'but as I think myself obliged to consider them as Men, I am certainly obliged, also, to use my best endeavours to prevent their being treated as beasts by our unchristian Countrymen, who deny them the priviledges of human nature, and, in order to excuse their own brutality, will scarcely allow that Negroes are human beings. The traceing their descent therefore is a point of some consequence to the subject, in which I am now engaged for their defence.'[93] Sharp, deeply religious, even fanatically so toward the end of his life, eventually followed a far different path from that of Clarkson and Wilberforce.

Even less concerned with the origins of black people than Wilberforce and Clarkson were the blacks in Britain working to free their own brethren. In 1787, while the settlers were being shipped from England, the Abolition Committee was meeting; and while Equiano was recovering from his insulting dismissal, Ottobah Cugoano published his *Thoughts and Sentiments on the Evil of Slavery*. It was Cugoano, under his English name of John Stewart, who alerted Sharp to the kidnapping of a black man named Harry Demane, the same man who Sharp rescued only to see him work for the slavers in Sierra Leone. Like Equiano he saw himself as by necessity a public person, working for the end of slavery even though he himself was now considered a free man.

It is generally acknowledged that Cugoano's book is not completely authentic – his writing ability was not at the level the book demonstrates, and whole sections of it appear to be paraphrases from Clarkson's *Essay on Slavery*.[94] But it was a nonetheless heartfelt and successful plea for the rights of black people, and 170 people subscribed to it, including Reynolds and Nollekens.

Along with the letters composed by the 'Sons of Africa', Cugoano unabashedly sent letters of his own to Edmund Burke, the Prince of Wales and George III. He was well acquainted with Sharp, to whom he also wrote on such matters as the black settlers from Nova Scotia ('Pardon the liberty taken in troubling you with this few lines but as there is Several Ships now going to new Brunswick I could wish to have your answer that I might be able to gived [*sic*] the black settlers there some kind of an answer to their request . . .') and blacks needing help in England.[95] He also indicated the difficulty of his own position as a black man in England: 'I have, within this last three months been after upwards of fifty places but, Complexion is a Predominant Prejudice for a man to starve for want in a christian Country will be a folly.'[96] Like Sharp's comment that he was 'far from having any particular esteem for the Negroes', Cugoano's statement is a hard reminder that even with an English wife and influential friends, the life of a black person in England was a difficult one.

In his book he gave 'particular thanks . . . to every one of that humane society of worthy and respectful gentlemen, whose liberality hath supported many of the Black poor about London', as well as to the British government which co-operated with them. Even so, he found fault with the handling of the Sierra Leone expedition, from the lack of prior agreement about the settlement's boundaries with the resident Africans, to the treatment of the settlers before they left England. According to him, 'they were to be hurried away at all event, come of them what would; and yet, after all, to be delayed in the ships before they were set out from the coast, until many of them have perished with cold, and other disorders, and several of the most intelligent among them are dead, and others that, in all probability, would have been most useful for them were hindered from going . . . .'.[97] Even then they faced dangerous slave traders when they arrived in Sierra Leone. Unless the slave trade itself were abolished even this charitable expedition could meet a disastrous end.

The real difficulty with the attempt to abolish the slave trade stemmed from the smugness with which the English embraced the supposed freedom of their own air, while enjoying the rewards of slavery elsewhere. The *Daily Universal Register* of 8 January 1785 wrote that slavery '[c]annot be censured in language too severe. It is shocking to humanity, cruel, wicked, diabolical'. After a paragraph condemning America's tolerance of slavery on its shores, it concluded by saying that in 'Britain, a negro becomes a freeman the moment he sets his foot on British ground'.[98] This was a fallacy which impeded progress against slavery on West Indian 'British ground', as people like Cugoano well understood, even when he had difficulty expressing it in writing. And it was against this attitude that Wilberforce and others struggled in their Sisyphean efforts to roll the rock of abolition up the Parliamentary hill.

The campaign demanded joint action. When Wilberforce's first motion failed in 1791, it was launched again early in 1792, with the dissemination of pamphlets against the trade, another information-gathering and speaking tour throughout England by Clarkson, and the encouragement of petitions. When Wilberforce gave notice of the motion, the 'machinery went like clockwork . . . the petitions began to pour in – 312 from England, 187 from Scotland. Only five were presented from the other side – even Liverpool abstaining.'[99] It would seem that such strong public opinion must sway the law makers but it did not. After a series of failures, and because of poor health, Clarkson went into a nine-year retirement but re-emerged in the winter of 1805–6. Pitt, with more issues to deal with than African slavery, was out of office and back in again during the protracted attempt to end the trade. Its activists were becoming as old and tired (Fox and Pitt were near death in 1806) as its opponents, and all felt ground down by the battle.

Slowly, however, a series of positive changes occurred. The Royal family began to disagree among themselves about the justice of slavery. A bill to prohibit the importation of slaves into recently annexed British colonies or into foreign colonies passed in the winter of 1805–6. The tide was turning, and a rejuvenated Wilberforce, backed by Fox, reintroduced his bill.

At long last, when Fox stood in the Commons for the fifteenth moving of the resolution in 1806, the year of his death, it carried by a wide margin of 114 to 15. In the Lords the vote was 41 to 30. A series of clauses were introduced by William Grenville on 2 January 1807, declaring that as of 1 January 1808 the slave trade was to be 'utterly abolished, prohibited and declared to be unlawful'.[100] It was read a second time on 23 February, passed over-whelmingly, and received a third reading on 16 March. The Lords passed it on 23 March, and the King agreed on 25 March. Wilber-force's biographer reports that at the final vote in the Commons the 'House was on its feet, giving Wilberforce an ovation such as it had given to no other living man . . . Insensible, as he afterwards confessed, to all that was passing around him, he sat bent in his seat, his head in his hands, and the tears streaming down his face.'[101]

This was a momentous occasion, and during the struggle for its achievement many of its hardest workers had fallen. Pitt died on 23 January 1806. Fox also died in 1806, just before abolition of the trade. Granville Sharp died in 1813 and of the older genera-tion was one of the few to see his greatest mission accomplished. Jonathan Strong, whose plight had begun it all, had died long before, on 17 April 1773, less than a year after the Somerset case and nearly thirty-five years before the end of the trade which had brought him to England.

As profound a victory as the end of the trade was, slavery itself was still firmly in place, with other countries willing to risk the embargo enforced by the British navy. The fact was, as a number of subsequent historians have noted, that slavery did not end by unflagging work and good intentions alone, but because the trade was nearing the end of its commercial worth, related to the need to stem the overproduction of sugar.[102] Nor did the abolitionists work in a vacuum, for the cause was also supported by English radicals and others. Fryer describes a mass meeting in Sheffield in 1794, in which thousands of workers unanimously called for the end of the slave trade and emancipation of the slaves.[103] Slave emancipation did not finally take place until 1833, and in the intervening years black English radicals joined whites in support-ing the rights of workers, and some were jailed and executed for their actions. They 'claim[ed] their rights as Englishmen', the black radical William Davidson announced in court in 1820, shortly before his conviction for his part in the Cato Street con-spiracy in which radicals plotted the murders of cabinet ministers in revenge for the deaths of eleven unarmed protesters. Davidson, along with four white men, was hanged and beheaded in front of a crowd outside Newgate gaol.[104] His involvement in political activism shows how far black people had become involved in British political and social movements in nearly 300 years in England.

As horrible as West Indian slavery was, and was to continue to be for some time after the abolition of the slave trade, and as difficult as life could be for black English people, one need only recall the continuing saga of American slavery to gain some sort of perspective. In the United States some slaves managed to move to the north and free themselves, yet they continued to experience there an oppression that was far less common in Britain.

In the mid-nineteenth century, the former slave Harriet Jacobs sailed from New York to London as nurse to her employer's children. Writing as Linda Brent, Jacobs published her memoirs in 1861 and revealed the truth behind the assertions of black female sexual abuse by white masters. In order to prevent the sale of her children, she hid for seven years in a tiny attic space that bent her over, froze in winter and scorched her in summer. Never again in good health, she nevertheless succeeded in sending her children north and in eventually escaping there herself.

When she arrived in London she stayed in the Adelaide Hotel where '[f]or the first time in my life I was in a place where I was treated according to my deportment, without reference to my complexion. I felt as if a great millstone had been lifted from my breast. Ensconced in a pleasant room, with my dear little charge, I laid my head on my pillow, for the first time, with the delightful consciousness of pure, unadulterated freedom.'[105] When she visited some rural poor in Steventon, Hampshire, she refuted the pro-slavery claim that the slaves of the Americas and West Indies were happier and better off than the poor people of Britain:

I had heard much about the poor in Europe. The people I saw around me were, many of them, among the poorest poor. But when I visited them in their little thatched cottages, I felt that the condition of even the meanest and most ignorant among them was vastly superior to the condition of the most favored slaves in America. They labored hard; but they were not ordered out to toil while the stars were in the sky, and driven and slashed by an overseer, through heat and cold, till the stars shone out again. Their homes were very humble; but they were protected by law. No insolent patrols could come, in the dead of night, and flog them at their pleasure. The father, when he closed his cottage door, felt safe with his family around him. No master or overseer could come and take from him his wife, or his daughter. They must separate to earn their living; but the parents knew where their children were going, and communicate with them by letters . . . There was no law forbidding them to learn to read and write; and if they helped each other in spelling out the Bible, they were in no danger of thirty-nine lashes . . .[106]

Jacobs claimed that during the ten months she resided in England, she never once saw even 'the slightest symptom of prejudice against color. Indeed, I entirely forgot it, till the time came for us to return to America.'[107]

There had been by Jacobs' time many generations of blacks in England, the descendants of slaves (and often of whites too) who were never slaves themselves. They 'no longer thought of themselves as constituting a distinct black community. They were part of the British poor', Fryer writes. Perhaps because the importation of black slaves slowed and finally ceased, and because the existing black English population commonly intermarried with whites, black people themselves once again acquired a kind of exoticism and sympathy when they were enslaved elsewhere. American blacks like Frederick Douglass and William Wells Brown, who visited England to gain support for American emancipation, found themselves embraced. Even as late as 1852 Brown noticed that one could encounter a dozen black college students in an hour's walk in central London.[108] Beethoven wrote his 'Kreutzer' sonata for a black pianist named George Bridgtower, who performed it with Beethoven by his side.[109] Black performers frequently toured England in the nineteenth century, as did prize fighters and orators. When Harriet Beecher Stowe (whom Abraham Lincoln is rumoured to have called 'the little lady who started this great [civil] war') published her novel *Uncle Tom's Cabin* in 1852, Victorian England went as mad for its memorabilia as their ancestors had done for the Wedgwood medallion.

What became of the many thousands of black people who

remained in England after the abolition of the slave trade? Like the children and grandchildren and great-grandchildren of Francis Barber, they married and raised families and worked – in England. They became, in short, English people, even though the 'records of their lives are obscure and scattered, and they have for the most part been forgotten by their descendants. But there must be many thousands of British families who, if they traced their roots back to the eighteenth or early nineteenth century, would find among their ancestors an African or person of African descent.'[110]

Their descendants live among us.[111] From London to Liverpool they walk the same streets as their ancestors, with lineage that goes back, for some, even to the sixteenth and seventeenth centuries. They have intermarried and become inextricably entwined in England's past and present. While individuals have doubtless been long forgotten, theirs is nonetheless an unbroken living legacy, a continual and very English presence.

Notes

Chapter 1: Paupers and Princes

1. Peter Fryer, *Black People in the British Empire: An Introduction* (London: Pluto Press, 1988), xiv
2. Quoted in Nigel File and Chris Power, *Black Settlers in Britain 1555–1958* (London: Heinemann Education Books, 1981) 6, from 'Acts of the Privy Council, xxvi, 1596–7, 16, 20, and 21,' and 'Licensing Caspar van Senden to deport Negroes' (1601) in *Tudor Royal Proclamations, 1588–1603*, ed. J.L. Hughes and J.F. Larkin (New Haven: Yale University Press, 1969), 221
3. James Walvin, ed., *Black and White: The Negro and English Society 1555–1945* (London: Allen Lane the Penguin Press, 1973) 9
4. Walvin, *Black and White* 9, referring to J.A. Rogers, *Nature Knows No Color-Line* (New York: 1952) 161
5. File 6
6. File 6
7. Stuart Hall et al., *Policing the Crisis* (London: Macmillan, 1978) 140
8. Folarin Olawale Shyllon, *Black People in Britain 1555–1833* (London: Oxford University Press for The Institute of Race Relations, 1977), 13
9. I have used a microfiche copy of the original hand-written and hand-corrected text. Part of a series called *Three Centuries of English and American Plays*, it was filmed by the Redex Company from a manuscript housed in the Larpent Collection, Huntington Library, San Marino, California, and loaned by the Cleveland Public Library in Cleveland, Ohio
10. Walvin, *Black and White* 24
11. *Gentleman's Magazine*, XXIX (1749), 240
12. Quoted by Wylie Sypher, 'The African Prince in London,' *Journal of the History of Ideas*, Vol. II, No. 2 (April, 1941), 244
13. Sypher, 'The African Prince in London, 237
14. *Memoirs of the Late Captain Hugh Crow of Liverpool* (London: Longman, Rees, Orme, Brown and Greene, 1830) 300

15. Christopher Fyfe, *A History of Sierra Leone* (London: Oxford University Press, 1962) 11, and Walvin, *Black and White* 51
16. *Gentleman's Magazine*, Vol. XX (1750), 272
17. Walvin, *Black and White*, 80
18. Walvin, *Black and White* 71
19. Richard B. Schwartz, *Daily Life in Johnson's London* (Madison: University of Wisconsin Press, 1983) 53
20. Schwartz 77
21. John Latimer, *Annals of Bristol in the Eighteenth Century* (Bristol, 1893), 174
22. 'The Black Man' in *All the Year Round*, 6 March 1875, 491
23. William Combe, *Devil Upon Two Sticks in England*, Vol. II (London: Printed at the Logographic Press, 1791), 96–7
24. Charles Dunster, *St. James's Street* (London: 1790), 14–15
25. Fryer 32. *The Character of a Town Misse* (W.L., 1675), 7
26. 'The Black Man,' 493
27. 'The Black Man,' 493
28. 'The Black Man,' 493
29. 'The Black Man,' 489
30. Shyllon 4–5
31. Fryer, *Staying Power* 75
32. Walvin, *The Black Presence* 14
33. Willan 255, quoted in M. Dorothy George, *London Life in the Eighteenth Century* (Chicago: Academy Publishers, 1984) 95
34. *A Narrative of the Most Remarkable Particulars in the Life of James Albert Ukasaw Gronniosaw, an African Prince, as Related by Himself* (Leeds: Printed by Davies and Booth, at the Stanhope Press, Vicar-Lane, 1814) 23
35. Gronniosaw 25
36. Gronniosaw 25
37. Gronniosaw 32
38. Benjamin Silliman, *A Journal of Travels in England, Holland and Scotland . . . in the Years 1805 and 1806* (New Haven: 1820), I, 272
39. Samuel Estwick, *Considerations on the Negroe Cause, Commonly So-Called, Addressed to the Right Honourable Lord Mansfield, Lord Chief Justice of the Court of King's Bench* (London: 1773), 94
40. *London Chronicle*, XXXIII (13–16 March 1773), 250
41. Philip Thicknesse, *A Year's Journey through France and Part of Spain*, (W. Brown, 1778), II, 108
42. David Dabydeen, *Hogarth's Blacks* (Manchester: Manchester University Press, 1897) 18

43. Elizabeth Helme, *London and It's [sic] Environs Described* (London: Printed for R. & J. Dodsley's in Pall-Mall, 1761), Vol. 3, 218

44. Walvin, *Black and White* 61

45. Walvin, *Black and White* 49

46. *London Chronicle*, XV.1116 (14–16 February 1764) 166

47. *Candid Reflections Upon the Judgement lately awarded by the Court of King's Bench, in Westminster-Hall, On what is commonly called the Negroe-cause* (T. Lowndes, 1772), 47

48. Thicknesse 108. Also quoted in Fryer, *Staying Power* 70 and numerous other places

49. Sir John Fielding, *Extracts from such of the Penal Laws, as Particularly relate to the Peace and Good Order of this Metropolis* (T. Cadell, 1768) 144–5

50. *Annals of Bristol* 249 and elsewhere

51. For more information on the conditions of eighteenth-century life see the following: Rosamond Bayne-Powell, *Eighteenth-Century London Life*; Jay Barrett Botsford, *English Life in the Eighteenth Century (As Influenced From Overseas)*; M. Dorothy George, *London Life in the Eighteenth Century*; John Latimer, *Annals of Bristol in the Eighteenth-Century*; Richard B. Schwartz, *Daily Life in Johnson's London*

52. Mary Eyre Matcham, *A Forgotten John Russell, Being Letters to a Man of Business 1724–1751* (London: Edward Arnold, 1905) 334

53. J. Jean Hecht, *Continental and Colonial Servants in Eighteenth Century England* (Northampton, Massachusetts: Smith College Studies in History, Vol. XL, 1954) 43

54. M. Dorothy George, *London Life in the Eighteenth Century* 109

55. Aleyn Lyell Reade, *Johnsonian Gleanings*, Part II, 'Francis Barber, The Doctor's Negro Servant' (London: Arden Press, 1912) 6

56. Reade 35

57. Reade 27

58. Barbara Tuchman, 'In Search of History,' in *Practising History* (New York: Ballantine Books, 1982) 19

59. Richard Holmes, *Footsteps: Adventures of a Romantic Biographer* (New York: Elisabeth Sifton Books, Viking, 1985) 208

Chapter 2: High Life below Stairs

1. Philip C. Yorke, ed., *The Diary of John Baker* (London: Hutchinson & Co. Ltd., 1931), 66

2. *Baker* 72

3. *Baker* 67
4. *Baker* 71
5. *Baker* 74–80
6. *Baker* 75
7. *Baker* 80
8. *Baker* 85
9. *Baker* 83–7. Perhaps strangest of all was the discovery of 2 October 1755: 'This morning a negro child of Capn Dromgoole's found drowned in a tub of water, with its head down and heels up, how long they knew not; but brought to life by lighting a pipe of tobacco and sticking the small end in its fundament, a blowing it at the bowl' (85)
10. *Baker* 83
11. *Baker* 164
12. 'Home from School – or the Commencement of the Holidays,' George Cruikshank, published by S. Knights, Sweetings Alley Royal Exchange. From a private collection
13. *Baker* 112
14. *Baker* 114
15. *Baker* 114
16. *Baker* 115–16
17. *Baker* 117
18. *Baker* 117
19. *Baker* 118
20. *Baker* 122
21. *Baker* 152
22. *Baker* 157
23. *Baker* 136
24. *Baker* 182
25. *Baker* 132
26. *Baker* 167
27. *Baker* 167
28. *Baker* 181
29. *Baker* 163
30. *Baker* 101
31. *Baker* 133
32. *Baker* 206
33. *Baker* 155
34. James Northcote, *The Life of Sir Joshua Reynolds* (London: Printed for Henry Colburn, Conduit-Street, 1819), Vol. 1, 204–6
35. *Baker* 96
36. *Baker* 138

37. *Baker* 126
38. *Baker* 147
39. *Baker* 201
40. James Walvin, *The Black Presence: A Documentary History of the Negro in England, 1555–1860* (New York: Scholcken Books, 1972), 15
41. Aleyn Lyell Reade, *Johnsonian Gleanings*, Part II, 15.
42. *The London Chronicle*, 1764, XV, 166c
43. *The London Packet*, June 26–9, 1772, No. 418, 1c
44. *Baker* 192
45. Northcote, Vol. 1, 108–9
46. *Baker* 195
47. *Baker* 154
48. *Baker* 154
49. *Baker* 154
50. David Garrick, 'High Life Below Stairs,' in two acts, in *A Collection of the Most Esteemed Farces and Entertainments Performed on the British Stage* in 4 volumes (Edinburgh: Printed for C. Elliot, Parliament-Square, 1782), Volume III, 104–34
51. *The London Chronicle*, 1757, II, 263c. Quoted in Hecht, *The Domestic Servant Class in Eighteenth-Century England* (London: Routledge & Kegan Paul, 1956), 214–15
52. *Lloyd's Evening Post*, 1780, XLVII, 180c. Quoted in Hecht, *Domestic Servant Class*, 215
53. Hecht, *Domestic Servant Class*, 215
54. Edward Long, *The History of Jamaica*, Vol. I (London: Printed for T. Lowndes, in Fleet-Street, 1744), 178
55. *The Gentleman's Magazine*, Vol. XXIV, October 1764
56. *The London Chronicle*, October 19–22, 1765, 387a and 387b
57. *The London Chronicle*, 1764, XVI, 317a. Quoted in Hecht, *Continental and Colonial Servants*, 43
58. Sir John Fielding, *Extracts from such of the Penal Laws, as Particularly Relate to the Peace and Good Order of This Metropolis* (London, 1769), 144
59. Philip Yorke, Introduction to *Baker*, 15
60. *Baker* 186
61. *Baker* 278
62. Sir John Hawkins, *The Life of Samuel Johnson LL.D.*, ed. Bertram H. Davis (London: Jonathan Cape, 1962), 138
63. Hester Lynch Piozzi, *Anecdotes of the Late Samuel Johnson, LL.D., during the last twenty years of his Life*, ed. S.C. Roberts (Cambridge: at the University Press, 1925), 136

64. George Birkbeck Hill, ed., *Boswell's Life of Johnson* (Oxford: The Clarendon Press, 1934), Vol. 3, 201
65. Boswell, Vol. III, 200
66. Quoted in Hill, Appendix A, 477
67. Boswell, Vol. III, 203
68. Reade 12
69. Reade 12
70. Reade 13–14
71. 'A Negro boy, about nine years of age, in a gray Searge suit, his hair cut close to his head, was lost on Tuesday last, August 9, at night, in S. Nicholas Lane, London' [1659]; 'A Black boy, twelve years of age, fit to wait on a gentleman, to be disposed of at Denis's Coffee House in Finch Lane, near the Royal Exchange' [1709]; 'Negro 22 years – run away – middle Size, with English stammering speech; cut on forehead; Jerusalem Arms, West Indies, 1706 on Left Arm; 1 guinea for Return, or voluntary Pardon' [1712]; 'Mr Pryne, the Bristol postmaster, undertakes to pay two guineas and expenses for the recovery of Captain Stephen Courtney's negro aged about 20 having three or four marks on each temple and the same on each cheek' [1715]; 'A healthy Negro Girl aged about fifteen years; speaks English, works at her needle, washes well, does household work, and has had the smallpox' [1761]; 'Ran away from his Master, a Negro Boy, under 5 feet high, about 16 years old, named Charles, he is very ill made, being remarkably bow legged, hollow Backed and Pot-bellied; he had when he went away a coarse dark brown Linen Frock, a Thickset Waistcoat, very dirty Leather Breeches, and on his Head an Old Velvet jockey Cap' [1768]. All quoted in James Walvin, *The Black Presence*, 79–80
72. Boswell, Vol. 1, 349–50
73. Piozzi 136
74. Boswell, Vol. 2, 116
75. Hawkins 138
76. *Annals of Bristol* 12
77. Reade 29–30
78. Hawkins 304
79. Quoted in Reade, Vol. IX, *A Further Miscellany*, 208
80. *Letters of Samuel Johnson*, Birkbeck Hill, ed., ii. 227. Quoted in Reade 31
81. Reade 31
82. Piozzi 136–7
83. Piozzi 165
84. Boswell, III, 92

85. Boswell, II, 386
86. Boswell, II, 222
87. Boswell, II, 376
88. Boswell, I, 27
89. Quoted in Reade 51
90. Boswell, IV, Appendix F, 444
91. Boswell, IV, 401–2
92. Henry Angelo, *Reminiscences of Henry Angelo, with Memoirs of his Late Father and Friends, Including Numerous original anecdotes and curious facts of the most celebrated characters that have flourished during the last eighty years* (London: Henry Colburn, New Burlington Street, 1828), Vol. I, 21
93. Reade 69
94. Reade 72
95. *Primitive Methodist Magazine*, Vol. X, 1829, 82. Quoted in Reade 72
96. Vita Sackville-West, *Knole and the Sackvilles* (London: William Heinemann Ltd., 1931), 191
97. Sackville-West 196
98. Sackville-West 81
99. Sackville-West 155
100. Shyllon, *Black People in Britain* 41. Quotations are from Thomas Whitehead, *Original Anecdotes of the Late Duke of Kingston and Miss. Cudleigh, alias Mrs. Harvey, alias Countess of Bristol, alias Duchess of Kingston* (London: 1792), 86–9
101. See Violet Biddulph, *Kitty, Duchess of Queensberry* (London: Ivor Nicholson and Watson Ltd., 1935), for a more complete biography of the Duchess
102. Angelo 447
103. Angelo 449
104. Angelo 449
105. Angelo 451
106. *The Morning Post, and Daily Advertiser*, No. 1482, Tuesday, July 22, 1777, 2a
107. Angelo 452
108. Ignatius Sancho, *Letters of Ignatius Sancho (An African to which are prefixed Memoirs of His Life by Joseph Jekyll, Esq., M.P. with an Introduction by Paul Edwards)* (London: Dawsons of Pall Mall, 1968), 5. First published posthumously by Miss F. Crewe in 1782, and by William Sancho in 1803
109. Sancho 31–3
110. Sancho 88

111. Sancho 34
112. Sancho, November 29, 1778, 171–4
113. Joseph Jekyll, *Sancho* ii
114. Jekyll iv
115. Sancho 25
116. Sancho 34–5
117. Sancho 38
118. John Thomas Smith, *Nollekens and his Times*, ed., G.W. Stonier (London: 1949), 14–15. Quoted by Paul Edwards in his Introduction to *Sancho*, v. First published 1828
119. Smith, Vol. II, 15, 21. Quoted in Fryer, *Staying Power*, 76
120. Anon., *Memoirs and Opinions of Mr. Blenfield* by the author of *Tales of Sympathy* (London: Printed for W. Lane, Leadenhall Street: 1790), Vol. I, Chap. 5, 44–54. Folarin Shyllon, in *Black People in Britain*, 200, was the first to point out that Sancho '[w]ithout a doubt . . . inspired the figure of Shirna Cambo.'
121. Sancho 238
122. Sancho 27
123. Sancho 150
124. Sancho 133
125. Sancho 99
126. Sancho 125–6
127. Sancho 120–1
128. Sancho 101
129. Sancho 149
130. Shyllon, *Black People in Britain* 200
131. Sancho 70-2
132. M. Dorothy George, *London Life in the Eighteenth Century*, 142
133. Sancho 146
134. Sancho 125–7
135. Nollekens, Vol. I, 27
136. *Memoirs and Opinions of Mr. Blenfield* 207–8
137. Shyllon, *Black People in Britain* 191
138. 'Gillespie,' 'Some Old Tobacconists,' in *Tobacco*, June 1, 1888. Quoted in Shyllon, *Black People in Britain* 201
139. Hecht, *Colonial Servants* 47

Chapter 3: What about Women?

1. Edward Hall, *Henry VIII*, ed. Charles Whibley, 1904, Vol. i., 15–17. Quoted in Eldred D. Jones, *Othello's Countrymen: The African*

in *English Renaissance Drama* (London: Oxford University Press, 1965) 28

2. *Othello's Countrymen* 29
3. *Othello's Countrymen* 29–30
4. *Staying Power* 3
5. *Staying Power* 7
6. *Staying Power* 76
7. *Hogarth's Blacks* 23–4
8. *Hogarth's Blacks* 32
9. Winthrop Jordan, *White Over Black: American Attitudes Toward the Negro 1550–1812* (New York: W.W. Norton, 1977) 4–11
10. James Walvin, *England, Slaves and Freedom* (London: Macmillan Press Ltd., 1986) 48
11. Walvin, *Black and White* 54
12. John MacDonald, *Memoirs of an Eighteenth-Century Footman, Travels (1745–1779)* (New York and London: Harper & Brothers) 122 and 166
13. Fryer 76
14. Quoted by Fryer, 76. Definition in brackets is his
15. Fryer 76
16. Fryer 76
17. Jane West, *Advantages of Education* . . . (London and New York: Garland Publishing Inc., 1974) 140–1
18. Helena Wells, *Constantia Neville; or, the West Indian* (London: Printed by C. Whittingham, Dean Street, Fetter-Lane, 1800) 61
19. West 77–8
20. West 110
21. West 320
22. William Roberts, ed., *Memoirs of the life and correspondence of Mrs. Hannah More*, second ed. (L.B. Seeley & Sons, 1834), II, 235
23. *Bristol Journal*, December 8, 1792. Quoted by Shyllon, *Black People* 170
24. James Walvin, *Black and White* 52. Quoted from *Cursory Remarks upon the Rev. Ramsay's Essays* . . . (London, 1785) 117
25. *The Annals of Bristol* 344
26. Fryer 23. This case has been widely discussed
27. Granville Sharp, unpublished letter book, 14
28. Granville Sharp, letter book, 19
29. Granville Sharp letter book, 20–1, York Minster Archives, Coll. 1896/1
30. Fryer 118

31. *New Times*, no. 9146, November 9, 1827. Quoted in Fryer 131
32. Reginald Coupland, *Wilberforce: A Narrative* (Oxford: at the Clarendon Press, 1923) 214–15
33. Fryer 32
34. *St. James's Evening Post*, 1726, no. 1695, March 19–22, 2b. Quoted in Hecht 49
35. John Thomas Smith, *Nollekens and His Times*, ed. Wilfred Whitten (London: John Lane the Bodley Head, 1920), 32–3
36. *Nollekens* 84
37. *Nollekens* 343–4
38. *Nollekens* 99
39. *Nollekens* 202
40. *Nollekens* 89–90
41. *Nollekens* 177
42. *Nollekens* 330
43. *Nollekens* 79
44. *Nollekens* 80
45. *Nollekens* 50
46. *Nollekens* 98
47. *Nollekens* 342–3
48. *Nollekens* 70
49. *Nollekens* 299
50. *Nollekens* 348
51. *Nollekens* 348
52. *The History of Mary Prince*, in *The Classic Slave Narratives* ed. Henry Louis Gates, Jr. (New York: New American Library, 1987), 189
53. *The History of Mary Prince* 191
54. *The History of Mary Prince* 194
55. *The History of Mary Prince* 209
56. *The History of Mary Prince* 218
57. *The History of Mary Prince* 218
58. *The History of Mary Prince* 219
59. *The History of Mary Prince* 230
60. *The History of Mary Prince* 233
61. Gene Adams, 'Dido Elizabeth Belle: A Black Girl at Kenwood,' in *Camden History Review* (London: 1984) 10
62. Peter Orlando Hutchinson ed., *The Diary and Letters of His Excellency Thomas Hutchinson, Esq.* (London: Sampson Low, Marston, Searle & Rivington, 1886) Vol. 2, 276–7
63. Hutchinson 276–7
64. Adams 13
65. *The London Times*, 9 June 1788, 555

Chapter 4: Sharp and Mansfield

1. E.C.P. Lascelles, *Granville Sharp and the Freedom of Slaves in England* (London: Humphrey Milford, and Oxford University Press, 1928), 112
2. Lascelles 114
3. Prince Hoare, *Memoirs of Granville Sharp, Esq.* (London: Henry Colburn, 1828), second edition, 35
4. Hoare 41
5. Sharp quoted in Hoare 43
6. Hoare 45
7. Lascelles 115
8. Lascelles 121
9. Lascelles 124–6
10. Edmund Heward, *Lord Mansfield* (London and Chichester: Barry Rose, 1979), 1
11. James Oldham, *The Mansfield Manuscripts and the Growth of English Law in the Eighteenth Century*, (Chapel Hill and London: The University of North Carolina Press, 1992), Vol. I, 9
12. Oldham 6
13. Oldham 10
14. Oldham 16
15. Oldham 20
16. Oldham 21
17. Quoted in Oldham 41
18. Richard Cumberland, *Memoirs*, 2:344–6, quoted in Oldham 41
19. Hoare 49
20. Letter book, 93
21. Hoare 49–50
22. Granville Sharp manuscripts in the New York Historical Society, BV Sec. Slavery, hereafter cited at NYHS
23. Sharp NYHS
24. Sharp NYHS
25. Sharp NYHS
26. Hoare 53
27. Sharp NYHS
28. Sharp NYHS
29. Sharp NYHS
30. Sharp NYHS
31. Sharp NYHS
32. Sharp, *A Representation of the Injustice of Tolerating Slavery*, 6. Holt's pronouncement was in Salkeld's Reports, Vol. II, 666

33. Sharp, *A Representation* . . . 13
34. Sharp, *A Representation* . . . 13
35. Sharp, *A Representation* . . . 43–4
36. Sharp, *A Representation* . . . 74–5
37. Sharp, *A Representation* . . . 77
38. Sharp, *A Representation* . . . 92
39. Sharp, *A Representation* . . . 109
40. Hoare, Vol. 1, 65
41. Letter book, 17 May 1768
42. Letter book, 5 February 1772
43. Toni Morrison, *Beloved* (New York: Alfred A. Knopf, 1987), 71
44. Granville Sharp, 'A Report of the Case of Lewis (a Negro) ag. Stapylton, with Remarks by G. Sharp), Sharp materials, NYHS
45. Hoare 84
46. Hoare 87
47. Hoare 87
48. Lewis proceedings, 5
49. Lewis proceedings, 12–13
50. Lewis proceedings, 15
51. Lewis proceedings, 16
52. Lewis proceedings, 30–1
53. Lewis proceedings, 41
54. Thomas Clarkson, quoted in Stuart 9
55. Hoare 79–80
56. Lewis proceedings, 34
57. Lewis proceedings, 35
58. Lewis proceedings, 54–5
59. Lewis proceedings, 35–6
60. Lewis proceedings, 37
61. Lewis proceedings, 62
62. Lewis proceedings, 63
63. Lewis proceedings, 67
64. Lewis proceedings, 76
65. Lewis proceedings, 78–9
66. Quoted in James Oldham, 'New Light on Mansfield and Slavery', *Journal of British Studies*, Vol. 27, Number 1, January 1988, 47
67. Shyllon, quoted in Oldham, 'New Light . . .', 53
68. Lewis proceedings
69. Sharp, 'Remarks . . .', 8
70. Sharp, 'Remarks . . .', 12–13
71. Letter book, 92–3
72. Tuke 25

73. Henry George Tuke, *The Fugitive Slave Circulars*, A Short Account of the Case of Sommersett the Negro . . . (London: Stanford, Charing Cross, 1876), 23. Relies upon and partially reprints Capel Lofft's transcription of the case. A long and seemingly endless controversy over which transcript of the case is most valid still rages. Capel Lofft's is most frequently cited, despite its possible occasional unreliability.

74. Tuke 25

75. Sharp NYHS 185

76. Hoare, Vol. 1, 105

77. Hoare, Vol. 1, 110

78. NYHS 36

79. Lewis proceedings, 11

80. Lewis proceedings, 10

81. Sharp NYHS 189

82. 'Somerset's Case, and the Extinction of Villenage and Slavery in England', *Proceedings of the Massachusetts Historical Society*, Vol. 7, February 1864, 323–4

83. Edward Fiddes, 'Lord Mansfield and the Sommersett Case', *The Law Quarterly Review* (London: Stevens and Sons, 1934), Vol. 50, 499

84. Quoted widely. See H.T. Catterall, *Judicial Cases Concerning American Slavery and the Negro* (Washington, D.C., 1926–37.) Vol. 1, 3

85. Tuke 61. See also William M. Wiecek, '*Somerset*: Lord Mansfield and the Legitimacy of Slavery in the Anglo-American World', *The University of Chicago Law Review*, Vol. 42, no. 1, Fall 1974, 86–146, p. 94, note 25

86. Philip C. Yorke, *The Life and Correspondence of Philip Yorke, Earl of Hardwicke, Lord High Chancellor of Great Britain*, Vol. II (Cambridge: Cambridge University Press, 1913), 473

87. Hoare, Vol. 1, 106–7

88. Sharp NYHS 186

89. Hoare, Vol. 1, 113–14

90. London: Printed for W. Flexney, opposite Gray's Inn Gate, Holborn, 1773. Price one shilling.

91. *Morning Chronicle and London Advertiser*, 21 May 1772, 2a and c

92. *Morning Chronicle and London Advertiser*, no. 947, 5 June 1772, 2c

93. *Morning Chronicle and London Advertiser*, no. 944, Tuesday, 2 June 1772, 3c

94. *The Gazetteer and New Daily Advertiser*, Thursday, 4 June 1772, 1–3

95. *The Craftsman*, Saturday, 13 June 1772, 1a

96. *The Gazetteer and New Daily Advertiser*, no. 139508, Monday, 15 June 1772, 1a and b
97. *Middlesex Journal, or Chronicle of Liberty*, no. 499, June 9–11, 1772, 1
98. Hoare, Vol. 1, 125
99. Tuke 27
100. Tuke 56
101. Tuke 61
102. Tuke 61
103. Tuke 62
104. Tuke 63
105. Tuke 63–4
106. Tuke 72
107. *The Craftsman; or Say's Weekly Journal*, Saturday, 30 May 1772, 2b
108. *The Craftsman; or Say's Weekly Journal*, Saturday, 23 May 1772, 3d
109. Tuke 72
110. Letter book, 43
111. Tuke 71
112. Letter book, 109–10
113. Baker 233–4
114. *The Morning Chronicle, and London Advertiser*, Wednesday, 24 June 1772, 2b
115. Widely reproduced. However, Tuke's nineteenth-century version changes the word 'Man' to 'Black', an interesting switch from the original
116. *The Craftsman; or, Say's Weekly Journal*, Saturday, 27 June 1772, 2c
117. *The Morning Chronicle, and London Advertiser*, Wednesday, 24 June 1772, 2b
118. *The Middlesex Journal: or, Chronicle of Liberty*, number 504, Saturday, 20 June–Tuesday, 23 June 1772, 3c; *Bingley's Journal: or, the Universal Gazette*, Saturday, 20 June–Saturday, 27 June 1772, number 108, 2c
119. *Gentleman's Magazine*, 1772, Vol. 42, 307–10
120. *The Gazetteer and New Daily Advertiser*, Thursday, 25 June 1772, 1c, and Friday, 26 June 1772
121. *Morning Chronicle, and London Advertiser*, Wednesday, 24 June 1772, 2b
122. Hoare, Vol. 1, 137
123. 'Somerset's Case, and the Extinction of Villenage and Slavery in England', *Proceedings of the Massachusetts Historical Society*, Vol. 7, February 1864, 325–6
124. Jerome Nadelhaft, 'The Somersett Case and Slavery: Myth,

Reality, and Repercussions', *The Journal of Negro History* (Washington, D.C.: The Association for the Study of Negro Life and History, Inc.), January 1966, Vol. 51, no. 1, 193–208

125. William M. Wiecek, '*Somerset*: Lord Mansfield and the Legitimacy of Slavery in the Anglo-American World', *The University of Chicago Law Review*, Vol. 42, no. 1, Fall 1974, 86–146
126. Nadelhaft 195; Fiddes 509–10
127. Wiecek 108–9
128. Wiecek 108–9
129. Shyllon *Black People* 25, but widely reported and written about
130. Oldham, 'New Light . . .', 65–6, from National Library of Scotland, MS 5027

Chapter 5: The Black Poor

1. Quoted in Sidney and Emma Kaplan, *The Black Presence in the Era of the American Revolution*, revised edition, (Amherst: University of Massachusetts Press, 1989) 72–3
2. Kaplan 72
3. Quoted in Kaplan 73
4. Kaplan 73
5. Fryer, *Staying Power* 191
6. Fryer, *Staying Power* 192
7. Quoted in Kaplan 84–5
8. Kaplan 81
9. Kaplan 83
10. Fryer, *Staying Power* 192
11. Fryer, *Staying Power* 192
12. Public Record Office, London (hereafter PRO) AO.12.102
13. PRO AO.12.102, 156–7
14. PRO AO.12.102, 25–6
15. Fryer, *Staying Power* 192–3
16. *The Daily Universal Register*, Wednesday, 26 January 1785, no. 22, p. 3, col. 1
17. John Thomas Smith, *Vagabondia. Or, Anecdotes of Mendicant Wanderers through the Streets of London, With Portraits of the Most Remarkable Drawn from the Life* (Los Angeles: Sherwin & Freutel Publishers, 1970), 33. Facsimile of the edition of 1817
18. *Vagabondia* 33
19. *Vagabondia* 34
20. *Vagabondia* 34

21. PRO T.1.631/1304
22. PRO T.1.631/1304
23. PRO T.1.631/1304
24. John H. Hutchins, *Jonas Hanway 1712–1786* (London: Society for Promoting Christian Knowledge), 1940, 180
25. PRO T.1.631/1304, 17 May 1786
26. PRO T.1.631/1334
27. PRO T.1.634/2012
28. PRO T.1.632, 'Proceedings of the Committee for the Relief of the Black Poor', 7th June 1786
29. PRO T.1.632, 'Proceedings . . .' 7th June 1786
30. PRO T.1.632, 'Proceedings . . .' 7th June 1786
31. PRO T.1.632, 'Proceedings . . .' 7th June 1786
32. PRO T.1.632/354
33. Henry Smeathman, *Plan of a Settlement to be Made Near Sierra Leona, on the Grain Coast of Africa* (London: Sold by T. Stockdale in Piccadilly, G. Kearsley in Fleet Street, and J. Sewel in Cornhill, 1786), title page. PRO T.1.632
34. Smeathman 16–17
35. Smeathman 4–6
36. Smeathman 7–9
37. Smeathman 23
38. Smeathman 10–11
39. PRO T.1.632/1623, 'Proceedings . . .' 28th June 1786
40. PRO T.1.633/1707, 'Proceedings . . .' 10th July 1786
41. PRO T.1.633/1633, 'Proceedings . . .' 3rd July 1786
42. PRO T.1.633/1673
43. T.1.634/1814, 'Proceedings . . .' 15th July 1786
44. PRO T.1.634/1903, 'Proceedings . . .' 26th July 1786
45. PRO T.1.634/1964, 28 July 1786
46. T.1.634/1965, 'Proceedings . . .' 31st July 1786
47. T.1.634/1906, 31st July 1786
48. PRO T.1.634/2012, 'Proceedings . . .' 4th August 1786
49. PRO T.1.634/2012, 'Proceedings . . .' 4th August 1786
50. PRO T.1.638, 'Proceedings . . .' 24th October 1786
51. PRO T.1.638, letter from George Peters to George Rose, 24 October 1786
52. PRO T.1.635/2540, letter to George Rose from the Navy Office, 30 October 1786
53. *The Life of Olaudah Equiano*, ed. Paul Edwards, (Essex: Longman Group U.K., 1989) 50. Originally published 1789
54. *Public Advertiser*, 5 February 1788

55. *Public Advertiser*, 28 January 1788
56. *Public Advertiser*, 28 January 1788
57. *The Life of Olaudah Equiano* 162–3
58. PRO T.1.638
59. PRO T.1.635/2430
60. PRO T.1.635/2497
61. PRO T.1/2430
62. *Life of Olaudah Equiano* 163
63. *Life of Olaudah Equiano* 163–4
64. PRO T.1.638/2684
65. PRO T.1.641/11
66. PRO T.1.643/173, 'Proceedings . . .' 19th January 1787
67. PRO T.1.641/140, 'Proceedings . . .' 16th January 1787
68. *Public Advertiser*, Wednesday, 17 January 1787, p. 4, col. 1
69. *Public Advertiser*, Wednesday, 31 January 1787, p. 2, col. 1
70. *Public Advertiser*, 20 January 1787, no. 16433, p. 2, col. 4, *Extract of a letter from Plymouth, Jan. 13*
71. PRO T.1.644, letter dated 2 April 1787
72. *Public Advertiser*, Monday, 29 January 1787, no. 16440, p. 4, col. 1
73. *Public Advertiser*, Monday, 26 February 1787, no. 16464, p. 4, col. 2, *Extract of a letter from Portsmouth*, 22 February 1787
74. PRO T.1.643
75. Anna Maria Falconbridge, *Narrative of Two Voyages to Sierra Leone During the Years 1791–2–3* (London: 1794)
76. PRO T.1.643
77. *Public Advertiser*, Wednesday, 4 April 1787, number 16496, p. 3
78. *Public Advertiser*, Friday, 6 April 1787, p. 3, col. 4
79. *Public Advertiser*, Friday, 6 April 1787, p. 3, col. 4
80. *Public Advertiser*, Friday, 6 April 1787, p. 3, col. 4
81. *Public Advertiser*, Wednesday, 11 April 1787, no. 16502, p. 3, col. 4
82. *Public Advertiser*, Saturday, 14 April 1787, no. 16585, p. 2, col. 3 & p. 3, col. 4
83. *Public Advertiser*, Wednesday, 11 April 1787, no. 16502, p. 3, col. 4
84. PRO T.1.646/1295
85. Paul Edwards, in *The Life of Equiano*, mistakenly records the requested amount as the astronomically high £321.4s
86. PRO T.1.647/1572

Chapter 6: The End of English Slavery

1. Christopher Fyfe, *A History of Sierra Leone* (London: Oxford University Press, 1968), 21
2. Hoare, Vol. 2, 83
3. Hoare, Vol. 2, 83
4. Stephen J. Braidwood, 'Initiatives and Organisation of the Black Poor 1786–1787' (paper presented to the International Conference on the History of Blacks in Britain, London, 28–30 September 1981), 12. Quoted in Fryer, *Staying Power*, 202
5. Fyfe 21
6. Fyfe 20
7. Fyfe 21
8. Fyfe 23
9. Fyfe 21
10. Fyfe 22–3
11. Fyfe 24–5
12. Anna Maria Falconbridge, *Narrative of Two Voyages to the River Sierra Leone During the Years 1791–1793* (London: Frank Cass & Co. Ltd., 1967), Letter II, Spithead, 12 January 1791, 15–16
13. Falconbridge, Letter III, Bance Island, 10 February 1791, 21–2
14. Falconbridge, Letter III, 64–6
15. Falconbridge, Letter VIII, Free Town, 1 July 1792, 150
16. *The Gentleman's Magazine*, Vol. 31, 'Parliamentary Proceedings of Lords and Commons' for 1791, August 1791, 735
17. *The Gentleman's Magazine*, Vol. 39, 363
18. James W. St. G. Walker, *The Black Loyalists: The Search for a Promised Land in Nova Scotia and Sierra Leone 1783–1870* (New York: African Publishing Company, Dalhousie University Press, 1976) 94–5
19. Hoare, Vol. 2, 157–9, letter from Sharp dated 5 October 1791
20. Walker 105
21. Walker 113
22. Walker 113
23. Walker 137
24. *The Gentleman's Magazine*, Vol. 62, October 1792, 1049
25. *The Gentleman's Magazine*, Vol. 63, January 1793, 80
26. Susana Smith, 12 May 1792, quoted in Christopher Fyfe, *'Our Children Free and Happy', Letters from Black Settlers in Africa in the 1790s* (Edinburgh: Edinburgh University Press, 1991), 24
27. 5 November 1792, Fyfe, *'Our Children Free and Happy'*, 27–28
28. Fyfe, *'Our Children Free and Happy'*, 36–7

29. Fyfe, 'Our Children Free and Happy', *30–1*

30. *Hoare, Vol. 2, 163–4*

31. *Falconbridge, Letter V, London, 30 September 1791, 126–7*

32. *Sharp to King Naimbanna, King of Robanna, 11 November 1791, in Hoare, Vol. 2, 164–5*

33. *Hoare 163–6*

34. *Hoare, Vol. 2, 166–7*

35. *Hannah More, 'The Black Prince', in Cheap Repository Tracts; Entertaining, Moral and Religious,* Vol. 1 (Boston: Printed and sold by E. Lincoln, Water-Street, 1803. Originally published in England, 1801–2), title page

36. 'The Black Prince', 173

37. 'The Black Prince', 185

38. Hoare, Vol. 2, 171

39. Fryer, *Staying Power*, 127 -8

40. Fryer, *Staying Power*, 128

41. Fryer, *Staying Power*, 128

42. Thomas Day, 'Fragment of an Original Letter on the Slavery of the Negroes; Written in the Year 1776, by Thomas Day, Esq.' (Philadelphia, 1784), a broadside

43. *London Chronicle*, 13–16 March 1773. Quoted in File 23

44. *Morning Post*, 22 December 1786. Quoted in File, Fig. 19

45. *Morning Post*, 29 December 1786. Quoted in File, Fig. 19.2

46. R. Coupland, *The British Anti-Slavery Movement* (London: Thornton Butterworth, Ltd., 1933) 66–78

47. Thomas Clarkson, *The History of the Rise, Progress, and Accomplishment of the Abolition of the African Slave-Trade, by the British Parliament,* in three volumes, (New York: John S. Taylor, 1836), Vol. 1, 176

48. Clarkson, Vol. 1, 194

49. David Richardson, *The Bristol Slave Traders: A Collective Portrait* (Bristol: Bristol Branch of the Historical Association, 1985), no. 60 in a series, 1

50. Ramsay Muir, *A History of Liverpool* (London, 1907), quoted in Frank J. Klingberg, *The Anti-Slavery Movement in England* (New Haven: Yale University Press, 1926), 78

51. Clarkson, Vol. 1, 225

52. Fryer, *Staying Power*, 56, quoting *House of Commons Sessional Papers of the Eighteenth Century*, LXIX, 125

53. Clarkson, Vol. 2, 28–32

54. Clarkson, Vol. 2, 224

55. Clarkson, Vol. 2, 267

56. Clarkson, Vol. 2, 33
57. Clarkson, Vol. 2, 10–12
58. *The Times*, 12 January 1792, 3d
59. *The Times*, 28 March 1792, 2d
60. *The Times*, 10 March 1792, 2b
61. Clarkson, Vol. 2, 296
62. Clarkson, Vol. 2, 297
63. These include Robert Bage's *Man as He Is* (1792); Barbauld's and Aiken's 'Dialogues between Master and Slave' in *Evenings at Home* (1792–4); the anonymously published *Berkeley Hall* (1796); William Combe's *Devil Upon Two Sticks in England* (1791); Edward Dubois' *Saint Godwin: A Tale of the Sixteenth, Seventeenth, and Eighteenth Centuries* (1800); William Godwin's *Political Justice* (1793); *St. Leon. A Tale of the Sixteenth Century* (1799); Elizabeth Hamilton's *Letters of a Hindoo Rajah* (1796) and *Memoirs of Modern Philosophers: A Novel* (1800); Elizabeth Helme's *Duncan and Peggy* (1794), *Farmer of Inglewood Forest* (1796) and *Henry Willoughby: A Novel* (1798); *Human Vicissitudes: or, Travels into Unexplored Regions* (anonymous, 1798); Elizabeth Inchbald's *Nature and Art* (1796); Charlotte Lennox's *Euphemia* (1790); Anna Maria Mackenzie's *Slavery, or The Times* (1793); *Memoirs of the Life and Travel of the Late Charles Macpherson, Esq. in Asia, Africa, and America* (anonymous, 1800); *Memoirs and Opinions of Mr. Blenfield* (anonymous, 1790); Dr John Moore's *Mordaunt* (1800); 'No Rum – No Sugar! Or, the Voice of Blood, Being Half an Hour's Conversation, between a Negro and an English Gentleman, Shewing the Horrible Nature of the Slave Trade . . .' (1792); Miss Peacock's *Posthumous Daughter: A Novel* (1797); S.J. Pratt's *Family Secrets* (1797); J.F. de Saint-Lambert's ('George Filmer') *Zimao, the African* (1800); the amazingly prolific Charlotte Smith's *Desmond* (1792), *Letters of a Solitary Wanderer* (1801), *The Old Manor House* (1793), and *The Wanderings of Warwick* (1794); Henry Summersett's *Aberford* (1798); Ann Thomas's *Adolphus de Biron* (1794); G. Thompson's *Sentimental Tour* (1798); George Walker's *Theodore Cyphon: or, the benevolent Jew. A Novel* (1796) and *The Vagabond* (1799); Helena Wells' *Constantia Neville; or, The West Indian* (1800); Jane West's ('Prudentia Homespun') *Advantages of an Education. Or, The History of Maria Williams. A Tale for Misses and Their Mammas* (1793); Joseph Wildman's *Force of Prejudice* (1799)
64. 'S.S.' in *Gentleman's Magazine*, Vol. 61, November 1791, 1046–7
65. Clarkson, Vol. 2, 41
66. Clarkson, Vol. 2, 252

67. Clarkson, Vol. 2, 253
68. Clarkson, Vol. 2, 265
69. Clarkson 274
70. Shyllon, *Black People*, 199, but widely quoted. Hume refused to believe that Africa had ever produced anything or anyone of intellectual, artistic or scientific interest.
71. *Public Advertiser*, 28 January 1788. See Shyllon, *Black People in Britain 1555–1833*, 231, for more on this
72. Shyllon, *Black People*, 236
73. *The Life of Olaudah Equiano*, introduction by Paul Edwards, xii. The letter is from Sharp to his niece Jemima, 22 February 1811
74. Quoted in Shyllon, *Black People*, 267
75. 'The Address of Thanks of the Sons of Africa to the Honourable Granville Sharp, Esq.', 15 December 1787, quoted in Shyllon, *Black People*, 268
76. Shyllon, *Black People*, 269–70
77. Shyllon, *Black People*, 269–70
78. Reginald Coupland, *Wilberforce: A Narrative* (Oxford: Clarendon Press, 1923), 108
79. Quoted in Coupland, *Wilberforce*, 93
80. Quoted in Coupland, *Wilberforce*, 119–30
81. Coupland, *Wilberforce*, 116
82. Robert Bisset, *The History of the Negro Slave Trade, in Its Connection with the Commerce and Prosperity of the West Indies, and The Wealth and Power of the British Empire, in Two Volumes*, (London: M'Dowell, Pemberton Row, Gough Square, 1805)
83. Coupland, *Wilberforce* 108
84. *The Times*, 10 November 1791, 2c
85. Coupland 114
86. Fryer, *Staying Power* 101
87. Coupland, *Wilberforce* 220
88. Shyllon, *Black People* 270
89. Winthrop Jordan, *White Over Black*, 248
90. Footnote to 'Of National Characters', 1753–4, quoted in Jordan 253
91. Jordan 248
92. Sharp letter book 158, 19 October 1772
93. Sharp letter book 159
94. See Paul Edwards' introduction to Cugoano's book (London: Dawsons of Pall Mall, 1969) for a detailed discussion of this
95. Paul Edwards, appendix to *Thoughts and Sentiments on the Evil of Slavery*, xix–xxiii

96. Edwards xxiii
97. Cugoano 140
98. *The Daily Universal Register*, Saturday, 8 January 1785, 3c
99. Coupland, 'The British Anti-Slavery Movement' 94
100. Coupland, 'The British Anti-Slavery Movement' 109
101. Coupland, *Wilberforce* 341
102. Fryer, *Staying Power*, 207. Fryer discusses the work of C.L.R. James, Eric Williams and others in this context
103. Fryer, *Staying Power* 211
104. Fryer, *Staying Power* 217–15
105. Harriet Jacobs, *Incidents in the Life of a Slave Girl* (Boston: published for the author, 1861. A reprint of the original by AMS Press, New York, 1973), 275
106. Jacobs 267
107. Jacobs 278
108. Fryer, *Staying Power* 436
109. Fryer, *Staying Power* 428
110. Fryer, *Staying Power* 235
111. *The Times Magazine*, 12 November 1994

Bibliography

In addition to the sources listed below, a large number of newspapers and magazines were used and are indicated in the notes. Unpublished sources include papers from London's Public Record Office (abbreviated as PRO in the notes), and various papers of Granville Sharp housed at the New York Historical Society and the York Minster Library.

Adams, Gene, 'Dido Elizabeth Belle: A Black Girl at Kenwood', in *Camden History Review*, London, 1984

Angelo, Henry, *Reminiscences of Henry Angelo, with Memoirs of his Late Father and Friends, Including Numerous original anecdotes and curious facts of the most celebrated characters that have flourished during the last eighty years*, London: Henry Colburn, New Burlington Street, 1828

Barbauld, Mrs and Mr Aiken, Dialogues between 'Master and Slave' in *Evenings at Home*, New York: Geo. A. Leavitt, (Publisher) undated. Written 1792–5 and originally published in London

Behn, Aphra, *Oroonoko or, The Royal Slave*, New York: W.W. Norton & Co., 1973

Bisset, Robert, *The History of the Negro Slave Trade, in Its Connection with the Commerce and Prosperity of the West Indies, and the Wealth and Power of the British Empire*, Vols. 1 and 2, London: M'Dowell, Pemberton Row, Gough Square, 1805

'The Black Man,' in *All the Year Round*, 6 March 1875

Boswell, James, *Boswell's Life of Johnson*, George Birbeck Hill, ed. Oxford: The Clarendon Press, 1934

Candid Reflections Upon the Judgement lately awarded by the Court of King's Bench, in Westminster-Hall, On what is commonly called the Negroe-Cause, London: T. Lowndes, 1772

Carlyle, Thomas, 'Occasional discourse on the nigger question, 1849,' in *Critical and Miscellaneous Essays*, Vol. vii, London, 1872

Bibliography

Clarkson, Thomas, *The History of the Rise, Progress, and Accomplishment of the Abolition of the African Slave Trade, by the British Parliament*, Vols. 1–3, New York: John S. Taylor, 1836

Combe, William, *Devil Upon Two Sticks in England*, London: Printed at the Logographic Press, 1791

Coupland, Reginald, *Wilberforce: A Narrative*, Oxford: Clarendon Press, 1923

Crow, Hugh, *Memoirs of the Late Captain Hugh Crow of Liverpool*, London: Longman, Rees, Orme, Brown and Greene, 1830

Cugoano, Ottobah, *Thoughts and Sentiments on the Evil of Slavery*, London, 1787

Curtin, Philip D., *The Atlantic Slave Trade: A Census*, Madison: University of Wisconsin Press, 1969

Dabydeen, David, *Hogarth's Blacks: Images of Blacks in Eighteenth Century English Art*, Manchester: Manchester University Press, 1987

Day, Thomas, 'The Dying Negro. A Poetical Epistle, supposed to be written by a Black, (who lately shot himself on board a vessel in the river Thames;) to his intended wife.' London: Printed for W. Flexney, Holborn, 1773

—— 'Fragment of an Original Letter on the Slavery of the Negroes; Written in the Year 1776.' Philadelphia, 1784

Dunster, Charles, *St. James's Street*, London: 1790. File, Nigel and Chris Power, *Black Settlers in Britain 1555–1958*, London: Heinemann Education Books, 1981

Equiano, Olaudah, *The Life of Olaudah Equiano*, ed. Paul Edwards, Essex: Longman Group UK, 1989

Estwick, Samuel, *Considerations on the Negroe Cause, Commonly So-Called, Addressed to the Right Honourable Lord Mansfield, Lord Chief Justice of the Court of King's Bench*, London, 1773

Falconbridge, Anna Maria, *Narrative of Two Voyages to Sierra Leone During the Years 1791–2–3*, London, 1794

Fiddes, Edward, 'Lord Mansfield and the Sommersett Case', in *The Law Quarterly Review*, London: Stevens and Sons, 1934

Fielding, Sir John, *Extracts from such of the Penal Laws, as Particularly relate to the Peace and Good Order of this Metropolis*, T. Cadell, 1768

Fryer, Peter, *Black People in the British Empire: An Introduction*, London: Pluto Press, 1988

——*Staying Power: The History of Black People in Britain*, London: Pluto Press, 1984

Christopher Fyfe, *A History of Sierra Leone*, London: Oxford University Press, 1962

Bibliography

Garrick, David, *High Life Below Stairs*, in two acts. In *A Collection of the Most Esteemed Farces and Entertainments Performed on the British Stage*, Vols. 1–4, Edinburgh: Printed for C. Elliot, Parliament-Square, 1782

George, Dorothy, *London Life in the Eighteenth Century*, Chicago: Academy Publishers, 1984

Godwin, William, *St. Leon. A Tale of the Sixteenth Century*. New York: Arno Press, 1972. Originally published 1799

Gronniosaw, James, *A Narrative of the Most Remarkable Particulars in the Life of James Albert Ukasaw Gronniosaw, an African Prince, as Related by Himself*, Leeds: Printed by Davies and Booth, at the Stanhope Press, Vicar-Lane, 1814

Gundara, Jagdish S. and Ian Duffield, eds. *Essays on the History of Blacks in Britain, From Roman Times to the Mid Twentieth Century*, Aldershot: Avebury, Ashgate Publishing Ltd., 1992

Hall, Stuart, et al., *Policing the Crisis*, London: Macmillan, 1978

Hawkins, Sir John, *The Life of Samuel Johnson LL.D.*, ed. Bertram H. Davis, London: Jonathan Cape, 1962

Hecht, J. Jean, *Continental and Colonial Servants in Eighteenth Century England*, Northampton, Massachusetts: Smith College Studies in History, Volume XL, 1954

—— *The Domestic Servant Class in Eighteenth-Century England*, London: Routledge & Kegan Paul, 1956

Helme, Elizabeth, *London and It's [sic] Environs Described*, London: Printed for R. & J. Dodsley's in Pall-Mall, 1761

Heward, Edmund, *Lord Mansfield*, London and Chichester: Barry Rose, 1979

Hoare, Prince, *Memoirs of Granville Sharp, Esq. Composed from His Own Manuscripts . . .* London: Printed for Henry Colburn and Co., 1820

Holmes, Richard, *Footsteps: Adventures of a Romantic Biographer*, New York: Elisabeth Sifton Books, Viking Press, 1985

Husband, Charles, ed., *'Race' in Britain: Continuity and Change*, Second Edition, London: Hutchinson University Library, 1987

Hutchinson, Thomas, *The Diary and Letters of His Excellency Thomas Hutchinson, Esq.*, Peter Orlando Hutchinson, ed., London: Sampson Low, Marston, Searle & Livingston, 1886

Jacobs, Harriet, *Incidents in the Life of a Slave Girl*, Boston, Massachusetts, 1861

James, C.L.R., *The Black Jacobins: Toussaint L'Ouverture and the San Domingo Revolution*, Second Edition, New York: Random House, 1963

Jonson, Ben, *Masque of Blackness*, 1605

Jones, Eldred, *Othello's Countrymen: The African in English Renaissance Drama*, London: Oxford University Press, 1965

Jordon, Winthrop, *White Over Black: American Attitudes Toward the Negro 1550–1812*, University of North Carolina Press, 1968

Kaplan, Sidney and Emma, *The Black Presence in the Era of American Revolution*, Amherst: University of Massachusetts Press, 1989

Klingberg, Frank J., *The Anti-Slavery Movement in England*, New Haven: Yale University Press, 1926

Lascelles, E.C.P., *Granville Sharp and the Freedom of Slaves in England*, London: Oxford University Press, 1928

Latimer, John, *Annals of Bristol in the Eighteenth Century*, Bristol, 1893

Little, K.L., *Negroes in Britain*, London: Kegan Paul, 1948

Long, Edward, *The History of Jamaica*, Vol. I, London: T. Lowndes, in Fleet-Street, 1744

Lowenthal, Leo, *Literature and Mass Culture: Communication in Society*, *Vol. 1*, New Brunswick and London: Transaction Books, 1984. Notes are from Chapter 3, 'Eighteenth Century England: A Case Study', originally published as 'The Debate over Art and Popular Culture: Eighteenth-Century England as a Case Study', *Common Frontiers of the Social Sciences*, ed. Mirra Komarowsky, Free Press, 1957, co-authored with Marjorie Fiske

Matcham, Mary Eyre, *A Forgotten John Russell, Being Letters to a Man of Business 1724–1751*, London: Edward Arnold, 1905

Memoirs and Opinions of Mr. Blenfield, London: Printed for W. Lane, Leadenhall Street, 1790

Montgomery, James, *Poems on the Abolition of the Slave Trade*, New York: Garland Publishing, 1978. Originally published London, 1809

More, Hannah, 'The Black Prince' in *Cheap Repository Tracts; Entertaining, Moral and Religious*, Vol. 1, Boston: Printed and sold by E. Lincoln, Water-Street, 1803. Originally published in England, 1801–2

—— *Memoirs of the life and correspondence of Mrs. Hannah More*, ed. William Roberts, L.B. Seeley & Sons, 1834

Morgan, Kenneth, *Bristol and the Atlantic Trade in the Eighteenth Century*, Cambridge: Cambridge University Press, 1993

Morrison, Toni, *Beloved*, New York: Alfred A. Knopf, 1987

Muir, Ramsay, *A History of Liverpool*, London, 1907

The Negro's Friend, or the Sheffield Anti-Slavery Album, Sheffield: Printed and sold by J. Blackwell, Highstreet and Miss Gales, Hartshend. Also by Longman, Rees, Orme, Brown, and Green, London, 1826

Nadelhaft, Jerome, 'The Somersett Case and Slavery: Myth, Reality, and Repercussions', in *The Journal of Negro History*, Washington, DC:

The Association for the Study of Negro Life and History Inc., January 1966, Vol. 51, no. 1, 193–208

'No Rum – No Sugar! Or, the Voice of Blood, Being Half an Hour's Conversation, between a Negro and an English Gentleman, Shewing the Horrible Nature of the Slave Trade, and Pointing out an Easy and Effectual Method of Terminating it, By an Act of the People.' London: Printed for L. Wayland, Middle-Row-Holborn, 1792

Northcote, James, *The Life of Sir Joshua Reynolds*, London: Printed for Henry Colburn, Conduit-Street, 1819

Oldham, James, *The Mansfield Manuscripts and the Growth of English Law in the Eighteenth Century*, Chapel Hill and London: The University of North Carolina Press, 1992

—— 'New Light on Mansfield and Slavery' in *Journal of British Studies*, Vol. 27, no 1, January 1988, 45–68

Piozzi, Hester Lynch, *Anecdotes of the Late Samuel Johnson, LL.D., during the last twenty years of his Life*, ed. S.C. Roberts, Cambridge: Cambridge University Press, 1925

Porter, Dale, *The Abolition of the Slave Trade in England, 1784–1807*, USA: Archon Books, 1970

Prince, Mary, *The History of Mary Prince*, ed. Thomas Pringle, in *The Classic Slave Narratives*, ed. Henry Louis Gates, Jr. New York: New American Library, 1987

Reade, Aleyn Lyell, *Johnsonian Gleanings*, Part II, 'Francis Barber, The Doctor's Negro Servant', London: Arden Press, 1912

Richardson, David, *The Bristol Slave Traders: A Collective Portrait*, Bristol: Bristol Branch of the Historical Association, 1985. Number 60 in a series

Rogers, J.A., *Nature Knows No Color-Line*, New York: J.A. Rogers, 1952

Sackville-West, Vita, *Knole and the Sackvilles*, London: William Heinemann Ltd., 1931

Sancho, Ignatius, *Letters of Ignatius Sancho*, ed. Paul Edwards, London: Dawsons of Pall Mall, 1968

Schaw, Janet, *Journal of a Lady of Quality; Being the Narrative of a Journey from Scotland to the West Indies, North Carolina, and Portugal, in the years 1774 to 1776*, edited by Evangeline Walker Andrews and Charles McLean Andrews, New Haven: Yale University Press and London: Oxford University Press, 1922

Schwartz, Richard B., *Daily Life in Johnson's London*, Madison: University of Wisconsin Press, 1983

Sharp, Granville, *The Law of Retribution*, London: W. Richardson for B. White, 1776

—— Letter Book, unpublished. York: The York Minster Library.

—— Manuscripts, unpublished. New York: The New York Historical Society

Shyllon, Folarin Olawale, *Black People in Britain 1555–1833*, London: published for the Institute of Race Relations by Oxford University Press, 1977

—— *Black Slaves In Britain*, London: published for the Institute of Race Relations by Oxford University Press, 1974

Silliman, Benjamin, *A Journal of Travels in England, Holland and Scotland . . . in the Years 1805 and 1806*, New Haven: 1820

Smeathman, Henry, *Plan of a Settlement to be Made Near Sierra Leona, on the Grain Coast of Africa*, London: Sold by T. Stockdale in Piccadilly, G. Kearsley in Fleet Street, and J. Sewel in Cornhill, 1786

Smith, John Thomas, *Nollekens and his Times*, ed. G.W. Stonier, London, 1949

—— *Vagabondia. Or, Anecdotes of Mendicant Wanderers through the Streets of London, With Portraits of the Most Remarkable Drawn from the Life*, Los Angeles: Sherwin & Freutel Publishers, 1970

'Somerset's Case, and the Extinction of Villenage and Slavery in England', *Proceedings of the Massachusetts Historical Society*, Vol. 7, February 1864

Southerne, Thomas, *Oroonoko* in *The Works of Thomas Southerne*, Robert Jordan and Harold Love, eds., Oxford: Clarendon Press, 1988. Originally performed and published 1695–6

Sypher, Wylie, 'The African Prince in London,' *Journal of the History of Ideas*, Vol. II, No. 2 (April, 1941): 237–47

—— *Guinea's Captive Kings*, Chapel Hill: University of North Carolina Press, 1942

—— 'The West-Indian as a "Character" in the Eighteenth Century,' in *Studies in Philology*, Vol. XXXVI, No. 3, 503–20, Chapel Hill: The University of North Carolina Press, July 1939

Thicknesse, Philip, *A Year's Journey through France and Part of Spain*, W. Brown, 1778

Tuchman, Barbara, 'In Search of History,' in *Practicing History*, New York: Ballantine Books, 1982

Tuke, Henry George, *The Fugitive Slave Circulars, a Short Account of the Case of Sommersett the Negro*, London: Stanford, Charing Cross, 1876

Walker, James W. St. G., *The Black Loyalists: The Search for a Promised*

Land in Nova Scotia and Sierra Leone 1783–1870, New York: African Publishing Company, Dalhousie University Press, 1976

Walvin, James, ed., *Black and White: The Negro and English Society 1555–1945*, London: Allen Lane the Penguin Press, 1973

—— *The Black Presence: A Documentary History of the Negro in England, 1555–1860*, London: Orbach & Chambers, 1971

—— *England, Slaves and Freedom, 1776–1838*, London: Macmillan Press Ltd., 1986

—— *A Short History of Slavery and the Slave Trade*, London, 1982

—— *Slavery and British Society 1776–1846*, Baton Rouge: Louisiana State University Press, 1982

Wells, Helena, *Constantia Neville; or, the West Indian*, London: printed by C. Whittingham, Dean Street, Fetter Lane, 1800

West, Jane, *Advantages of Education . . .* , London and New York: Garland Publishing Inc., 1974

Wiecek, William M., '*Somerset*: Lord Mansfield and the Legitimacy of Slavery in the Anglo-American World', *The University of Chicago Law Review*, Vol. 42, no. 1, Fall 1974, 86–146

Williams, Eric, *Capitalism and Slavery*, New York: Capricorn Books, 1966. Originally published by University of North Carolina, 1944

Yorke, Philip C., ed., *The Diary of John Baker*, London: Hutchinson & Co. Ltd., 1931

Zweig, Paul, *The Adventurer*, New York, 1974

Index